UNCLE
MAME

Also by Eric Myers

Screen Deco: A Celebration of High Style in Hollywood
(co-authored by Howard Mandelbaum)

Forties Screen Style: A Celebration of High Pastiche in Hollywood
(co-authored by Howard Mandelbaum)

UNCLE MAME

The Life
of Patrick Dennis

Eric Myers

St. Martin's Press ≋ New York

To Charles Busch . . .
who always has the best ideas

c.\

www.stmartins.com

Design by James Sinclair

Library of Congress Cataloging-in-Publication Data

Myers, Eric.
    Uncle Mame : the life of Patrick Dennis / Eric Myers.—1st ed.
      p.   cm.
    Includes index.
    ISBN 0-312-24655-2
    1. Dennis, Patrick, 1921-1976. 2. Novelists, American—20th century—
Biography.   3. Gay men—United States—Biography.   I. Title.

   PS3554.E537 Z78 2000
   813'.54—dc21
   [B]   00-031739

First Edition: November 2000

10 9 8 7 6 5 4 3 2 1

CONTENTS

Part Four

ACKNOWLEDGMENTS

Historians of popular culture face a common dilemma: the subjects they are researching are often not considered "important" enough to have engendered any kind of serious documentation by scholars. I found this to be the case with Patrick Dennis. Aside from the newspaper and magazine interviews he occasionally granted when a book was published, there remains little mention of him in critical or historical texts. The veil of silence that seemed to drop over him after his death inspired me to seek out his story. The result was an article I contributed to the April 1997 issue of *Quest* magazine, which in turn led to this book.

With little in the way of research material, I depended on the recollections of those closest to Pat as my primary sources of information. Pat's immediate family—his widow, Louise Tanner, and his children, Michael and Betsy Tanner—opened their hearts, their minds, and their memories to me, sharing thoughts that were often funny, sometimes painful, and always fascinating. Louise Tanner was introduced to me by her wonderful friends Elaine Adam and Vivian Weaver, who also allowed me to interview them about their pal Patrick and the wild days they shared at the Council on Foreign Relations. Elaine and Vivian were in turn introduced to me by our mutual friend Lita Weinrib, without whom this book would not have been possible.

Pat was lucky to have a long, long list of friends who adored him. Unfortunately, at least a dozen of those closest to him had passed away before this project was initiated. The information they might have contributed can only be imagined, but I am terribly grateful to those surviving friends of Pat's who took the time to speak with me. Interviews with nearly one hundred people formed the backbone for this book, and I'd like to thank each of those individuals:

Cris Alexander and Shaun
  O'Brien
Marilyn Amdur
Lydia Anderson
David Anton
Abe and Nan Badian
Nancy Bequette
John Bowab
John Boxer
Carlisle Brazy (Connick)
Jacques and Glendora Brazy
Peggy Brooks
Kirk and Barbara Browning
Dr. William G. Cahan
Carmen Capalbo
Peggy Cass
Jerome Cavanaugh
Ross Claiborne
John Condit
Ricky Dalton
Bill Diebold
Frank and Bita Dobo
Michael Dobo
Professor Norman Dorsen,
  NYU Law School
Barbara Harned Dorsett
Emi Fors
Robert Fryer
Dean Fuller
Gregor Gamble
Jean Garay
Violet Gershenson
Tom and Patty Godfrey
Dody Goodman

Murray Grand
Charles Gurney
James Harvey
Nancy Hoffman
Isabelle Holland
Robert Hutchings
Marjorie Jackson
Sister Joanna (formerly Susan
  Hastings)
J. B. Johnson
Hervey Jolin
Webster Jones
Katie Kelley
Pansy Kimbro
Ring Lardner Jr.
Paula Lawrence
Janet Waldo Lee
Robin Little
Arthur Loeb
Cordelia Godfrey Longstreth
Jean Montague Massengale
Mildred B. Jones Mathers
E. G. McGrath
William McPherson
Dr. John Mock
Carlos Montes
Gordon Muchow
Julian Muller
Anne Noggle
Mary Pease
David Peterson
Nina Quirós
Abigail Rosenthal
Lucy Rosenthal

Roger Ross	Katherine Walch
James Sherburne	William Weaver
Joy Singer	Robert Weisel
Patty Sommer	Forrest Williams
C. B. Squire	Phyllis Williamson
Alan Stark	Clinton Wright
Keith Stevenson	Katherine Deane Wright
William Stump	Thew Wright
Robert and Elizabeth Valkenier	Lyonel Zunz
Jac Venza	

In addition, many people who never actually knew Pat acted as conduits to some of the individuals above or helped to provide other information on Pat. They include Elliott Stein, Bruce Feldman, Hilary Knight, Michael Brittain, Lorraine Sattler, James Ireland Baker, Louise Kaufman, Robert Hofler, Steve Ross, Frank Andrews, the late Robert Mackintosh, Ray Powers, Gwin Chin, Libby Lyon, Marilyn Rogers, Jane A. Johnston, Robert Plunket, Leslie Goodwin-Malamuth, Richard Amdur, Elizabeth Bishop, Carol Townsend and Kathy Miehls of Evanston Township High School, Eden Juron Pearlman of the Evanston Historical Society, Eleonora Golobic of the American Field Service research library, Peter Swords, Robert Bryan, Tim Page, Anthony Chetwynd, Arturo Aldama, José Luis Ibañez, and Jerry Herman.

The following friends offered invaluable encouragement and support: Brooks Peters, Paul Rudnick, Scott Rudin, Howard and Ron Mandelbaum, Cyndi Stivers, Brian Kellow, Harry Clein, Bruce Goldstein, Richard Tyler Jordan, Peter Mintun, Eric Bernhoft, Jim Moon, and John Chapman.

Thanks are due my sister and brother-in-law, Fredricka and Tony Laurian, who provided me with a cabin in the woods overlooking Lake Tahoe for a week to begin work on this book. Completion also took place far from my hectic New York home, in surroundings of great restfulness and tranquillity, courtesy of the Asolare Foundation in Lexington, North Carolina, and the Vermont Studio Center in Johnson, Vermont.

My agent, Edward Hibbert of Donadio & Olson, tirelessly worked to find a good home for the book. I'm deeply grateful to my editor,

Keith Kahla of St. Martin's Press, for taking me under his wing. Keith's assistant, Teresa Theophano, handled a thousand and one details and crises with unfailing aplomb and good humor. Robert Wyatt deserves a special thank-you for his early vote of confidence, his input, and his ceaseless encouragement. Copy editor Steven Boldt and production editor Robert Cloud, each with a fine eye for detail, have made invaluable contributions.

And to the handful of hard-core Patrick Dennis fans who have helped keep his name alive in the quarter century since his untimely death, my gratitude and the hope that he may finally begin to emerge from the shadows of neglect.

—ERIC MYERS
New York City
May 2000

PROLOGUE

It took William Makepeace Thackeray to concoct Becky Sharp, Jane Austen to invent Emma, and Oscar Wilde to conceive Lady Windermere. Memorable ladies all, and their creators are equally celebrated. Auntie Mame is even better known and more beloved by the general public, but how many people remember the man who gave her to us?

In the quarter century since his death, Edward Everett Tanner III (also known pseudonymously as Patrick Dennis and Virginia Rowans) is in danger of slipping through the cracks of history. During the mid-1950s and early 1960s he was one of the most widely read authors in the United States and enjoyed the unprecedented status of having three books on the *New York Times* bestseller list simultaneously. Now, when he is remembered at all, it is chiefly for *Auntie Mame*. People assume that the book is based on fact—that young Patrick really was raised by a madcap New York aunt—when in reality, he grew up rather conventionally as part of an upper-middle-class family in the Chicago suburb of Evanston, Illinois. Once he left those confines, however, he led a life as unusual—and as poignant—as that of any fictional character he could have created.

Auntie Mame was only one of Tanner's sixteen novels. The book made him a millionaire and has earned its place as a perennial pop classic of American fiction. Millions of readers worldwide turned Auntie Mame into one of the most beloved ladies in twentieth-century popular literature. "The madwoman of Washington Square" was an eccentric New Yorker who adopted her orphaned young nephew, Patrick, led him through a series of kooky misadventures, and gave him an upbringing that administered a swift symbolic kick in the pants to

Eisenhower's America. The warmth, style, and joie de vivre of this big-hearted eccentric earned her a place somewhere between Holly Golightly and Lorelei Lee in the pantheon of unforgettable female characters in American fiction. Here's Patrick Dennis giving his first impressions of life with his auntie:

> Auntie Mame's days were spent in a perpetual whirl of shopping, entertaining, going to other people's parties, being fitted for the outlandish clothes of the day—and hers were even more so—going to the theater and to the little experimental plays that opened and shut like clams all over New York, being taken to dinner by a series of intellectual gentlemen, and traipsing through galleries of incomprehensible pictures and statues. But with all of her hectic, empty life, she still had plenty of time to devote to me. I was dragged along to most of the exhibitions, the shopping forays with her friend Vera, and to whatever functions Auntie Mame thought would be Suitable, Stimulating, or Enlightening for a child of ten. That covered a wide range . . .

A hit stage play, a hit movie, a hit musical, and a movie—not exactly a hit—of the musical proved Auntie Mame's durability over the years, with a parade of Mames that included Rosalind Russell, Greer Garson, Bea Lillie, Angela Lansbury, and Lucille Ball. It seems that every actress of a certain age played or wanted to play Auntie Mame. And at one time or another virtually all of us have wished that we had a real Auntie Mame in our lives.

Novels such as *Auntie Mame, Little Me,* and *Genius* have made Tanner a modern American counterpart to such revered British wits as P. G. Wodehouse, Ronald Firbank, and Evelyn Waugh. Tanner was really the first American writer to popularize High Camp, and to introduce that elusive esthetic into mainstream fiction. Funk and Wagnalls defines *camp* as "a comical style or quality typically perceived in banal, flamboyant, or patently artificial gestures, appearances, literary works, etc., that intentionally or unwittingly seem to parody themselves." Although the term made its way through theatrical and homosexual enclaves as early as the 1930s, it wasn't until the mid-1960s that it became common currency. In her pioneering 1964

Partisan Review essay, "Notes on Camp," Susan Sontag wrote: "The whole point of camp is to dethrone the serious." And nobody dethroned the serious like Tanner. The man had a keen way with a social scalpel. He used camp to puncture the pretensions of the Ozzie and Harriet era.

Tanner was one of the last and best practitioners of a literary genre that is now virtually extinct: the light comic novel. In the age of the Internet, cable TV, and the VCR, literature has been freighted with heavy baggage it was not always meant to assume. Throughout the first two-thirds of the century, American novelists such as Thorne Smith, Cornelia Otis Skinner, Max Shulman, Anita Loos, and Patrick Dennis delighted hordes of readers with novels designed only to entertain— and perhaps satirize a social stratum or two. Tanner never really took his own work seriously; he attributed his success mainly to the huge numbers of travelers and invalids who devoured his books. "They seem to be constant companions to the bedpan and the steamer basket," he playfully confessed.

And yet Tanner continues to influence new generations of writers. Feminist commentator Camille Paglia told the *New York Times* that *Auntie Mame* was her Bible: "I read it periodically. I consider it one of the greatest books of my life. . . . I have no respect whatsoever for what is called the serious novel of the postwar era. This book, on the other hand, has a kind of magic insight into sex and gender and society in the period since World War II." Novelist, screenwriter, and Obie-winning playwright Paul Rudnick (*Jeffrey, In and Out*) is a longtime fan of Tanner's work. "He was like Cole Porter," says Rudnick, "in that he was one of the first writers who had a camp sophistication that crossed over. That probably was not something he intended. He simply wrote about what he loved. That pleasure became infectious, and the world responded. I think sometimes he's either dismissed or merely enjoyed because his books are so purely entertaining, but they're also major social history. You could really create a time line from Edith Wharton through Patrick Dennis to Tom Wolfe. If you want to get *really* pretentious about it, you could go all the way back to Molière. They were people who were fascinated by the social mores of their time, and they were excellent reporters. Patrick Dennis really makes you feel sometimes that you're eavesdropping or reading someone's diary, or opening someone else's mail. And there's nothing more delicious than that! It's literature that attains the pleasure of gossip."

Brilliant, quirky, and utterly charismatic, Tanner was as much an eccentric as Auntie Mame herself. Although both Tanner and his books were uproariously funny, and he was beloved by those close to him, his life was marked by an underpinning of frustration and melancholy. "You know, he was really a tragic clown," said his widow, Louise. Ultimately, Tanner was forced to turn his uncompromising insight onto himself.

Nearly thirty years have passed since Pat Tanner walked away from his typewriter for good. As we move further and further away from his era, it's becoming clear that his legacy risks being forgotten or even ignored. The man and his work are badly in need of rescue.

PART ONE

Edward Everett
("Pat") Tanner III,
aged 4 (1925)

ONE

Kid Stuff

Chicago's leafy, peaceful, upper-middle-class suburb of Evanston, Illinois, forms the backdrop for the opening scene of the novel *Love and Mrs. Sargent* by Virginia Rowans. In 1961, when the book was published, Ms. Rowans had already written three other novels. Her alter ego, Patrick Dennis, had written four, including the runaway bestseller *Auntie Mame*. Neither Ms. Rowans nor Mr. Dennis ever actually existed, but together they formed the pseudonymous literary persona of Evanston's own Edward Everett Tanner III, known to his friends simply as Pat.

Evanston today looks much the way it did when Pat Tanner was growing up there in the 1920s and 1930s. Its compact downtown borders the southern edge of Northwestern University, which still retains its Gothic-spired, halls-of-Ivy design. The broad, shady streets of the residential districts are lined with two-story Victorians, low-slung Prairie School bungalows, and opulent mansions built by trade barons at the end of the last century. The town exudes a quiet, comfortable feeling that inspires nostalgia: it's a bit like the setting of a Booth Tarkington novel, or an MGM backlot set for an Andy Hardy movie.

The entire east side of the 1500 block of Asbury Avenue, between Lake and Davis Streets, was unfortunately demolished in the early 1960s by the Methodist Church for a low-rise office complex, but the west side of the street has changed little over the past eighty years. At 1574 Asbury Avenue, a vaguely Prairie-style two-story house still stands, although it has recently suffered an ignominious frosting of gray stucco. There is no plaque on the house to mark it as the childhood home of the author of *Auntie Mame*.

This comfortable, upper-middle-class residence had a picture window fronting the street and a large solarium in the rear. On the side was a garage, a late-1920s addition, with space for two cars. Inside the house, everything was smartly upholstered in black sateen with brilliant turquoise welting, the result of a stylishness that always came naturally to Pat's mother, Florence. Although she had been born and raised in the much smaller town of Ottawa, Illinois, sixty miles southwest of Chicago, Florence Thacker had always been known for vast quantities of chic and charm that made her a hit in Chicago social circles. "She could charm the birds right off the trees," Pat often said of her.

Florence was one of three women in the house at 1574 Asbury Avenue. There were also Pat's sister, Barbara, born ten years before him, and his grandmother, Samantha Thacker, Florence's mother, who doted on him. Another lady known for her charm, Samantha was already a bit senile by the time Pat was born, and she got progressively dottier. Young Pat quickly learned how to take full advantage of Grandma's increasing memory loss. One day when she took ten-year-old Pat and a group of his friends into the Loop for a matinee, Pat convinced her upon exiting that they had not yet gone inside and seen the show. He then steered her and his pals straight into the Rivoli burlesque house next door, where they all happily spent the rest of the afternoon enjoying a lengthy anatomy lesson. Grandma never knew the difference.

The women in Pat's house adored him, and his sister, Barbara, became his best friend. But Edward Everett Tanner Jr. was clearly displeased by his son. He had been hoping for something quite different. Imposing, athletic, and decidedly masculine, Edward Tanner wanted a son in his own image and never ceased to remind Pat of that fact.

Born into a prominent family in Buffalo—his uncle Alonzo Tanner had been Grover Cleveland's law partner—Edward Tanner II grew up in a household with close ties to the nascent Christian Science movement. His mother, Mary Williams Tanner, was one of the best friends of Christian Science founder Mary Baker Eddy. Pat would often mention what a frequent guest Mary Baker Eddy had been in Mary Tanner's home—especially whenever Eddy was hiding out while recuperating from clandestine medical treatments. "I think that might have contributed to Pat's contempt for religion," Pat's widow, Louise, once said with a note of dryness. Mary Williams Tanner eventually succumbed to cancer when she refused all medical care. Pat described his paternal grandmother as an individual "whose only redeeming feature was that she was a Democrat."

Once grown-up, Edward left Buffalo and worked his way into the Midwest. In Ottawa, Illinois, he met Florence Thacker at a dance at the boat club. Although a farming community, Ottawa had a rigid class system, and the local boat club was the equivalent of a yacht club anywhere else. Florence had a young daughter, Barbara, by a marriage that had ended in a divorce—a rarity in that time and place. However, this did not deter Edward from proposing to Florence and accepting young Barbara as his own daughter. Edward would prove a better father to Barbara than to Pat—he did not carry the same expectations for her—and Barbara adored her new daddy. As far as she was concerned, Edward would always be her real father.

The family moved to Evanston, and Edward became a successful Chicago commodities dealer. He dealt in futures and commodities and maintained a seat on the Board of Trade until the Great Depression tightened its grip in 1932. During World War I, he had distinguished himself as a pilot and a flying instructor. Well into adulthood, he kept up his athletic pursuits; he excelled in many sports and was a duck hunter and champion swimmer. In most ways, he was the antithesis of the dreamy, artistic kid he considered himself stuck with for a son. Pat was decidedly *not* the kind of boy who liked to go out and toss the football around.

Evanston, a bastion of Presbyterianism, had a strict social structure, and the Tanners placed fairly close to the upper crust. Staunch Republicans, they proudly hosted a fund-raiser for Alf Landon when he was running for president. Pat's childhood friends remember Florence as a somewhat society-minded but genuine person, while their image of his father is of a cold, distant, and vaguely threatening man. When it came to parties and the social circuit, however, Ed and Florence Tanner knew how to bring out the flashiest, most entertaining aspects of their personalities. They made a dazzling couple, brimming with charm and wit. Always a popular pair of guests, they knew how to keep a party moving.

The Tanners' sense of humor was always evident in the Christmas cards they chose to send. After the 1929 stock market crash, they mailed out their season's greetings on canceled stock certificates. By the time Pat was in his teens, he was designing the Tanner family Christmas cards in full color and writing the Tanner-specific greetings in pithy doggerel. (Pat never liked having religious holidays shoved down his throat. When a high school friend sent him a card reading "Let's put the CHRIST back in Christmas," Pat did up his own card in reply: "Let's put the NO back in Noel!")

Pat always liked to say that he was born in the same bed in the same room in the same Chicago hospital as writer-actress Cornelia Otis Skinner *(Our Hearts Were Young and Gay)*, but in a different year. Skinner was born some twenty years before Pat, who was born May 18, 1921. (Pat became friendly with Ms. Skinner later on, and she was a frequent dinner-party guest of Pat and Louise's years later in New York City. According to Louise, "Pat always thought she was a terrific camp.") Although he was named Edward Everett Tanner III, Pat received his nickname before he was born. When Florence's petite waistline expanded alarmingly with what was obviously going to be a huge and actively kicking baby, Ed Tanner started calling the unborn child Pat after the Irish heavyweight boxer Pat Sweeney. Sweeney was an enormous bruiser, a dirty fighter who was known for kicking his opponents. When Pat Tanner finally entered the world, he weighed in at a full eleven pounds.

From the very beginning, Pat seemed fascinated with the adults who surrounded him and was constantly observing situations and eavesdropping on gossipy conversations that would eventually find their way into his books. "And did you know she's having an affair with her doorman?" Florence would be whispering to a neighbor while five-year-old Pat would be petting the dog and taking it all in. Before long he was learning how to shock, *épater les bourgeois*, a pastime with which he would amuse himself all his life. As early as his grade-school years, he had a favorite morning ritual: He would sit in the picture window at the front of his house reading *Ballyhoo*, the 1920s equivalent to *Playboy*. Once he was certain that all of his classmates had taken shocked notice of him on their way to Dewey Elementary School, he'd finally leave the house and be in his classroom at 9 A.M. sharp with a sly grin on his face.

Meanwhile, Pat was developing a fascination for all things theatrical. His best childhood buddy was Gordon Muchow, a boy of the same age who lived around the corner. Gordon was also stagestruck, and he and Pat used to dress up in costumes whenever they could and stage backyard extravaganzas. Soon Pat put up a theater in his basement, replete with primitive lighting and sheets for curtains, and he and Gordon would put on skits that Pat wrote. Other kids in the neighborhood always got recruited for the casts. On one occasion Pat and Gordon collaborated on a play that they called *The Prince Who Found Happiness*. Pat directed and Gordon was the star. For the two of them, it was quite a production, and they wanted to perform it for a bigger audience. When Health Day came around at Dewey Elementary School, it was the perfect opportunity to stage the show there. Pat made the simple addition of one final line for the King: "And now, we will all go have a feast of green vegetables!" And that, of course, made the production an appropriate entertainment for Health Day.

It wasn't the only time that Pat and Gordon performed at school. When they were both ten, they did an Apache dance, with Gordon dressed as a French streetwalker and the much taller Pat as a *maquereau* tossing him around the Dewey Elementary School auditorium. Saturday afternoons, the two friends would often go down to the library to read the theater magazines. Sooner or later, Gordon would usually run off to play baseball with the rest of the neighborhood boys, but Pat always declined. "I kind of felt sorry that he didn't get involved in that more," says Gordon, "but it didn't bother him at all. I'd be with him, and the other guys would say, 'Come on, we're getting up a game,' and I'd go over, and he'd go off by himself and do something on his own." According to Gordon, Pat's lack of interest in athletics never caused him to be bullied or ostracized. He was well liked and accepted by everyone. "But," Gordon points out, "when he walked, he kind of rose up on his toes, and some of the guys would kid him about that. He walked that way, and I walked sort of like a duck—you know, flat-footed. I imagine the two of us walking down the street looked kind of funny."

The two boys liked nothing better than the chance to dress up in costumes and act out various characters. In a 1931 snapshot the two ten-year-olds are pursuing their favorite activity: Gordon Muchow is wearing a cowboy outfit and imitating Tom Mix, while Pat, who towers over him, is garbed in an evening gown, posing as a pigeon-breasted society dowager in supreme Margaret Dumont style.

Gordon had a clubhouse in his backyard where he used to build model airplanes and play Ping-Pong. When Pat would come over, he wouldn't join in with the model-airplane building or at Ping-Pong, but he kept Gordon and the other neighborhood kids amused with a constant stream of stand-up comedy and movie-star impersonations. "I think he always had a great empathy with women; a great understanding and a great interest in women," says Gordon. "This sensitivity to the female viewpoint was almost everywhere, in almost everything that he did in those skits of ours. And he was awfully good at it. He would repeat a performance that he'd just seen in a movie or a play. My dad loved him. He'd come over to the house, and my dad would always encourage him to put on these skits for us. I remember that Pat was *always* impressed by the female parts. He'd imitate the way an actress entered a nightclub, for example. The one that really sticks in my mind was an imitation of a telephone operator at a switchboard. That came from a movie. It was one of my dad's favorites; he'd always ask for it." Twenty-five years later, it would turn into a memorable moment in both the novel and the play of *Auntie Mame*.

Pat and Gordon often went to see the theater productions of the summer school of nearby Northwestern University. Northwestern was then and remains one of the most prestigious theater schools in the country. For both boys, that was a formative experience; they felt lucky to have such good theater so close to their front door. By the time they were eleven, Pat and Gordon were taking the el into the Loop and spending the day seeing one movie after another, an endless parade of early talkies in magical movie palaces like the Oriental and the United Artists and the Chicago.

As the Busby Berkeley era of movie musicals took hold, a tap-dancing vogue swept the country. Everyone, especially stagestruck children, wanted to take tap-dancing lessons. One out-of-work dancer, hit hard by the Depression, began giving tap lessons after school to the students at Dewey Elementary for a quarter apiece, and Pat and Gordon signed right up. Not every child had a quarter to spare, but the

teacher would usually let everyone stick around and take lessons anyway. Sometimes Pat would even come up with a quarter for a kid who
couldn't afford it. "Pat had more money than I did," says Muchow, "and
he was very generous with it. We liked malted milks and things like
that, and if I didn't have the money, he'd always buy one for me. He got
a bike—oh, a wonderful bicycle. And when we entered seventh grade,
it was a new school a couple of miles away. He used to give me a ride
to school every morning, with me sitting on the handlebars of his bike.
He was always very, very nice. To everybody."

Often when Pat came to visit Gordon, Gordon's sister Phyllis would
be doing household chores such as washing the dishes or scrubbing
floors. Before long, Pat had nicknamed her Cindy, for Cinderella. He
enjoyed chatting with Phyllis and going over her movie-star scrapbooks
with her. "We always adored him because he was so much fun and so
smart; very up-to-the-minute on everything," Phyllis says, laughing,
today. "He even gave me tips on how to wear my eyeliner!"

Dispensing beauty advice was the kind of behavior that caused
some of Pat's adult neighbors to refer to him as effeminate. His young
friends, however, weren't as quick to label him. Instead, they tended to
think of him as grown-up, sophisticated, and artistic. They perceived
him as one of their own, if perhaps a bit of an oddball. And a bit of a
schoolmarm: even as a boy, he insisted on using somewhat florid English and didn't hesitate to correct anyone who trifled with the language.
"You don't *loan* things, you *lend* them. *Loan* is a noun, not a verb."

"Every single day, as long as I knew him, it was a play," says David
Peterson, who was a close friend of Pat's from kindergarten days. "He
woke up in the morning and said, 'This is what we'll be today.' He loved
to surprise people, shock people, create a situation for himself that
others could join. A neat guy. He *was* the personification of Mame.
Delightful, carefree, didn't hurt anybody, but didn't want to be run-of-
the-mill either. He loved doing the oddball kind of thing. There were
about ten of us who started kindergarten together and remained
friends through high school. We had a wonderful, wonderful, fun
childhood."

Pat indeed made sure he had plenty of good times outside the
house. What happened *inside* was something he rarely discussed. "He

didn't speak of his family often," explains Peterson. "He never discussed his problems with his father. His life was too much make-believe, and that was too serious."

Painfully, cruelly serious. The older Pat got, and the more pronounced his interests and personality became, the less Ed liked him. Ed started calling his son a "pansy."

Pat's childhood friends remember his mother with great fondness as charming, sophisticated, and friendly. A volunteer librarian at Dewey Elementary School, Florence got to know many of them. Gordon Muchow particularly liked her. "She let us have the run of the house," he says. "We could do whatever we wanted; if we needed more sheets for curtains for the basement theater, she'd let us have them." (Another friend, however, remembers Pat's father blowing up at Pat when he asked for ten dollars' worth of lighting equipment for the theater.)

"My grandmother Florence did a lot for people," says Patrick's niece Susan, now Sister Joanna Hastings of the Dominican Sisters of the Perpetual Rosary in Milwaukee. "She always welcomed new neighbors by taking food over to their homes the day they moved in, so they wouldn't have to cook. She even did that when they moved to the Gold Coast. And she was a hospital volunteer. During the First World War she drove an ambulance for a Chicago hospital, and she liked it so much that the hospital kept her on as a volunteer nurse. She continued to do that during the Second World War, and after. When I had my tonsils out, there she was at my bedside, working at the hospital in her gray uniform."

The Tanners weathered the first few years of the Great Depression fairly well, but by 1932, Ed had a huge cash flow problem. He had generously lent large sums of money to friends and colleagues who had been much harder hit by the Depression than he. Few of his friends were able to repay him, and he eventually spent all of his operating capital bailing them out. To repay his own debts and break even, he was forced to sell his seat on the Chicago Board of Trade. The Tanners' flashy lifestyle—which included a sixteen-cylinder Cadillac with chauffeur—had to change.

Ed was able to keep the house, but expenses had to be reined in. He found work in property appraisals, but his reduced circumstances started taking an emotional toll. Ed and Florence had always been party people who enjoyed a good drink—Roaring Twenties types out of an F. Scott Fitzgerald novel—but in 1932 Ed began drinking heavily, a habit that would continue the rest of his life. It could not have been easy on the rest of the family. Fortunately, Pat had allies in his mother and his older sister. Barbara had been an only child for the first ten years of her life and was thrilled when Pat was born. She adored Pat from the moment he came into the world, and as Pat grew older, he would always refer to his sister as his best friend. Pat looked up to Barbara; she was one of the few people whose word meant something to him. But by 1935, Barbara had married and moved out, leaving Pat and Florence to deal with Ed's drinking bouts alone.

TWO

Growing Pains

Pat and Florence shared a sneaky, subversive sense of humor that helped them cope with Ed's alcohol abuse. The two devised some clever ways of getting back at him.

One night Ed came home thoroughly soused after going swimming at the Chicago Athletic Club. He walked in the door, threw himself on the sofa, and promptly passed out. It had already happened too many times, and Pat and Florence were getting sick of it. "Let's do something to make him sorry he did this," said Florence. They promptly got out a bottle of nail polish and painted all of his toenails bright red.

When Ed finally came to, he faced quite a surprise. For days afterward, Florence and Pat would innocently ask him, "Haven't you been swimming today?" And Ed would mumble, "Uh, no, I didn't feel like it." Of course he had no idea how the nail polish had got on his feet in the first place, nor how to get rid of it.

But Ed's drinking, and his sullen resentment of Pat, were not the only problems Pat and Florence had to face. Not until Pat was ten did he find out his mother had been married before, and that his beloved Barbara was really his half-sister. At fifteen, Pat learned a nastier family secret: his father had been keeping a mistress for years and had no intention of terminating the relationship. The news undoubtedly soured his feelings toward his father that much more. Florence was living with this burden of knowledge as well, which could not have been easy on Pat. As the years went by, Florence would develop a drinking problem of her own. It's not at all surprising that Pat eventually followed suit.

There were still good times to be had outside the house, and Pat did his best to forget his unhappy home life and enjoy his friends. By playing the court jester, he was able to create an atmosphere of fun around himself that counteracted the gloom he endured at 1574 Asbury Avenue. Pat developed a pattern he would repeat throughout his life: he used his humor and sophistication as a shield, rarely allowing others to break through into his more guarded zones. He had no problems discussing his mother with his friends; he was fond of her and loved her sense of humor. But his father was a subject he almost never brought up.

Pat was now growing up in a world of cotillions and "fortnightlies"—formal dances for teenagers held biweekly at the Evanston Women's Club. Under the hawkeyed supervision of one Miss Jessie Pocock, young Evanston boys in suits and white gloves waltzed with the town's subdebs while their parents watched from a balcony and Miss Jessie circulated, instructing boys to go over and invite the wallflowers to dance. Pat, a good dancer and adept conversationalist, was quite popular with the young ladies of the cotillion.

Mildred B. Jones Mathers met Pat at an eighth-grade cotillion when they were both twelve. They formed a close friendship and didn't lose touch until they were in their forties. "We were like two comedians," she says. "We played off each other's lines. I think Pat kept himself this way on purpose as a defense mechanism, so people wouldn't ask questions, so that everybody would always be happy and like him and he'd like them. He was always making jokes and so was I; I think I understood what he was doing, so I never broke the barrier and he didn't either. But there had to have been troubles in his life when he was young for him to be the way he was. You read people, and you know when they're hurt, and when they're not like other people. You knew the minute you met Pat that he was looking for friends and that he did not have that support at home. He was fearful and looking for acceptance. He was like a puppy. He wanted you to love him; he wanted you to make a fuss over him."

"I wonder," says one friend who prefers to remain anonymous, "whether Pat wasn't concealing his own sexual desires from himself. These days, that may be hard for young people to imagine. But the internalization of the fear and disgrace that existed at that time—and even today, I'm sure—well, there was really no place for a person to turn. And with a father like his—my God. I didn't know the father very well, but just between us, I never liked him. He was a ramrod, a man who would have had no sympathy at all for what he would have regarded as a terrible thing. He would have been part of the new right-wing Republican cause if he were alive today. Pat generally couldn't stand him." Ed Tanner was known to spout his bigoted opinions quite freely, which may have contributed to turning Pat into a staunchly liberal Democrat. Years later, Pat would use him as the model for two of his most flagrantly prejudiced characters: Mr. Upson in *Auntie Mame* and the reactionary table guest in *Guestward Ho!*

As Pat entered adolescence, his love of the theater grew stronger and became a mainstay for him. He was particularly fascinated with scenic design and began thinking that he wanted to make it his life's work.

As a teenager, Pat joined the Boy Scouts, which may seem like an odd step for a kid who was anything *but* the all-American boy. However, skits and playlets made up a huge part of the activities of Evanston's Troop 5 and gave Pat a chance to write, design, and act. Webster Jones, one of the boys in the troop, became friendly with him. "He was utterly unlike anyone else I knew," says Jones, "and he was the life of any party he went to. Pat was three grades ahead of me in school; I used to see him walking to school, bobbing up and down. But the first time I really got to know him was in the Boy Scout troop at the Episcopal church called St. Mark's. When I got in the troop, Pat was treasurer. Then he quit the troop within a year. That was in 1936. Even after he got out of the troop, he was very helpful in aiding us on plays. Pat would draw the set designs for us and help us with makeup and costumes. One time I needed a skit for the patrol. I went over to his house and said, 'Pat, I need a skit for next week.' He sat down at the typewriter and typed this thing right out."

Here's an excerpt from that example of Pat's juvenilia, dated 1937:

STATION ANNOUNCER: Ladies and gentlemen, this is station PDQ, the mighty voice of the Black and Blue network. And now we present the Brown Brothers Hour.

MUSIC IS HEARD ("Flat Foot Floogie")

PROGRAM ANNOUNCER: Good evening, ladies and gentlemen. The Brown Brothers, makers of Brown Brothers Cough Drops in six delicious flavors—strawberry, raspberry, cherry, orange, lemon and *tutti frutti*—present The March of Crime, or, A Year With Troop Five. Remember, if you ever have a splitting headache, a splitting cough, or a splitting cold, just split a dime and buy a box of Brown Brothers Cough Drops. Remember, they aren't Brown Brothers without the long red beards on the box. Brown Brothers' delicious drops are good for man or beast. They have been known to cure athlete's foot, neuralgia, heartburn, constipation, stiff muscles, dandruff, falling hair, tired eyes, barber's itch, that sluggish feeling, hangover, stomach ulcers, brain tumors, cancer and, er, ah, oh yes—coughs and colds. Just listen to one of the letters which we have received from one of our thousands of enthusiastic users: "Gentlemen: We represent Miss Minnie Klotz of Sprinkle, Indiana. After taking your lemon drops Miss Klotz was confined to the hospital"—oh, pardon me, wrong letter. Here it is: "Dear Brown Brothers, Your cough drops have made my life a paradise. Thank you for the generous check you sent me. Sincerely, Isabella Gaulstone."

That was one of the tamer skits. A bit more risqué was the one he wrote for another Scout troop at the Evanston YMCA. One of its lines, spoken by an eleven-year-old boy in front of an audience full of parents, was "I'd like to introduce Mr. and Mrs. Bates and their little son Master Bates."

Pat evidently enjoyed his years as a Boy Scout. His theatrical talents kept him popular and in demand. He was also clearly fascinated with observing the activities of his troop's scoutmaster, who was molesting several of the boys. Those who were molested, and those who were aware of what was going on, apparently kept quiet about it. "Most of us in the troop did not realize M——e was a homosexual," says Webster Jones. "I'm sure that M——e affected some of the Scouts in that troop. He liked to take three or four of us to the movies on a Friday or Saturday night. He just liked to have us around, but I never saw him misbehave on any of these outings."

One boy who was "affected" by the scoutmaster was John Mock, now a psychotherapist in Philadelphia. Mock, who is openly gay, was aware of his own orientation at that time and says, "M——e made a pass at me, and we did have one encounter when I was still a Scout, about thirteen or fourteen. I found him repulsive; I found his collection of semen in a milk bottle gross. M——e got the message; my comment when he showed me this trophy was 'how interesting' or something like that, but I beat a hasty retreat and never let him get close to me again. Unfortunately he was very good at making inroads on several other members of the Scout troop who were my age or a little younger. He was able to seduce them far better than I was. I was still very inhibited. So far as I know, there was never any scandal, he was never caught, and he continued being scoutmaster."

Whether the scoutmaster ever made Pat one of his conquests will never be known, but Dr. Mock strongly feels that no sexual encounters ever took place between Pat and the scoutmaster. "First of all," he says, "I don't think Pat would have been his type. And I'm sure Pat saw through him. I would be inclined to think that Pat would have spurned him; their personalities were so different."

Mock, who has recently been writing his memoirs, was impressed enough by Pat to include lengthy passages on him. Here is one in which he paints a detailed picture of the teenaged Pat that delineates the almost unnerving insight that would make Pat such a successful writer and social observer:

Troop 5 did provide me a social life. I mingled congenially, but with a certain dissembling, for my fellow Scouts seemed ordinary and only intermittently stimulating. There was one notable exception: Pat. He was, without question, one of the most singular individuals I've ever encountered. "Encountered" because Pat was difficult to know, and an intriguing enigma. He was a lucid, eccentric figure in the troop, prowling catlike on the perimeter. His being there at all was puzzling, as if he hied from some alien realm with a purpose that was always obscure. Not once did he allow me into his mysterious world, past or present. He was more pressingly curious about me, more adept at subtle probing. And within prudently prescribed limits, I was more open. The fact that Pat could plug deeply into my personality, discern hidden places of which I was unaware, influencing me to move in uncharacteristic directions, made him both a fascinating and unsettling companion. His face was pleasant but unremarkable at that time, without distinctive features. He was tall, willowy, and deceptively thin, for his body had a softness, a reptilian absence of bony definition, that exuded a peculiar, genderless physicality I found faintly repellent. Pat had an idiosyncratic brilliance, a wry perspective of the passing scene, a quirky wit. In conversation he was often vague and preoccupied, as if making contact with only a fraction of his consciousness, while the remainder was away on another plane. His eccentric talents were awesome and disconcerting, especially his exceptional powers of observation and extraordinary recall. A paradoxical spirit amongst the ho-hum conservatism of Troop 5, Pat was urbane, ironic, insidiously iconoclastic, and fecund with imaginative seditions for routing the prevailing stodginess.

The Tanners frequently took summer trips to visit Florence's family two hours away in Ottawa, Illinois. Often Pat would stay for a month or two on the farm that his uncle owned. The city mouse always seemed to be enjoying himself, but he definitely did things his own way. Pat's uncle expected him to do some work while he was at the farm, but Pat was decidedly not interested. He preferred to spend his time at the farm with his aunt Neida, who had majored in theater at Northwestern University and shared his interests. She was active in her church drama group, and Pat loved helping her put on productions. He was constantly sketching costume and set designs and writing new skits for the church. Soon the entire community knew him; he rapidly became a young local celebrity. Neighbors would often spot him behind the barn directing his cousins and their pals in rehearsals of his latest skits. When the locals would see the skits at church, many of them realized that they had served as inspiration for some of Pat's characters.

Tom Godfrey, one of Pat's many Ottawa cousins, stayed in close touch with Pat till the end of Pat's life. "He was just this exotic guy," says Tom. "Because he was in the country, he would insist on going barefoot. He'd stumble through the stubble fields after the grain was cut and get his feet all slashed up. My uncle would raise hell with him, but he did what he did. And he was just enough older that he had all kinds of fascinating things he would show us. Just what kind of things? Well, we won't go into that. . . . But he was very artistic; very theatrical; always lots of fun."

In 1934, Pat became a freshman at Evanston Township High School. Evanston Township is considered one of the country's best public high schools; it regularly places in the top 5 percent. Pat, however, would always struggle with his studies; his grades were rarely outstanding, and he had particular difficulty with math. His English scores, not surprisingly, were considerably higher. What meant the most to him, though, was the chance to join the drama club, immerse himself in theater, and meet plenty of other kids who shared his great love. Pat was fortunate to find a new group of stagestruck friends, because his childhood buddy, Gordon Muchow, was losing interest in the theater and drifting more toward scientific pursuits.

Evanston Township High School benefited from being in such close proximity to Northwestern University. The two schools had a kind of lend-lease program under which student teachers doing their training at Northwestern were allowed to teach some classes at Evanston Township. Stacy Keach Sr. was one of these; he took the reins of the school's drama department. Keach was an enormously inspiring mentor to his students at Evanston Township, who still speak glowingly of him and his influence after all these years. Pat was especially thrilled by the environment that Keach created and threw himself into acting, designing, writing, and even publicity. "Pat was good in designing," says Katie Stockbridge Kelley, who was also in the drama club. "He *wasn't* much of a carpenter or electrician, as I recall. But he kept us in stitches as *we* did it. He was always entertaining."

Katie's mother had been an actress; she had even understudied Maude Adams in James M. Barrie's *The Little Minister*. An elderly retired woman who had been Fannie Brice's wardrobe mistress also lived at the house as a boarder. So the Stockbridge home was sympathetic to Katie and all of her drama club friends, including Pat. Pat spent many hours there during his high school years rehearsing shows and devouring all the theater lore he could. As usual, he provided plenty of entertainment. "Pat would do off-the-cuff monologues and soliloquies," says Katie, "right off the top of his head. Once he had the audience with him, they just thought it was wonderful. He had an unlimited source of subjects. The man was *smart,* way beyond his age."

Pat and his drama club buddies soon became involved in the children's theater program at Northwestern University. High school drama students who showed promise were often cast in the plays or allowed to work backstage. For the Evanston Township kids, it was a huge thrill as well as a chance to get early professional experience. Pat was cast in several roles, including the Mad Hatter in *Alice in Wonderland.* He became completely enraptured and caught up in the theater at Northwestern and gave it more than anybody expected.

He also started writing for the school paper. For the most part, he contributed to "Judy," the regular humor column, which was named after Punch's wife. Most of what he wrote centered on the students and teachers at Evanston Township, although occasionally his jokes got a bit risqué and had to be cut. He also did a few theater reviews for the paper. Here are his thoughts on the pre-Broadway tryout of the Cole Porter musical *You Never Know* from 1938:

You Never Know struck me as neither very good nor very bad. Based on *Candlelight,* a passé comedy of bad manners, Cole Porter's latest opus brings to Chicago such stars as Clifton Webb, Lupe Velez (with her black tresses stained copper), naive Toby Wing, Rex O'Malley and, last but not least, leather-lunged Libby Holman Reynolds, whose chief duties are moaning two torch songs, wearing expensive clothes, being on stage for the finale and backing the production with part of her Smith Reynolds Tobacco fortune.

The story deals with Gaston (Clifton Webb), a humble valet who disguises himself as his master, and who becomes entangled with fiery Lupe Velez, the personal maid who is masquerading as her mistress. The rest is history.

The music, none of which can be played on the radio until *You Never Know* opens in New York City next fall, is up to the usual Cole "Night and Day" Porter standard. The best tunes are "Candlelight," "You Never Know" and "Maria."

The dancing is divided among Clifton Webb, whose graceful flitting is reminiscent of a cross between Gregory Whitson and

Pavlova, a second-rate tap dancer called April, and six glorified chorus boys known as "The Debonairs." The only sensational routine appears in the Gendarme number at the first [scene] of the second act.

Hollywood's contributions seem to be the real stars of the show. Toby (most photographed girl in the movies) Wing, as Ida Courtney, the beautiful and not-so-dumb blonde, is superb, while Senorita Velez carries the rest of the play. Indeed, if it were not for Lupe, who girates [sic] through two hours of rollicking horse-play and whose sidesplitting impersonations of Katherine [sic] Hepburn, Simone Simon, Shirley Temple, Gloria Swanson and exotic Dolores Del Rio bring down the house, *You Never Know* would be a dull musical at its worst.

Time proved the seventeen-year-old Pat right on this one. Cole Porter himself referred to *You Never Know* as the worst production he had ever been associated with, and the show ran a disappointing seventy-eight performances on Broadway.

When not studying or rehearsing, Pat spent his free time with his drama club chums. It was the height of the swing era, and Pat and his pals loved to dance. He would meet with friends like David Peterson and Katie Kelley after school, and they would dance away the afternoon to music on the radio; on weekends everyone would get together for dance parties or trips downtown to the Aragon Ballroom. Often on a Friday night, Pat and his friend Anne Noggle would take the elevated into the Loop to a club called Ye Olde Cellar, where a weekly rumba contest took place. The kids had a curfew, so Pat would bring along a large alarm clock and set it on their table. When it went off, they went home. The club's adult patrons thought the two of them were adorable.

Pat and his friends also delighted in giving parties based on specific themes. One of the most elaborate was a circus party for which Pat drew beautiful color posters as decorations. Everyone came dressed as a different circus character—there was a balloon salesman, a ringmaster, a belly dancer. Pat showed up in a pink leotard and handlebar mustache as the Man on the Flying Trapeze. Webster Jones threw a party with a casino theme, and Pat spent days designing even more impressive posters for each game, including roulette, blackjack, and bingo. "We had a floor show," says Webster, "and Annie Noggle and Pat performed. The floor show consisted of a friend of mine on piano and drums, Pat and Annie doing the conga, an opera singer, a magician, and so forth. Pat and Annie led the conga line out the side door, around the yard, and through the front door. My dad said afterwards, 'Never have a party like this again. The house *vibrated!*' "

It all seems terribly innocent now. Pat's gang rarely even tried to get drunk—it was actually frowned upon as a stupid thing to do. If anyone got hold of booze, got crocked, and disgraced himself or smashed up his parents' car, he was basically shunned by the group. Nevertheless, David Peterson's parents were remarkably permissive when it came to parties. Maybe they were certain that David's drama-group friends were basically decent kids. "I had an agreement with them," he explains. "They would go to visit relatives out in Hinsdale, Illinois, and they would leave at noon on Saturday and promise not to come home until three on Sunday. So I could have a big party and tear up the place as much as I wanted, but it had to be back in immaculate condition when they got home. Pat and a few others would stay over and we'd clean house the next morning."

Once David Peterson went to Pat's house for dinner. Afterward, Pat was walking him to the bus stop and decided it was David's turn to give a party again. "All right," said David. "What kind of party shall I give?" Pat suggested a formal tea. He said he'd write up a script for the party and they'd all do a reading. Saturday afternoon came around, and everyone gathered at David's, where, in the backyard at a card table in sweltering summer heat, Pat read a ninety-page play he had written. "He had played hooky from school most of the week in order to type it," says David. "The play was about all of us, ten or fifteen years hence, and it was absolutely hysterical. We all got such a big bang out of it."

Pat claimed to be able to read palms, which made him a hit at every party. He probably learned from a cheap booklet ordered from the Johnson-Smith catalog, but those who had their fortunes told by him said he had great faith in palm-reading and did it with the utmost seriousness. In his memoir, John Mock remembers a local church bazaar for which Pat built an elaborate tent, dressed up as a Gypsy hag (replete with scarves and spangles), and spend an entire day playing seeress. "He was seated cross-legged in the shadowy recesses of the tent," writes Mock, "intoning his revelations in a strange accent vaguely suggestive of some Middle European kingdom, fingers and hands hovering and weaving graceful accompaniment, then suddenly flinging his arms wildly in florid punctuation. A long line stretched outside his makeshift den, for word spread quickly about his arcane flair, his cunningly outrageous patter."

Pat was never known to have gone steady with anyone—of either sex—during his high school years. "I don't think he was ever a boyfriend to anybody," says Millie B. Jones Mathers, "although he talked about girls, and every Christmas he'd give them all lipsticks. He was very attentive and had been brought up with very good manners. In dancing school he'd always hold you just right. He was just a fun person to be with."

Indeed, Pat's physical response to women was far from cold. He developed a particularly deep friendship with Anne Noggle, who was one of his favorite dancing partners. Anne shared Pat's somewhat iconoclastic attitude and flair for the well-timed shock effect. "Pat and I became the closest of friends," says Noggle. "We weren't really boyfriend and girlfriend, but we used to play around a lot when we were kids. He used to say that our dancing was 'a vertical accomplishment of a horizontal desire.' I thought Pat had originated that phrase, but I recently read it somewhere, so maybe it wasn't his own. But when we were dancing, he would say that, and you know, he'd get a little hard-on now and then. He never wore underpants when he was a kid; nothing. I said, 'How can you stand wool pants?' When you danced with him, you knew damn well he didn't wear underwear. He was—right there! And I would tease him. We'd be seated at a table after a dance, and I'd know somebody who was coming by and introduce them. There Pat would be with his erection, and he couldn't get up to greet them because he didn't have any underpants on. Those baggy pants would have stood out like a tent! He'd get so mad at me!"

Anne's mischievous streak definitely matched Pat's. "At parties," she says, "we made a point of going to the bathroom together so we could shock the other people there. So now you know the kind of pranks we pulled off. It was a different world then; we lived in a sort of Ginger Rogers–Fred Astaire world, trying to ignore the poverty and the bad things about that time. And so everything was gaiety and mirth. I mean gaiety in the ordinary sense. You know, the other would cross my mind now and then, and then I would think, 'Absolutely not,' knowing him when we were young. Because I can tell you truthfully that he was attracted to women as well as men."

Toward the end of their high school years, many Evanston boys took part in a rite of passage, a trip to a sleazy dance bar located in a western suburb frequented largely by organized-crime figures. At the bar, male patrons would lean up against a wall while dime-a-dance girls would rub their bodies against them. John Mock, Pat, and several of their acquaintances borrowed a car and made the trip, although Pat was the only one not committed to seeing it through. Mock writes:

> Throughout the drive there he was a dissident element, questioning our foolishness, urging us to reconsider and turn back, the disapproving, clucking monitor of our tense and rapid chatter. His motives for joining us—"I'm just going along for the ride"—were as elusive and eccentric as he himself was. Pat had a penchant for "experience collecting"—within limits. When we clambered out at the club's parking lot, he remained alone in the back seat, wrapped in disdain, to await our return. . . . One trip to the wall was enough for me. I was aching and sore and not even modestly stimulated. Afterwards, in the car, one boy raved about his several encounters. The rest of us, subdued, a bit embarrassed, muttered our agreement: "exciting, amazing, incredible, felt really great!" Obviously, we were all as uncomfortable as hell. Pat's forbidding figure loomed in the back seat. I felt his dark Jovian frown. His muted sniffs and snorts rendered better than any words his lofty black-browed judgment of our juvenile capers.

Pat owned a primitive home recording device that, in that pre-audio-cassette era, utilized three-minute wax discs. Anne Noggle has held on to sixteen discs that she and Pat recorded together during the late 1930s and early 1940s. Some of the discs are popular songs that Pat transcribed off radio broadcasts for dance purposes—numbers like "Perfidia" and "La Cucaracha." Others feature Pat, Anne, and their friends singing, imitating such stars as Marlene Dietrich, Nelson Eddy, and Jeanette MacDonald, and generally cutting up. Several discs are of Anne reciting various versions of a comic monologue, obviously written by Pat, of a blowsy, drunken nightclub chanteuse boring a society swell between sets:

Scotch, Charlie, I'll mix it myself. . . . Oh, hello, Roddy. I'm really stinking tonight. . . . Did you hear me slur on "Je Vous Adore"? And did you hear that nasty man say, "Throw her a fish"? I was simply livid. I tell you, I couldn't have been more furious. Another Scotch, Charlie. Have you got a cigarette or something? I'm so damn mad I could spit. Thanks awfully. Roddy, you're such a man-about-town . . . tell me, do you know Audrey Upjohn? I had lunch with Franny Penny at the Stork Club this afternoon. Franny's such a slut, and I daren't dream about what she must say about me . . . but a half hour with her is positively the equivalent of a college degree. . . . Anyway, she was telling me that Audrey Upjohn has been modeling at Bendel's ever since her father was sent to Sing Sing. She says he borrowed money from his stockholders or something, and that he's so crooked they'll have to *screw* him into his grave. I can just see the society page of the *Times*. Charlie, another Scotch. . . . By the way, darling, did you *see* her doing that exhibition rumba at the Bundle's benefit? I thought she'd swallowed a washing-machine motor . . . and she had on a white jersey job that every shopgirl in town has. I got more applause for my number, that one Gogo St. John wrote for me. It goes, "At night I walk the avenuuue, the city streets are bathed in bluuuue"—Cholly Knickerbocker simply adored it, but that ghastly Walter Winchell said that if my singing didn't improve, walking the avenue would be the only way I could make a dime. . . . Another Scotch, Charlie.

And so on. There's also a solo comedy sketch with Pat in a pinched falsetto portraying the spinsterish leader of a troop of Girl Scouts on a hiking trip in the woods, singing marching songs ("Maids of the Wood, March On!") and cautioning the girls to be careful not to use poison ivy as toilet paper. On another disc, Pat leads a group of friends in a ditty he wrote himself: "Who Put the Snatch on the Lindbergh Baby (Wasn't That a Nasty Thing to Do?)"

Who put the snatch on the Lindbergh baby?
Wasn't that a nasty thing to do?
Little Charles Augie was playing with his doggy.
He didn't do nothin' to you—
Lindy went and flew the ocean.
Is that the proper way to show your devotion?
So, who put the snatch on the Lindbergh baby?
Was it you, you, or you-ou?

Of particular interest are several audio letters from Pat to Anne in which he discusses the skits he's writing for her and the plans he's got in store for the two of them for the weekend. Pat keeps making disparaging references to the sound of his voice, but the voice is in fact quite pleasant—a firm baritone with broad Jimmy Stewart–esque Midwestern vowels. These are probably the only extant recordings of Pat's voice, as he never did television or radio interviews. Talk to those who were close to Pat during his adulthood, and they'll tell you that the voice turned into something quite different as time went by. It became more theatrical, more pointed in tone, and perfect for the utterance of laconic bons mots.

Pat graduated from Evanston Township High School in 1938. By that time, his family's economic picture was improving and the Tanners had been able to give their daughter a beautiful wedding when Barbara married Jack Hastings in 1935. Pat's home life was more stressful with his sister out of the house. He had not made any college plans, and he had to find some legitimate work and a reason to be anywhere but home. The best thing that happened to Pat at that time was Finale Productions, a small business venture on which he embarked with his friends from the Evanston Township High School drama club.

Finale Productions was a group of talented Evanston Township kids who offered local organizations their skills at staging amateur theater. Millie Mathers, Anne Noggle and her sister Mary, and David Peterson were all part of it, as were other friends of Pat's. If a church, school, or theatrical group in the greater-Chicago area wanted to stage a show and didn't know how to go about it, they'd hire Finale and its members would direct, design, and produce the whole show, as long as the organization provided the script and most of the actors. It was meant to be remunerative, but most of the Finale members actually wound up working as volunteers out of their sheer love of theater. It was all good practice for the careers many of them hoped to achieve.

Pat threw himself into the work and loved it. It was another chance to perform and to do the set designing that he hoped would become his profession. He did design most of the sets for Finale Productions—but made sure to leave the hammering and nailing to everyone else. Nobody complained; in fact, everyone else enjoyed the running entertainment Pat provided while *they* built the scenery.

Even though he had outgrown the Boy Scouts, Pat still stayed in close touch with the members of Troop 5 and kept writing skits and designing sets for them. Theater, in all its aspects, remained his chief refuge from the gloom at home, just as it had been during his high school years.

Pat's grandmother Samantha, her brain addled with advanced senility, died in 1939. With Samantha deceased and Barbara married, Florence and Ed now no longer needed a large house. In addition, Ed's financial situation was improving as the country began to rise out of the Depression. Florence and Ed decided to leave Evanston and move with Pat to a magnificent apartment building on Chicago's Gold Coast at 3202 Lakeshore Drive. The Tanners would now be living in high style on the ritziest street in town.

THREE

"A Great Big Town on a Great Big Lake"

A chapter of Pat's 1966 novel *Tony* is set in an elegant Georgian apartment building known as Lochby Court, located on Chicago's Lakeshore Drive. Here is how Pat described it:

> The trip up the Drive from the top of the bus was impressive, with Lake Michigan coldly gray pounding against the shore to my right, the massive apartment buildings, equally cold and gray to my left. Eventually the driver called out "Belmont!" and I disembarked. There, spread out before me, was Lochby Court in all its eighteenth-century splendor and there, too, standing at one of the gate posts was the groom I had seen in the photograph, impressive in his bottle green tailcoat and white buckskin breeches. As I crossed the street a woman came out of the front door swathed in brown fur. Was it mink? Was it sable? "Do you think you can get me a taxi, Henry?"

Lochby Court was modeled on 3202 Lakeshore Drive. The large, luxurious red-brick building was also home to Chicago's ex-mayor Thompson. Directly across the harbor from Lincoln Park, it boasted a large circular driveway in front and a huge garden in back with a playground for children, as well as lawns and flowerbeds that extended all the way to the end of the block. With all that space, and at only three stories, 3202 Lakeshore Drive almost inevitably fell prey to the wrecking ball in the early 1960s and was replaced by a generically hideous high-rise.

The Tanners' new living quarters were elegant, with a long entrance hall, living room, octagonal dining room, two bedrooms, and two bathrooms. Evanston was now a twenty-minute el ride away, and although Pat enjoyed being nearer to the theaters and movie palaces of the Loop, he remained as close as ever to his friends in the old neighborhood. His social life with them continued as if he'd never moved, and he regularly took the el out to visit and to attend the weekend parties that he loved. He also remained an active member of Finale Productions.

Pat and Anne Noggle stayed especially close, and they continued to spend many nights out on the town dancing. "I remember clearly the night we went to the Pump Room," she says. "He had five dollars, which was a lot then, but not enough for the Pump Room. Pat could not get the family car that night, and I had an old Model A Ford. By that time they'd moved to Chicago. Pat came out to Evanston on the elevated to get me, and he had his tuxedo with him, but he didn't want to wear it on the elevated. He confessed later that he changed his clothes in Evanston after he got off the el! He went into an apartment building and down the back stairway, where it was really dark, and he changed into his tuxedo there. He confessed all of this to me later. He said he wouldn't have been caught dead in that elevated in a tuxedo!

"So we drove downtown in my Model A, and we drove up to the Pump Room. He pulled the car over to the curb, got out, opened my door, handed the keys to the attendant, and said, 'Please park the car.' And as we went in, I said to him, 'Pat, they won't know how to work the spark!' And he said, 'Never mind!' and we just went on in! Xavier Cugat was playing there. We sat at the bar and had a Coke and nursed it all evening and danced. It was really fun. We did a lot of fun things."

Anne Noggle also remembers a friendship they formed with a young artist couple in Chicago: "We met them when they were painting murals up high on a wall. We liked them right off. We would talk to them, and they'd hardly get any work done, we'd talk so much. They lived on the North Side of Chicago; didn't have much money, but they were good artists. We'd go there, and while they painted things, we would lie on the floor, and I'd take all the female roles, and he'd take all the male roles, and we read everything of Noël Coward and George

Bernard Shaw. It was just wonderful. I've often yearned to do that sort of thing as a grown-up. What a nice thing it is to read those plays."

Pat frequently visited his sister and her family—her husband, Jack, and her two young daughters, Susan and Patty. "I always looked up to my uncle Pat," says Susan (now Sister Joanna Hastings). "One afternoon when Patty and I were very young children, and he was about nineteen, he came to stay with us for a few hours while my parents went out. He was dressed to go to a dance later that evening, and I remember how elegant he looked as he came striding down the block toward us, with his coat flapping in the wind. He was to take us and leave us with the neighbors when he was ready to leave. We didn't want him to go; we grabbed his thumbs and hung on to him and *pleaded* with him to stay. I don't remember how we did it, but he stayed with us. My mother said they came home about ten o'clock that night, and there he was, in full evening dress in the living room, and we were all sitting in a chair and he was reading to us. He had stayed the whole evening."

The closest Pat ever came to going to college was in the autumn of 1939, when he enrolled in classes at the Art Institute of Chicago. Never the scholar, he decided it was not for him. He dropped out in a matter of weeks. Years later, in a *Life* magazine profile, he would snipe, "I loathed school, and I'm not tempted to make up for it with adult education, which seems mostly a matter of therapy, centered on courses like Burn Your Own Initials on Your Belt."

As usual, Pat was using levity to mask deeper problems. Once enrolled in classes at the Art Institute, he had felt overwhelmed and concluded that he had little talent. His home life, meanwhile, remained unhappy, although he apparently made no effort to move out on his own. Uprooted from his old environment, and lacking the motivation to continue with college, he became mired in inertia. That situation would plague him, off and on, through the rest of his life.

Today Pat would undoubtedly have been diagnosed as clinically depressed and would have benefited from the advances made by psychiatry and psychopharmacology. But for the teenaged Pat Tanner in 1939, that was not an option. One can only imagine the intensity of Pat's loneliness; his feelings of rejection and alienation from a tyrannical father and from the society in which he lived. Unsure of his future, his talents, and his career; struggling with his conflicted sexuality; watching both his parents drift into alcoholism and mutual recrimination—Pat was not in a healthy environment for a young man already prone to depressive funks.

Mature-looking at nineteen, Pat was now desperately trying to learn how to drink. He soon discovered that his constitution required copious amounts of alcohol to produce even the slightest feelings of intoxication. "I went to a dinner party in Hubbard Woods," he wrote Webster Jones, "and drank a whole half-magnum of champagne all by myself while the ladies were powdering up for the brawl with still no effect. I really think there's something wrong with me." Regarding another party, he writes, "I drank and drank and drank and it didn't even hit me. I guess I'll have to give it up. It isn't accomplishing a damn thing. Honestly, Web, you'd be horrified at the amount of Scotch I can hold without feeling a bit different. I guess that's the reason I don't drink—I don't have to."

If only that had remained true throughout his life.

Finally, Pat got his first regular job. He went to work as a stockboy at Stebbins Wholesale and Retail Hardware Company at 15 West Van Buren, just off State Street. He despised the work. "The only time I remember seeing him unhappy," says David Peterson, "was during that job. He wrote me a letter—'Get me out of here! Get me another job!' I think his father had insisted that he had to take a job, so he took the first thing that came along." Still, Pat made the best of it. In a letter to Webster Jones dated April 18, 1940, he writes:

Would have loved to go to the cinema with you Friday but I've been employed for sometime and my afternoons now belong to the Stebbins Wholesale and Retail Hardware Company. Established 1860—also my mornings. It's a very good company. The "L" passes in front and it's right where the "nice" part of downtown leaves off and the naughty-naughty part begins. We can look out of our alley door almost any warm day and see the corps de ballet of the Gem Theatre and the State-Harrison Theatre and the Girlocade sunning at the stage entrance.

Some Friday night you and Johnny [Mock] must get up a group

of gay blades to come down about six, meet me for dinner, and all go on a tour to some of our neighboring burlies, Penny arcades, flop houses and pool halls and honky-tonks. . . . I can promise an educational evening! Then we can all get mermaids tattooed on our chests (next door to the Gem) and go home. What a night! Any Friday you say. Let me hear from you. So long.

For the world at large, Pat continued to present his happy-go-lucky, bon vivant persona. More than ever, he stood out from his Evanston pals as an exotic personality with a fey edge. In another letter to Webster Jones—who was quite emphatically heterosexual and very down-to-earth—he already sounds as campy as Auntie Mame:

So you're really on the ball about our little hike. I think it's lovely! Divine one might even say, mightn't one? Finding a summer home sounds très blah to me. Could we take Annie and a couple of bottles along just to liven up the party and make things more interesting? I'm sure she'd love to rough it with a passel of really attractive young men.

I've been working night and day down at the Outlet. It should let up soon though. Annie and I went down to see Eddie Duchin last Friday and had a high old time. We all must go out together some night. Why don't you hunt up another party for us to get invited to?

To Pat's somewhat naive young friends, his personality still did not register as stereotypically gay. Pat himself had not settled down on either side of the sexual fence, and he was even sporadically going steady with an attractive girl, named Dee Dee Kelly, who lived across the hall from him. On Tuesday nights, he and David Peterson would double-date with Dee Dee and David's girlfriend, Gracie Feldschneider, and go off to a Michigan Avenue nightclub for rumba lessons. The foursome soon became favorites of the waitresses. One night Pat announced to the entire staff that he and Dee Dee had just been married. All the waitresses pooled their resources and bought them a lovely wedding gift, and only several months later did Pat and Dee Dee fess up and tell them that it had all been a joke. Fortunately, none of the waitresses managed to spill a tray on them, but that night, Pat and Dee Dee left a sizable tip as penance.

In spite of the good times Pat was able to concoct for himself and his friends, his depression deepened. After working at Stebbins Hardware for nearly a year, despondent at age nineteen, he made the first of many suicide attempts. Taking one of his father's loaded .45s, he disappeared into his room and closed the door. Fortunately he was spotted by a family manservant, who broke in and stopped him.

Agnes Noggle, the mother of his friends Anne and Mary, came to the rescue. She worked at Columbia Educational Books, an enormous store on Michigan Avenue that stayed open till midnight, and found him a job there. Agnes, a matronly woman in her fifties, was completely swept up by Pat's charm and was a marvelous companion in humor for him. Pat affectionately dubbed her the Whore of Babylon, an appellation that she loved, perhaps because she had a bit of a crush on him. Pat found working at Columbia Educational Books far more congenial than Stebbins Hardware, and his four-to-midnight hours allowed him to go to parties till dawn and then sleep most of the day. Within a matter of months he was made manager of the store's department of old and rare prints, and within a few more months he was promoted to managing the textbook section. Mystery writer James Sherburne, a former Evanston Township High School classmate of Pat's, got to know Pat better through mutual friends who worked at the store. "I remember him as a very funny, very sardonic young man," says Sherburne, "who didn't have a terribly high regard for his employers or for the customers. He thought they were all ignoramuses." Once, having to wait on a particularly rude, insolent high school kid, Pat treated him with utterly excessive courtesy, to the boy's complete confusion and unease. When the boy had paid and went to pick up the books—which Pat had insisted on meticulously wrapping for him—Pat leaned over the counter, handed the package to him ceremoniously, then said slowly and softly, "And now, you rotten little bastard, until you learn some manners, I never want to see you in this bookstore again!" The boy, crestfallen, fled in a panic.

Pat rapidly became one of the store's most popular employees. He was a particular favorite with two sloe-eyed Jewish beauties, Jane and Eleanore Rosenberg, sisters who worked for him in his department. At one time, Pat seemed to be dating both of them. "Which one is Pat gonna leave the store with tonight?" became a popular guessing game among the other employees.

The Rosenberg sisters also loved playing along with Pat's humor. Columbia Educational Books was heavily patronized by parochial-school nuns ordering textbooks for their students, and Pat was always trying to pass the Rosenberg girls off to the nuns as Irish. He would introduce them as Bridget and Molly O'Hare, "me darlin' girls from Ireland." Whether the nuns believed him or not, Jane and Eleanore joined in the fun, affecting Irish accents and having a fine time with phrases like "Sure, Sister Mary, and it's a fine textbook you're speaking of." Sometimes Pat would take a nun out to lunch on his expense account at the nearby Palmer House hotel and soon have her giggling with his sly compliments ("Sister Mary, if you would even *consider* disrobing . . .").

In 1941, Pat hired seventeen-year-old Forrest Williams, an Evanston acquaintance, to work for him at the bookstore. The two became close friends. "From the time I came to know Pat," says Williams today, "I liked and admired him greatly. The fact that he was all of three years older—and at that age, that's a lot!—also made me feel rather special when I was around him. What struck everyone first, and often most, about Pat was his unfailing, almost nonstop wit. But he also impressed me at least as much as one of the kindest, most genuinely courteous of persons. Paradoxical, perhaps, because he was ever alert to the ridiculous in all of us; and that, of course, can stem from or lead to a certain dislike or cynicism. Yet, for all his enjoyment of exposing the ridiculous, he seemed to do so in a spirit of affection. And never impolitely. One felt that he always included himself in his spirit of parody and caricature. I first became explicitly aware of this mix of kindness and courtesy when we were on our way to dinner from the bookstore one evening. We had crossed Michigan Avenue and were in the Loop, where there were always a certain number of panhandlers, drunks, and homeless. It was rather cold, and we were both quite bundled up. A somewhat intoxicated and dilapidated man asked Pat, who was smoking, as usual, whether he had a cigarette. Pat inclined his head slightly and said, 'Of course,' as if he were responding to the most natural request from, say, Einstein. Despite the fact that he first had to unbutton his overcoat and reach through a tight scarf, he produced his cigarette case, flipped it open, and proffered it. By the time the man could thank him for the cigarette, Pat had given him a light. What struck me so was that all this was done as a complete matter of course, without a trace of condescension or even emphasis, as simply and naturally as if he were, say, buying a paper. Although I'm sure I've often been remiss since then, I took his example very much to heart."

Williams feels that this mix of kindness and courtesy is what he'd most like to be remembered about Pat. "It wasn't at all the stilted behavior of the so-called upper class," he explains, "but seemingly as much instinctual as deliberative. It was always present, even when he was caricaturing or making fun of people, which explains why one would rarely take umbrage. Whereas one often feels laughed at or put down by witty persons, Pat was one of those rare individuals who could make you feel that he is laughing at or with himself as well as you."

Still, Williams is aware—in retrospect—that problems lurked beneath Pat's whimsical persona: "This didn't occur to me at the time, but now I realize that he was always a little too funny, always a little too lighthearted. Always entertaining and amusing everyone else. There was a Pat behind the unfailing humor who wasn't apparent either to me or, I conjecture, to him. I'm inclined to think that it was a very understandable anxiety about sexual desires that he couldn't admit—indeed, I believe, was scarcely aware of, if at all. One has to understand the cultural and social milieu of the time to realize that the very notion of homosexuality seemed to my generation an absolute horror, a crime or terrible sin and inhuman perversion—and entirely deliberate and voluntary, to boot. Neither I nor Pat could have thought of him as homosexual, any more than as, say, a murderer. In addition to the times must be reckoned Pat's father, who wasn't the most tolerant parent I ever met. Someone—Auden?—said that behind every great man's achievement lies a great anxiety. I recognize now that today his manner would probably lead me—and him—to suppose that he was gay, and consider the possibility nobody's business but his own."

By December of 1941, Pat was engaged to a Southern girl named Isabelle Woolford, whom he had met while on a trip to Atlanta to visit his favorite cousin, Ned Hitt. In a letter to Webster Jones, the news is relegated to a couple of brief sentences toward the end:

Dear Webby,

I was so sorry not to have seen you over the Christmas holidays but I was terribly rushed up till Christmas Eve and then the Ballantyne-Augustines held a regular whooperdoo of a party and I had to sit up an hour afterwards in order to get out to Sister's house in Hubbard Woods for the annual Christmas tree, Tom and Jerries, state breakfast and vommitting. Christmas night I left for Atlanta. I took the 11:25 train out and since the two nights before had been entirely sleepless I trundled into my berth about midnight and didn't wake up till Tennessee about noon the next day and it being so late and the scenery so changed I popped into the aisle stark naked only to make a hasty retreat at the horrified gasps of a couple of totally uncharming schoolmarms who had, up to the time of my debut, been happily counting telegraph poles along the road bed.

I blew into Atlanta about seven (Eastern Time) and was whisked off to the tail end of a post-debutante cocktail party (I drank in Atlanta—When in Rome, etc.) then into my tails minus bathing and shaving and off to a dinner party and then to Dolly Hewlett's coming out at the Driving Club.

I had a perfectly marvelous time and had my picture taken twice. Once in full dress for the *Journal* and once in an old cashmere sweater and bare feet on the Hitt's badminton court. Each time with a drink and a little bleary-eyed but quite sober just the same. The Atlantans were a bit horrified at the bare-feet-for-badminton but the weather there was just like Northern October and besides I had no tennis shoes with me.

I got myself engaged too!

A wonderful girl named Isabelle Woolford who goes to Mount Vernon in Washington and the nuptials are scheduled to come off a year from this June. Congratulations are in order. Please Hurry to do so.

Had to turn down all the bids for Post-Christmas parties up here but what with the wonderful time I had down south it works out even.

Time to go home now. Write me soon.

Although the letter was written in late December 1941, three weeks after the bombing of Pearl Harbor and America's entry into World War II, there is no mention of this whatsoever. In another letter to Webster Jones that Pat wrote six weeks later, on February 19, 1942, he leads off with a report on his trip to the draft board:

Dear Webby,

Yesterday was Registration Day and I'm now the bewildered owner of a little card that says I'm six feet-two, have blue eyes, brown hair and Caucasian parents. The draft headquarters in our ward is situated on North Clark Street between Ricketts and a bowling alley and has all the ear marks of having once been a thriving brothel in long-gone days of peace and plenty. Most of the men registering were in the thirty-five to forty-four bracket. There were only a couple of youngsters there; the one ahead of me who was twenty-one and another poor kid with bad afflictions and definite traces of congenital gonorrhea. All in all it looked as if the Axis could land without a bit of trouble if the coughing queue of humanity waiting to be signed up was representative of American manhood. It's kind of depressing to be officially no longer seventeen-come-May now that I have to tote a draft card around with me. Now everybody—you in particular—will start spreading it around that I'm old enough to vote and could have cast a ballot for McKinley if so inclined.

The engagement is still on and I shall have a picture of Isabelle by the time you're home provided you don't rush and that lazy baggage gets around to picking out her favorite proof and forwarding the finished product. By the way, she's an aunt now. Charlotte, her sister, dropped her foal last Monday and they call it—a girl—Isabelle. Isn't that sickening? Well, what's in a name?

I trickled into Saks yesterday and sent the whelp what the nice lady in Infants' Wear assured me was the correct sized sweater for a seven and a half pounder. It looked as if it would cramp a two-month-old fetus but I guess it'll fit. I also made the horrible mistake of giving shipping instructions as follows: Miss Isabelle Ballenger (that's the baby's name), 2846 Vernon Drive, Atlanta

Georgia. Didn't give it another thought until Barrows Greenough said "Pat, I knew you were going with some girl from Atlanta named Isabelle but what's this about her having a baby and you sending it a sweater?" Not that it was any of his business, but I hurriedly made explanations that that was the baby's name and, to date, I'd sired no Child of Shame. If you hear any such gossip, just discount it as the disastrous results of my frivolity.

The more I see of babies the more anxious I am to claim a number of income tax exemptions for me own. Ah L'amour! With the above pink and blue thoughts I leave you for this evening.

Write soon,

Pat

By May, the draft board was still ignoring Pat, which was fine with him. Nonetheless, he was concerned. He did not relish the idea of combat, nor did he enjoy contemplating the possibility of being stationed in some dreary dump of an army base in the Deep South. There had to be some alternative for a twenty-one-year-old, able-bodied American male who was willing to serve the cause.

There was.

FOUR

Across to Africa

Autumn of 1942 arrived, and there was still no call from the draft board. But Forrest Williams, who was now eighteen, had heard about the American Field Service from a friend at Northwestern University. Williams and another friend, Henry "Budd" Selz, decided to enlist in the Field Service and asked Pat if he'd like to join up with them.

Then, as now, the American Field Service was not as widely known as it deserved to be. For conscientious objectors, for 4-F's, for fellows like Pat who wanted to participate in the war effort through means other than the military, the AFS was a viable option. Created before the U.S. entry into World War II, it was an all-volunteer group of combat ambulance drivers that was sponsored by the U.S. government as a wartime service with American and Allied army troops in the Africa, Europe, and India-Burma campaigns. By war's end, AFS units deployed on army orders of battle had conducted an estimated 714,000 ambulance patient evacuations, aiding 139,500 soldiers hit by enemy fire.

When America entered the war, AFS ambulance drivers were registered by the State Department under Article 10 of the Geneva Red Cross Convention as an American government responsibility and as members of the American army medical services. They were attached to Allied army units, but served primarily under U.S. War Department control or U.S. Army command.

The AFS attracted a diverse group of recruits with even more diverse reasons for joining up. "The Junior League at war" was how Pat impishly referred to it. There were men who were draft-classified 1-F, who did not quite meet the army's physical standards for overseas combat and risked being assigned to the most boring stateside military duties. Quakers joined up, and pacifists of all stripes. There were conscientious objectors, artists, writers. And amongst all of these groups was a fair sprinkling of homosexuals. In that pre-Stonewall era, some were fairly uncloseted, others less so. "The gay contingent was accepted," says journalist William Stump, who served with Pat in Africa. "It was a question of performance. If you performed, if you did your job and weren't afraid to get in the ambulance and get in harm's way, nobody gave a damn. And I think that with a lot of these young, college-age kids, it was the first time they'd ever *met* anybody gay. I knew one gay guy from a New England family; he became a great friend of mine, and he was as brave as you could imagine." Indeed, courage was a requirement for this tough job. AFS drivers were constantly out on the battlefield, dodging bombs and bullets alongside the soldiers.

Mixed in with the bulk of AFS volunteers, who were mostly of college age, was an older contingent that was anything but pacifistic—men who desperately wanted to see combat but were classified 4-F or were simply too old to be accepted into the service. Some had already served at the front in World War I. The result was a lively mix of pacifists and fire-eating militarists.

On October 27, Pat enlisted in the AFS along with Forrest Williams and Budd Selz. They were to stay in the United States until they received their marching orders. While waiting, Pat wrote Webster Jones:

I'm glad you got in the Naval Reserve. That should give you something like an ensignship or something when you graduate, shouldn't it? As for me, I'm strictly out of the Army. Budd and Forrest and I have all joined the American Field Service and should be off for Egypt anytime between now and God-knows-when. It's all very nice—glamorous—foreign—spell of the tropics—camel's breath and all of that. The Field Service sends ambulances and people like us to the British and Free French armies and there we stay for a year subject to reenlistment. We're under British jurisdiction and the allowance is twenty bucks a month. Uniforms, equipment and such are furnished by us.

We've already had our measurements taken for shorts and pith helmets and all that sort of thing and we've started on the necessary shots. Now all we have to do is get our passports and wait for a boat.

It costs like sin (which I've always found expensive) but we can't wait to take off. We may be trotting around to parties with you this Christmas or the three of us may be singing "God Rest Ye Merry Gentlemen" in the hold of some ship carrying explosives to Africa. That remains to be seen. However, I'll write you just before we set sail so you can comb the newspapers during the ensuing two or three months to see if we've been torpedoed.

Volunteers in the AFS had to pay a $250 fee for their own uniforms, equipment, and ambulance, and would receive a princely salary of $20 per month. If they came from wealthy families, this was usually not a problem; if they didn't, the better-heeled members of the community often offered to sponsor them. Pat did his best to contribute as much as he could on his own. He quit at Columbia Educational Books and took a far duller but better-paying job as the store manager at the Julius Zweig Printer's Exchange until he was called up. He also sold off most of his possessions, including his beloved record player/recorder and his tuxedos and tailcoats.

In December, Pat, Budd, and Forrest received word that they would shortly be sent to New York to embark on a troopship bound for Africa. By this time, Pat had managed to get himself engaged to not one, but three girls. In addition to Isabelle Woolford in Atlanta, he now claimed as fiancées his neighbor Dee Dee Kelly and Eleanore Rosenberg, of the two Rosenberg sisters he'd been dating while working at Columbia Books. The situation was worthy of a Feydeau farce, or a Patrick Dennis novel. Whether any of the women found out about the others is lost to history, but Pat ultimately escaped matrimony with all three.

When Pat, Budd, and Forrest got their orders, a furious round of farewell parties ensued. One of the last was given by Pat's old high school chum Katie Kelley and her family at their home in Evanston. He attended dressed in full Desert Fox uniform. "This was in the middle of winter," Katie Kelley says, "and in Pat walked in khaki shorts, boots, knee socks, and a pith helmet! He sailed through the party, finally saying, 'Ta-ta, ta-ta, I'm off!' And he walked out the door and went to Africa."

Forrest decided to stay on in Evanston and fly to New York the day before his embarkation. Pat and Budd, meanwhile, jumped on the next Twentieth Century Limited out of Chicago, ready to raise hell in the Big Apple with the two weeks' time they had left. Pat wrote Webster:

Budd and I finally fell on the Century absolutely dead until we found some odious West Point sprouts who thought, and quite foolishly, that anything as chic as the American Field Service should have rounds of drinks bought for them in exchange for harrowing tales of desert life. It was only after the fourth or fifth Scotch that Budd said we hadn't been to the desert yet and at that point all of West Point disappeared to wash its hands.

Gossip! On the train we spotted a dear young thing known to all of us (and if you think I'll give you her name to defame all over the North Shore you're badly mistaken) who was traveling in the company of a large gold wedding ring. She explained that the ring was just a prop to ward off traveling men and Army stallions and that she was going to visit her old and true school chum Marjorie in New York. Of course the next morning Marjorie appeared in an ensign's uniform and our little friend and Marjorie *and* the wedding ring spent a heavenly week together in the Commodore. The rare part is that Rose Ann Smith's room was right next to theirs and you know me with my listening-thru-walls-with-an-empty-water-tumbler tricks. Oh the conversations Our Mutual Friend and "Marjorie" had were choice! Oh the sin!

Pat had already been to New York several times and knew how to live what he called "*la vie* Riley" there. During his two weeks in the city, he and Budd saw all the plays they could squeeze in and went to club after club, including everything from the Village Vanguard to the Stage Door Canteen. By the eve of their embarkation, the two had decimated their savings and were left with barely ten bucks between them. Contributions from close friends and family members saw them through; Pat's mother, Florence, even sent her bridge winnings for the week.

Then Forrest Williams arrived from Evanston with a wad of bills in his back pocket, and the three chums were able to enjoy one last wild night on the town before embarking on the hospital ship *Atlantis* for Africa on the morning of January 16, 1943. Emblazoned with large Red Cross symbols and brilliantly lit up at night, the *Atlantis* at first inspired a secure feeling in everyone—until they learned that her sister ship had been sunk by submarines just a few weeks before.

The *Atlantis*'s unit of sixty-eight volunteers was bound for the British Eighth Army in the Western Desert in Egypt. It would be a long, three-and-a-half-week voyage across the Atlantic and down around the Cape of Good Hope to the port town of Durban in South Africa. Pat and the Evanston gang decided to make the best of it, turning the trip into one long party at sea. On the way over, they hooked up with another volunteer who was a kindred spirit: William Weaver, now esteemed as one of the premier translators of Italian literature into English and a leading chronicler of Italian history, art, and culture. "We regarded Pat as the most sophisticated member of our group, because he knew all the words to all the songs of *Pal Joey*," says Weaver. "I had never even *seen* a Broadway musical at the time; I had led a fairly sheltered, provincial life in Virginia and Washington. He was irrepressibly funny and witty and irreverent, and he livened things up considerably."

Pat and the boys staged a talent show midway through the voyage. Weaver, known at the time by his nickname Pinkie, did a mean Helen Morgan imitation seated atop a piano, and six-foot-two Pat stole the show as Carmen Miranda. "I don't think anybody who saw it will ever forget it," says fellow volunteer C. B. Squire. "Several of us helped him achieve this by piling huge amounts of fruit on top of his head. How he managed to carry this off, I don't know, but that was Pat!"

Everyone spent time reading and exchanging books on the voyage. One of the most popular of the recent bestsellers being passed around was Max Shulman's *Barefoot Boy with Cheek,* a comic take on life at a Midwestern college that was a huge success in 1943. "We all took turns reading it aloud," says Squire. "Pat was the only one who could read it without having absolute hysterics to the point of not being able to read anymore. He could read it as if it were the telephone directory. And of course that made it even funnier. I greatly admired that quality, because I couldn't read it without laughing so hard that I had to stop reading."

Squire remembers that Pat delighted in being the center of attention in a group—as an entertainer, not necessarily a ringleader. "Pat was sardonic," he explains, "with an absolutely razor-sharp sense of humor, but he was not vindictive in using his wit. Sometimes you could carry on a conversation with him for several minutes without being absolutely certain whether he was being serious or not. This I found, in my youth, rather confusing. I don't think it would bother me quite as much now. But you never were quite sure with Pat."

C. B. Squire, Fred Wackernagel Jr., and "66 Contributing Editors" got together and started producing a weekly typewritten shipboard newsletter called *Daze at Sea*. Vol. I, no. 1, carried the following item:

HAIR RAZING . . . If heads look a bit shaggy on Deck A, don't blame it on the ship's hairdresser. Edward Everett Tanner III, Squad 7, is the cause. Basing his barbering knowledge on his Aunt Mary's dog Poo, a French Poodle that he trimmed, Tanner started in at his trade yesterday. Customers to date: two. Customers satisfied: one. A bit of angry feeling arose after Henry Selz examined Pat Tanner's results in a mirror. But Forrest Williams, the other customer, apparently is satisfied. Pat declaims that anyone finding the ship's hairdresser too busy will find him ready and willing ("able" may be the word for Tanner, at your own discretion).

And a Society Page item of issue number three, which sounds very much like Pat's handiwork, read:

PINK PUNCH . . . Definitely the social event of the season was the *très gay* birthday *fête* last Tuesday evening in honor of Norman E. (Binghamton Polo and Squash) Dailey in the Cotillion Room of William F. ("Pinkie") Weaver's new yacht *Atlantis*. The party included the Village Vanguard contingent, with a smattering of the gayer Stork Club sons of habitués from B2. The décor, strikingly different, centered around a sumptuous canopy of puce mosquito netting from the sea-going trousseau of H. Oldfield

("Bud") Selz, which was festooned with garlands of pink *papier de toilet*. The charming hosts were attired in full Arf Ess uniforms, and gloves were worn by all. The receiving line comprised, in addition to Messrs. Dailey, Weaver and Selz, Edward E. ("Pat") Tanner XFV, F. Thayer ("Goldilocks") Sanderson and Bernard ("Silent Don") Skalski, all from Group 7 except Dailey and Weaver. Refreshments were served.

The volunteers on board the *Atlantis* were saddled with a much older leader appointed from within their ranks who, although a decent sort, was decidedly humorless. His second-in-command was a would-be martinet, and both were calculated to bring out the prankster in Pat. "Well," Pat would huff, "their motto is to make this war as *disagreeable* as possible!" The leader decided that the men needed toughening up and forced them to perform fifteen minutes of calisthenics on deck every morning. One of the exercises was running in place. As Pat began the exercise for the first time, he couldn't help humming Offenbach's "Can Can" at the top of his lungs and doing high kicks. Suddenly everybody else started humming and kicking along with him. The leader was apoplectic, but all he could do was give in. Eventually he threw up his hands and was forced every morning to make the best of the situation, saying, "Okay, kids, 'Can Can'!" and then letting the men hum and kick away while he did a silent slow burn.

After three and a half weeks at sea, the *Atlantis* finally arrived in Durban, South Africa, on February 11, 1943. "It was a gay old trip, every inch of the way," Pat wrote Webster Jones. "Met lots of interesting people—good and bad but all interesting."

Pat and the other members of Middle East Unit 37 would sit in Durban for three weeks awaiting their next movement. A resort city, Durban offered few cultural attractions aside from eating and going to the movies. Pat and his friends did a lot of both. One of the movies they saw was MGM's 1940 hit *Waterloo Bridge,* starring Robert Taylor and Vivien Leigh. "There was that great moment," says William Weaver, "where Vivien Leigh confesses her past to Lucile Watson, and Lucile Watson says to her something like, 'Do you mean there's been another man?' And Vivien Leigh answers, 'Lady Margaret, you *are* naive!' And this became a great favorite line in the whole American Field Service. 'Lady Margaret, you *are* naive!' became repeated in a whole lot of situations, especially by Pat!"

The other big highlight of the stay in Durban was a trip to a reptile farm on the outskirts of town. Pat and his pals posed for a photo holding a giant boa constrictor that had just swallowed a whole small pig. "The pig was quite visible inside the boa constrictor," says Weaver. "You could see the pig's outline, even his little trotters."

The men of AFS Unit 37 left Durban on another ship for another three-week voyage, up the east coast of Africa to the city of Taûfiq, near Suez. In Taûfiq, Pat and the boys underwent the AFS version of basic training, which was little more arduous than a high school gym class. Essentially, AFS basic training meant learning how to drive an ambulance under battlefield conditions and how to maintain and repair it. Pat enjoyed it thoroughly. "I, as never changed a tire (or tyre—as ever you prefer) before in my life," he wrote his sister, Barbara, "am on speaking terms with every known organ of any automobile. Things are no longer Things, they're carburetors, or differentials or crank cases. Oh, it's fascinating! Not that I'd like to sit up nights all the rest of my life performing general hysterectomies on old motors or anything but it really does give one confidence in the horse as a means of locomotion."

After training, the volunteers received a week's leave in Cairo, following which Unit 37 was dissolved and Pat, Forrest Williams, Budd Selz, and William Weaver were assigned to a platoon with the British army. "Here I sit in the Middle East," Pat wrote Webster Jones on April 9, 1943. "We had a marvelous leave in Cairo and the more I see of the world the more certain I am that wild horses couldn't drag me back to America. This corner seems to be the Garden Spot but now that I think of it I'd even like to go back to Europe and settle down. Well, not settle down exactly but sort of roam around that particular section and this one. You can take your rolling lawns and leafy suburbs and give them right back to the Garden Club. Excepting possibly Atlanta, I'm thru with every thriving little metropolis west of Fifth Avenue. And Fifth Avenue jars me a little too."

The British army posting was brief, and the boys found themselves newly attached to a Greek brigade within weeks. They were based in Lebanon, where no fighting was taking place, and their duties were about as strenuous as a stay at a health spa. When the AFS volunteers had patients to transport in their ambulances, it was usually to the dentist or the VD hospital. "This is our daily program," wrote Pat to Barbara:

6:00 Get up—brush teeth—dress—make Budd get up
6:30 Eat breakfast (Eggs, cheese, bread, marmalade, tea with lemon)
7:00 Go to barber for shave and eau de cologne
7:30 Work
1:00 Lunch (varied)
2:00 Go swimming
4:00 Tea, literary, letter writing and officers' social hour
7:00 Cocktail hour
8:00 Dinner (also varied)
9:00 Officers' social hour

That's my day. It's easy work. It's lovely. It's fun.

Now for the Confessional:

I just don't know what the hell I'm going to do after the war. I just can't go home and go to work. What with the food and shelter and such all being supplied so that there's nothing to have to worry about except doing each little duty each day, it's going to make a psychological mess of your little brother. Anyway I'll have to think fast before the war's over (an event for which I'm not in the least anxious) and get some nice nation to give me a nice comfy position someplace.

If you had any sense, dear, you'd slip your husband something in his coffee and leave that Evanston urinal the minute his insurance money starts coming in. Good God, that there are places in this neck of the woods where you can live like Lady Mendl on nothing a month would slay you! I'm all for evacuating the whole family. Why, the girls would be speaking three languages this very minute. . . .

My life, as usual, is just one gay extravaganza. We have the old French-type straddle latreens which flush automatically every four minutes. Well you know me, my first time astride the damned things went off and delivered the most breath-taking goose of ice water since those old seltzer-bottle skits in the Vanities. . . .

Pat often found himself hospitalized during this period with bouts of sandfly fever. The hospital stays annoyed him endlessly, but he always managed to turn each one into a party. During one convalescence, he wrote Webster Jones:

Budd and I are still together. We're attached to the Royal Greek Army and we haven't felt as socially prominent since the year we made our debuts. It's just the best little army in the whole Middle East and I wouldn't dream of being with another. We're learning Greek and lots more French and when my year's up I'm seriously considering getting a commission and citizenship from Greece. That remains, however, to be seen.

Bill Manning, one of Budd's Alpha Delta chums, is in the neighborhood and being very efficient. He's a good man but suffers from an Edmund Lowe-&-Victor McLaglen complex of "Here come the Arabs! Up and at 'em boys! Ready, aim, fire!" which is just a little ludicrous in this territory where there hasn't been a shot fired since the Crusades.

At the moment I'm tucked away in a cozy little hospital with nothing in the world wrong with me except the natural fury at being here. This is my third day—no, the fourth day—and I couldn't feel better at a Christian Science Revival Meeting. Since there's so very little to do outside of reading and writing I've settled down to becoming the Peck's Bad Boy of the Officers' Ward.

It's a neat little roomful, too. Two captains and a lieutenant with arthritis and a ballistics expert with mal de bowel. We chitchat about cricket scores and panzer movements and bowel movements and amputations and all sorts of jolly froth like that. Every now and again—just to break the monotony—one of the arthritis victims will rise from his couch of pain and hobble over here to let me feel his tortured member while he waggles that aching limb over my bed with gay abandon and terrifying moans. Then the ballistics expert will launch into a little oration on the hospital cuisine showing a most remarkable vocabulary of four-letter words.

Budd and Pinkie show up twice a day wearing my clothes and usually smuggle in some food and cigarettes or they'll bring Georgous to shave me or station Galainis (our No. One batman—those sweet Greeks have given us four) outside the balcony so I can scream down gentle commands in Greek and send him out scurrying about for cakes and bananas. In the afternoons I usually hold a reception for twenty or thirty Greek officers and the hospital staff is getting so that it just can't cope with me. I'm certain my discharge is cinched.

That takes care of the local dirt. It's time now for a nice, long enema. Write me soon and let's have piles of really good gossip.

A few days later, Pat wrote to his sister, Barbara:

Today, dearest-sister-a-b'y-ever-had, bein June Thirteenth and your birthday (although I never can remember whether you're sixty-six or sixty-seven this year) is, I think, a very appropriate day to write. Your sending me a letter dated on my birthday also makes it appropriate and my being again in the hospital with, again, sand-fly fever makes it still more appropriate since writing letters kills time and time is what I've got plenty of.

That was a rather involved sentence but I'll try to improve as the letter goes on. . . .

Now let's get on with the world-shaking events that are taking place in our young lives:

SICK REPORT:
I'm sort of making a Personal Appearance tour of the Middle Eastern hospitals which, I regret to say, lack somewhat the chic

to be found in St. Luke's or the Maternity Wing in Evanston. This is my second hospital this week—sand fly fever, nothing serious, don't get excited, there's a dear—and I'm feeling just a bit *de trop* trussed up here in these pale blue flanellette pyjamas without a damned thing wrong with me. However, I return to my own little Greek Brigade Wednesday if the heavens fall. . . .

SOCIAL COMMENT:
Our social life—Budd's and mine—is still quite as ripping as ever. The Greeks live for the moment they can come into our tent and practice English and Colonel Daskarolis even went so far as to buy a whole leather-bound set of Shakespeare to improve his. We're still the belles of the Brigade without half trying and I wouldn't be in another army for anything in the world. All of which brings me to the next item:

BREAK THE NEWS TO MOTHER DEPARTMENT:
Well, ducks, this is it. Due to a new ultimatum posted to the A.F.S. by that great American Institution, the Draft Board, Field Service men will have to do one of the following things:

(1) At the end of a year's service just sign up again (no month's leave to America, that means)

(2) Go back to America and get drafted. Which means that you can't sign up for any Fun-Army like the French or Greek or English or even the American over here. You just have to go home and get drafted.

Not that I'd stand a Chinaman's chance of getting into the Home Guard in the U.S. but it's just one of those little technical regulations which, may I add with some indelicacy, gripes my arse.

Not that I'd be caught dead in America but I did think it might be fun to pop in for a month and maybe get married and then I was all set for the Royal Greek Army and a quiet life in Alexandria after the war.

Of course it's rather fortunate all around that I like the A.F.S. and don't sit around clenching my fists and talking about Action as is the lamentable case of any number of Field Service people with that indomitable Rover-Boys-in-the-Middle-East complex.

But after the Royal Greek Army to which, thank God, I am permanently attached, the American Army (even if my stomach, lungs and a number of other things could get me in) would seem like a ninety-nine-year sentence in hell.

Just tell Mamma, in your inimitable manner of quiet tact, that I won't be home for a month's visit next spring. A selling point on your side is that Elsie Williams has given Two Boys to The Cause and she hasn't even a husband or any grandchildren to call her own. Her daughter also died in Paris about twelve years ago. Watch your step, kid.

HOME FRONT:
Mamma keeps flooding the mails with good-natured gossip of the Red Cross. . . . Her letters are good fun, though, and practically devoid of sentiment. Occasionally she talks of thinking about me terribly hard on a certain date and being sure that the thoughts are radio-ed over here. She never, though, mentions receiving any cheery thoughts on the days when I think about home, so I guess there's not a hell of a lot in this telepathy stuff.

Pappa occasionally breaks down and sends a couple of pages of man-to-man stuff which just isn't like him. They're nice letters, though, and who's ever doing his typing now is to be congratulated. It's just when he uses the word "Fellah" that he sends an icy chill down my spine which lasts for days. I do wish you'd speak to him about this.

AND IN CLOSING MAY I ADD:
I have ten or twenty people to write and certainly can't waste the time of day chinning here with you.

I hope that your birthday and anniversary came and went without the gift of another Cadillac three feet too long for the garage from your adoring husband. A nice vacuum cleaner is so much more practical; "the sort of thing you can always use."

Your brats are well, up and around, and that you're not planning to have any more. Temperance, dear, temperance.

Give my love to your brats, by the way, and try to raise them by the Montessori Method or whatever new way is stylish now.

Dearest regards to your old man and to you. Be my V-Girl now and spread loads of sweetness and joy among the various members of the family. All of which I have to write and write now.

Love and kisses and happy birthday, your adoring little brother,

PAT

Shortly afterward, Pat received a telegram from his mother reading, "Don't worry dear, we understand." In another letter a month later, Pat reassured Barbara:

Remember, ducks, as far as Baby is concerned, war is *not* hell. I couldn't be more comfortable. The food's good. The social life simply ripping. Right now we're going to skip over to dear Major Birdwood's for the cocktail hour (he's from the Indian Army, very nice). The [censored] Minister of War promises to be here for dinner and the King himself later in the week. I simply must shine up my old tiara and practice a few deep curtsies.

Give my love to your whelps and tell them I'm deeply flattered at my inclusion in their evening prayers although it won't do this depraved young soul much good.

Determined as he was to be the entertaining social chronicler, Pat kept his letters home as light and frothy as possible. And since he hadn't seen any actual warfare yet, he had no problem maintaining that tone. Just as he rarely got down to serious heart-to-hearts in real life, he made sure his letters home were almost as frivolous as a Cholly Knickerbocker gossip column. But his experiences during the months he spent with the Royal Greek Army in Lebanon did inspire him to write a serious article for the *National Herald*, the Greek newspaper published in America in both Greek and English editions. Not counting his humor columns and theater reviews for his high school paper, this was twenty-two-year-old Pat's first published work. It appeared in the *National Herald's* Sunday edition of August 15, 1943 (see appendix).

Word of Pat's reporting spread to Evanston, where the story was excerpted in local publications. A proud Florence Tanner also circulated copies of her son's article all over town. That embarrassed Pat no end, and he wrote Barbara about "that ghastly Greek article which Mamma in undiscriminating pride seems to think Pulitzer stuff. . . . If only the dear Consul General gives me a commission I'll be quite satisfied and never write so much as my maiden name again."

Tiaras. Curtsies. Maiden names. It all sounds as if Pat was so comfortable with his sister, he had already come out to her. And yet, that was probably not the case. A man could straddle the sexual fence for a long time in that era without really admitting his confused feelings to himself or anyone else. It seems inconceivable to our jaded contemporary sensibilities that a young man could write and speak the way Pat did and not necessarily be perceived as gay, rather only as eccentric, exotic, and entertaining. And although Pat fell in with a coterie of sophisticated, upper-middle-class American volunteers in the AFS, only a few of these men went on to lead actively homosexual lives. Many of them were as campy as Pat was at that time, yet they settled down to marry and raise families in the suburbs after the war's end. "As far as I know," says William Weaver today, "Pat had *no* sex life at the time, and I certainly didn't. There was sex going on, but not with us, and we really didn't discuss it."

An insight into Pat's manner, and that of his AFS clique, can be gleaned from composer/playwright/novelist Dean Fuller (*Once Upon a Mattress*), who served alongside Pat during the last half of Pat's AFS term. "Kaufman and Hart had already written *The Man Who Came to Dinner*," explains Fuller, "so the Sheridan Whiteside character went through this group like wildfire. The other thing is that everybody at that time was reading Evelyn Waugh. There were copies of his books everywhere. No one reminded me more of Pat than the very, very gay undergraduate who stuttered in *Brideshead Revisited*. Everybody in the group called everybody else 'my dear,' which was something Pat had started. It was all sort of quasi-homosexual, although none of us, to my knowledge, was homosexual. But we were playing that Evelyn Waugh game. Still, Pat had very serious moments where he could drop the whole camp thing totally and be very convincing. He could have taught in a university without any problem at all."

Pat and his unit were transferred to a more remote posting in

Lebanon in mid-August of 1943. With even fewer responsibilities, and to fight the boredom, Pat and William Weaver concocted a little handwritten newspaper they dubbed *The Parish Monthly*. Its entire press run was one issue—painstakingly printed by Pat in pencil—and the only reader was Budd Selz. This parody of a parish publication was full of vaguely obscene news items about pastor William J. Clutchbreast and his flock. It also included a poem that was all full of double entendres, signed "Gwendolyn Clutchbreast, age 9"—the reverend's daughter— and a report from the Ladies' Aid society that involved all kinds of lascivious contributions to the rummage sale.

The easiest stretch of Pat's AFS stint would soon be over. The tough part was about to begin, and for that, he would need every ounce of the spirit and good humor that he possessed in such abundant supply.

FIVE

The Combat Zone

In the fall of 1943, Pat's unit received orders to report to Cairo, where it was assigned to the British army. Once arrived, they were to drive their ambulances all the way from Cairo to Tripoli, where they would wait to be taken by ship to serve on the battlefields of Italy.

During the long, long journey to Tripoli, Pat made up a ditty that everyone would join in and sing with great enthusiasm:

> *If a German raped your sister, would you* fight?
> *If a German raped your sister, is it* right?
> *Would you sit at home in your backyard without a word to say?*
> *If they cut off all the kiddies' hands in Topeka, U.S.A.?*

The trip took weeks, with all thirty ambulances in a painfully slow convoy traveling the south shore of the Mediterranean. The drivers would start out early each morning and keep going until midafternoon, when the heat became unbearably intense. Then they would stay overnight wherever they had stopped, sleeping on their stretchers under the stars or in their ambulances. Long, long afternoons and evenings were spent with nothing to do but gossip and tell stories and subsist on vile rations such as soy sausages and canned corned beef. The British army rations garnished about as much respect as British cuisine in general. Fresh fruit and vegetables were virtually nonexistent, but every now and then the drivers would see a bedouin by the side of the road holding up a melon for sale, and the ambulances would all come to a screeching halt.

A condiment called golden syrup—or gooey stroop—often came to the rescue of tired rations. The British equivalent of Karo syrup, it somehow improved the flavor of almost anything it was poured onto, including the dreaded soy links and canned meat. The boys also had the questionable pleasure of feasting on camel burgers. "Actually," says Weaver, "we were lucky if it really *was* camel. I got so sick off those camel burgers; I got worms the size of lead pencils and it took me months to get rid of them."

Finally they arrived in Tripoli, where they spent a month waiting before being sent across the Mediterranean to Italy at the end of 1943. There the group was dissolved and the men were reassigned to different British army units. Pat, Forrest, and Budd were able to stick together, while William Weaver, William Stump, and others were sent to serve elsewhere in Italy. Thrown in with a group of AFS drivers that he had never met, Pat instantly made new friends.

"I had already heard about Pat," says Dean Fuller. "Word had traveled that he was funny and larger-than-life, and that he could keep everyone amused. And that's a great talent. When I realized we were going to be in the same section, I thought, 'Well, this is going to be fun!'"

Fuller first met Pat shortly after Pat's arrival in Italy. "We were billeted at little cottages," Fuller says, "where there was no electricity and no heat except for a little charcoal brazier, which we all sat around. The first thing he said to me when we met was, 'Belly up to the brassiere!' That was typical."

By now, Pat had become the center of an all-Evanston coterie that included Forrest Williams, Budd Selz, and Bill Hooton. Dean Fuller soon became part of the little clique, as did Kirk Browning, who went on to become a television pioneer by directing such esteemed cultural fare as the NBC Opera, *Live from Lincoln Center,* and *Live from the Met.* Browning first got to know Pat during the journey through the desert to Tripoli. He and Pat became great friends, and Browning remembers him with real fondness: "Pat felt totally rewarded by having the challenges of our duties and meeting them. There was no neurosis about it at all. And whenever we did have a moment of surcease from those labors, we had such fun. I don't think there were many of the soldiers that enjoyed the kind of ridiculous irony of the way we lived. There were several friends who had very rich families who sent them wine and linen and glassware; the most inappropriate things. There were times we would get together and have candlelight dinners with lace tablecloths and terribly expensive paté—and we'd sit as though we were in the Stork Club! Pat adored the ridiculousness of sitting in the sand. You couldn't even take a bath; water was so short we had to bathe in gasoline! It's a wonder we didn't blow up, because we all smoked! We were given one canteen a day in order to brush our teeth and drink. The food from the British army was so appalling, but Pat never complained about any of that. We had such fun under pressure, creating an environment that was so out of key. Pat pulled those dinners together, he *loved* doing that kind of thing. It was such fun for him. When you were with him, it made perfect sense; it was the most logical thing; it wasn't at all outré! He was totally convinced that there was no reason not to be civilized. But at a moment's notice he could go onto the battlefield. He had that balance. He took his role in the Service very seriously, and he was very good at it. I can remember times when he had no sense of fear or of exposing himself to danger, he would do what he was ordered to and did it immediately. He was marvelous."

Between bombing raids in Italy, Pat and Kirk Browning tried collaborating as songwriters, with Pat writing the lyrics and Kirk the music. "I just don't know where those songs are now, and it kills me!" says Browning today. "Isn't that terrible? The hell with my music—Pat wrote the most wonderful lyrics! He was marvelous at tossing off those witty, faux-Coward cabaret lyrics. We never had the songs published; it was at the very end of the sheet-music era. But I think they may have been performed in New York at the Blue Room; I don't remember by whom."

At first, Pat was happy to be in Italy and attached to the British army, which fit in beautifully with his Evelyn Waugh attitude. He especially enjoyed the opportunity to wear the jaunty British army uniform—lemon yellow shirts, New Zealand battle-dress tops, officers' hats or berets—and to accessorize them according to his taste. "It was all kind of snotty, but it was fun," says Dean Fuller. "You basically wore the uniform of the army with which you served, but you modified it. A lot. There were no regulations about that."

On January 19, 1944, shortly after his arrival in Italy, Pat received the first of several wounds. While backing out onto a road with his ambulance full of wounded soldiers, he was struck in the back by shrapnel from an exploding shell. Fortunately the injury was slight and required no medical care other than a temporary dressing. Later, he received another superficial wound in the thigh. In the advanced dressing station, a medic moved to cut open Pat's shorts, as was customary for wounds below the waist. "You will *not!*" Pat snorted. "These shorts are from the finest apparel shop in Cairo!" The shorts remained intact. After he was treated and bandaged, he posed for a photo on the fender of his ambulance in full view of the German forward observers, saying, "I want them to see how a *gentleman* reacts to their artillery!"

Gentlemen like Pat were frequently forced to borrow toilet paper from each other on the battlefield, as it was always in short supply. Pat once asked Forrest Williams for some before heading into a thicket. Williams handed him a roll. Pat removed four pieces and handed the roll back. Thinking Pat was being overly considerate, Williams said, "Oh, take all you need, Pat."

"A true gentleman," sniffed Pat, "*never* needs more than four pieces of toilet paper!"

In February of 1944, Pat and his group were sent to serve at the battle of Monte Cassino, during which they had to endure the sight of Allied bombers systematically flattening the ancient, beautiful Monte Cassino monastery. He and the others spent many weeks living in the basement of a bombed-out bar in the rubble of the town of Sant'Elia downhill from the monastery. They were part of an advanced dressing station for Cassino casualties, transporting the wounded to the nearest medical unit. Most of their trips were made at night, when the German attacks tended to occur. It was dicey work, because any sign of movement or vehicle dust could bring on 88mm shell attacks. If an ambulance was driven slowly enough, the German forward observer could usually distinguish it and wouldn't target it—in the daytime, at least.

One night Pat got lost somewhere in no-man's-land. Instead of panicking, he turned off the ambulance and went to sleep in it until daylight. The next morning the pack of cigarettes that he always had on the dashboard for himself and the wounded—was gone. In its place was a little note reading only *Danke schön* and bearing a sketch showing the way back to Allied lines. Pat thought that was wonderful.

While holed up in the basement of the Sant'Elia bar, Pat fought boredom by enlisting Kirk Browning and Dean Fuller to help him concoct a new musical about nuns that would star Ethel Merman. The Act I finale was to feature a chorus line of nuns coming onstage, slipping in mud, and belting out a ditty called "I've Got a Dirty Habit." Somehow, the boys never got much further in their work than that.

Midway through the Monte Cassino bombing, some Polish forward observers decided to occupy the bombed-out roof of the bar as it afforded such a good view of the monastery and German troop movements on the southeast slope of the mountain. This was a risky move and did not entirely please Pat and his AFS friends, who could all have become shell targets if the Germans had spotted the Polish observers. But Pat, as usual, did enjoy demoralizing the German army with displays of insouciance and high style. He proposed that when one or more of the Polish observers were not busy at their posts, they should join the AFS drivers outdoors for afternoon teas. Thanks to Pat, a tea party was always ready and waiting each afternoon for his Polish friends.

The fighting raged on. Pat's sister, Barbara, generously sent him money, but he had nowhere to spend it. In a letter of April 14, 1944, Pat wrote Barbara:

Thank you, Pet, for the money you've been sending—but stop. Anyway, dear, I don't need the money. Food, however—little things like shrimps and caviar and Sherry Pralines and smoked turkey and chutney—does help me struggle along from day to day.

Now for the secrets and additional Don't-Tell-Mama stuff: Just believe I'll be home about the middle of next February— unannounced. It should be sort of fun to surprise the Parents although Poppa would probably have a mild stroke and la Mere would scream "Dar—ling!," trip on a rug, break her hip and be in a plaster pantie girdle for two or three years.

The last of the secrets is that . . . I shall probably wed little Miss Bitch-of-the-Earth during my leave.

There now, that's a lot to keep under your bangs. . . .

On April 22, 1944, Pat sustained a wound that luckily did not leave him disfigured. While driving his ambulance back to his post from a dressing station, he was suddenly pursued by enemy shellfire. A piece of shrapnel flew through the open window of the ambulance and tore into his left cheek. Bleeding profusely, Pat continued driving to his post, where he received emergency treatment and was then evacuated to a medical unit for removal of the shrapnel. Miraculously, no bones or teeth had been broken, but Pat lost nearly a pint of blood. He spent two weeks recuperating in a hospital and, even more miraculously, never developed any kind of scar from the incident. By early May, he was discharged from the hospital and back on the job.

Pat's duties were every bit as dangerous as those of any soldier. AFS drivers were dodging the same enemy fire as the armies in which they served, and their own casualty rates were high. Other drivers were not as lucky as Pat. During one battle, Pat and his partner were loading a wounded soldier on a stretcher into their ambulance. Pat had his head bent; his partner didn't. A flying bullet missed Pat's inclined head and went through his partner's head and killed him instantly.

Late June of 1944 found Pat back in the hospital with a bout of jaundice. As usual he hated being stuck there and spent his time reading, firing off letters home, and annoying the nurses. On June 28, he wrote Barbara:

This place is a trifle tarsome. I'm being treated like an ancient Lenox platter—something British, something foreign, something rare, something with which to be very careful. The nurses, whom I persist in calling Sister just to give them that old Continental lilt, make a point of enunciating ev-e-r-y-thing ve-ry clear-lee just so I won't have too much difficulty understanding the language, and it's not a good thing. I've had so many kinds of tests today I'm still not sure that I've any blood left. I've also had twelve different kinds and colors of pills. There are going to be more tests tomorrow only as an added attraction I can have black coffee and crackers (they mean biscuits) for breakfast in the morning instead of nothing which they served today. There are also tests for a week from today and a week after that. They think. One nice feature is that they know I'm a civilian and can get up and go whenever I feel like it which is going to be soon. Christ, in a decent (or British) trap the sister flops you into bed, sends

around a fat-free diet and gives you plenty of fluids. Then you're
well and don't have jaundice anymore. Not so with these amazing Ameddicans. I've lots of letters to write, though, and they'll
keep me busy for a couple of days. By then my (pardon the
expression) urine should be out of the sparkling burgundy category and my eyes white again. At that point I leave. I'll be
delighted to stop in every day or two to let them look me over but
I'm getting to the age where I can't just sink into retirement in
some veterans' home. Besides there's the Season going on up in
Rome and the Smart Set has invaded every worthwhile palazzo in
town. These nurses are very nice but give me la Principessa Gio-
vanna Collonna any day.

So you're out of stockings and into leg paint too? Well, love,
even if you were an ugly child you always did have a decent set
of gams. I never grudged you your stems and never will—unless,
of course, they get large or something unforetold like that.

Sister dear, I love you so. I'm always so proud when I think
that your only uniforms have been the Bungalow apron and the
Maternity wrap-around. We may have had differences during our
years—(my 16 and your 40) but you were mostly very sweet and
kind to me and bought me lots of sodas before Walgreens raised
them back up to fifteen cents, and you did send me that lovely
copy of "Bob, Son of Battle" when you were at Smith and it certainly was a stinker. And you have no ambition to join any
women's army and I just love you for it.

My, don't we sound Byronesque!

I do hope you have a Nice Restful Vacation. I know just the
spot for you: Lovely Lake Placenta in the heart of the Goldenrod
Belt. It's just so peaceful and quiet you can hardly believe yourself. Forty-eight miles from the nearest town and you just com-
mune with Nature. A really rustic little tarpaper cabin—two
rooms—with kerosene cooking facilities ("Our guests raved over
them in 1913—So Modern, they all said") and yards from the
back house. There's swimming and carp fishing galore in lovely
Lake Placenta. A few mosquitoes to be sure, where, pray, are
there not, but such a clean, active camp life and so completely
relaxing. There's a boat you can row too. Do look into this little

inland Desert Isle Where City Cares Are Shed Like Falling Leaves (a motto our Mr. Thruppy, who owns the land, conceived). It's a hundred dollars a week including transportation by buckboard from the station or, if you'd care to take it for the whole season, from Decoration Day to Labor Day, that is, you can have it for nine hundred and fifty in advance. And it does pay to be thrifty.

You'd better do as I say and call Mr. Thruppy before you go off to some old lodge where you have to wear attractive clothes all the time and expose your children, the darlins, to—who knows—perhaps even a bar.

No, Barbara dear, it's the rustic life for you. Always was. Give you the back woods and to hell with Bar Harbor.

You've stood about enough. Time to sign off and write someone Who Cares. The Noisse, a very bornee young lady from Rock Island, Illinoise, thinks I'm writing a book and even ventured to ask about it. I looked darkly over my most amazing set of Strassbourg frames and said, "Yais, an exposé." Since then service has been remarkably good.

Pat's sense of humor was certainly staying intact, in spite of his witnessing enormous destruction in Italy. By now he was on intimate terms with the human toll the war was taking on soldiers and civilians alike. After the Monte Cassino bombing, he and one of his ambulance partners, Turner Bullock, were invited to dinner by a grateful Italian family. They did their best to enjoy the meager repast until they realized what they were eating. The shape of a leg was the giveaway—it was the family dog.

Pat continued to keep his darkest emotions at bay through his whimsy and his highly developed sense of fantasy. "I think the reason I was so fond of Pat in the context of the war," says Kirk Browning, "was that he was so idiosyncratic. He was unlike anybody else that had ever served in that ambulance unit, and that was a very eccentric group! Pat was uncorrupted. He was very vulnerable, and he refused to harden himself to the primitive, hideous conditions of the life that we were living. There was something kind of poetic about it. The sad part of it was that he had to fantasize to keep his persona and what he wanted to be intact. It was impossible under the conditions in which we lived for him to have the kind of gentility and humor and the kind of conversations that he enjoyed because the conditions were just too antipathetic. So Pat's solution was to begin to fantasize and to create conditions that accommodated his sensibility, but were unreal. He would pretend to be in another place. He would pretend that we were other people than we were. He would assign us other roles than we had in reality. And we found it engaging and funny and charming because he carried it off with tremendous panache; he was wonderful. He would get up in the morning and suddenly all of us who happened to be there would be a family in a suburban house. He would be the father, somebody else would be his wife; others would be his children; he had a whole scenario. He would assign roles, and we would go along with it."

The long battle of Monte Cassino had finally ended in May, and the Allies entered Rome on June 4, 1944. By July, action in Italy slowed to the point where Pat, Dean Fuller, and Budd Selz all felt that they could do more good in France. They volunteered to join the French unit and were soon on their way to Naples, then on a boat across the Mediterranean to France.

The crossing took five days. Volunteer William Hannah reported in a written account of the voyage: "Not enough words of sympathy can be attributed to the brave lads parked on the afterdeck—Fuller, Tanner, Selz, Mayer, Addams, Boyd France, Hope, and Smith—for directly facing them is a bare, wooden framing built over the side of the ship, a platform serving an obvious purpose for all troops on board. Pat Tanner's philosophic attitude toward this imposition, however, does wonders in maintaining morale on the afterdeck."

Pat and the rest of Section One, American Field Service, disembarked in Saint-Raphaël, a small town on the Côte d'Azur between Cannes and Saint-Tropez. But they were in for some disappointments. During these waning days of the war, there was even less action in the south of France than in Italy, and service with the French army was quite different from service with the Greek or British army. For one thing, it was far less glamorous. By that time, the French army was almost totally Moroccan, and the officers were mostly white Frenchmen from Algeria, not Paris sophisticates. Since the American army supplied the French First Army, the uniforms were all American—cast-off American uniforms at that, with canvas puttees, and Pat did *not* appreciate them. It was all too serious, like the life of a real GI, and hardly Evelyn Waugh–ish enough to keep Pat amused.

Moreover, Pat did not have the same adoring coterie with him. Only Dean Fuller and Budd Selz remained from the old gang in Italy. He still lived up to his best Sheridan Whiteside standards, but his witticisms and flights of fancy could now only be appreciated by a few rather than many. To ease some of the boredom, he appointed himself *chef supérieur* for the company, fearlessly dousing the bland canned-stew rations with French cologne to liven them up, and launching omelette-making competitions. At one of the latter, he was given an omelette that had inadvertently been prepared with twice the normal amount of cheese. "Thanks," he murmured after downing it, then promptly threw up.

Pat continued doing his best to keep up his own spirits and those of his buddies, but the human devastation that he had witnessed back in Italy had already begun to send him on a downward emotional spiral. Making matters worse, he had an unhappy romantic affair with one of the other AFS volunteers. The name of the volunteer and the nature of the problems are unknown, but another suicide attempt ensued. Pat tried to asphyxiate himself by sitting in his ambulance within an enclosed space with the engine running. Fortunately, one of his buddies found him before any real damage had been done. Pat just laughed sheepishly, then turned off the ignition.

More and more, Pat was taking refuge in the fantasy worlds he had concocted for himself and his AFS buddies. Finally the day came when the suburban-family fantasy suddenly seemed real to him. He started it in the morning, but by afternoon, he had still not come out of it. There seemed to be no bringing him back to reality. Suddenly he began talking to Forrest Williams as if Forrest were right there—although Forrest had remained behind in Italy.

The October 10, 1944, diary of Section One volunteer Jeremy Addams reads: "Gray to Luxeil with the Section, leaving Tanner at 46th American General [hospital] in Besançon, he being in acute neurotic depression."

"It was very sad, Pat being taken away and put in a hospital," says

Kirk Browning. "I think it was a terrible blow to him. He had been a wonderful driver and was very good about handling his patients. But in Italy, when the war changed, and we saw the people, the civilians—it was too terrible, that tragedy. Pat just couldn't take it. The rest of us just steeled ourselves, but he had no carapace to put on."

Documents in the archives of the AFS form a paper trail that tells the rest of the story. Permission to reprint them in this book was not given because of their personal and confidential nature. The documents explain, however, that Pat was hospitalized at Besançon and diagnosed as having had a serious nervous breakdown, complicated by an unclassified psychosis. The condition, it was felt, manifested itself in an attempt to escape from reality into fantasy, which induced or resulted in amnesia. Pat claimed at that time to remember nothing of his stay in France beyond his sailing from Naples. His attending psychiatrist recommended that Pat be returned to the United States.

On October 18, 1944, Pat was provisionally released from the AFS for repatriation and honorable discharge. He spent the rest of the fall waiting in France to be shipped back.

Early in 1945, Pat was finally sent home to the United States, where he spent several months as a psychiatric patient at the veterans' hospital in Farmingdale, Long Island.

This unhappy ending to Pat's tour of duty in the American Field Service may, however, be seen in a different light. Dean Fuller, who witnessed Pat's breakdown in France, says, "The war wasn't as much fun anymore. And Pat decided—Pat started acting funny. I've always thought it was intentional. I think he was bored. Not scared—just bored. I was the one who took him to the psychiatric hospital, and he was making jokes at the time. But I remember him clinging to my hand as the orderly came in and said, 'This way, please.' He sort of clung to me for a moment—and then he went.

"I was the last one to see him before he went home. And I can remember him telling me, I guess in a letter a couple of weeks before he shipped out, that the first thing the American doctor said to him was 'How's your health?' Pat just exploded with laughter, which, of course, made the doctor think he was off his rocker. So he made jokes in the letter about wearing lampshades and so forth, and keeping the doctors and nurses amused, so he was definitely up to concert pitch. And he went home, and then he was fine. I think he just got tired of it, because he was a *very* hard worker, and there was no question about him doing his duty. I think it was probably true that he had nervous depression, but I saw him change. It just wasn't as much fun anymore, and he was no longer the center of attention, the way he had been in Italy. He didn't have his group around him. So if he did this deliberately, he did a good job, and I don't blame him for it at all. I'd forgive anybody wanting to be moved out of boredom. If I'd thought that he'd done that because he was afraid, I wouldn't feel the same. But he *never* was afraid. He *always* did what he was required to do."

Decades later, long after his death, Pat would be honored for the courage he had shown on the battlefield. In 1989, by a special U.S. Department of the Army decree, all seventy-two members of the American Field Service who had been wounded in World War II—including Pat Tanner—were awarded the Purple Heart.

PART TWO

Pat circa 1946,
shortly after his
arrival in New
York

SIX

New Boy in Town

Battered and impoverished London, humiliated Paris, shattered Berlin, discredited Rome—the old capitals towards which, before the war, Americans had so often looked with sensations of diffident inferiority, now seemed flaccid beside this prodigy of the West; visitors from abroad, who in former times had generally responded to New York with a sort of spellbound condescension, could hardly patronize Manhattan now. There seemed a momentous symbolism to the very stance of the place, and Manhattan was its own best logo: unmistakable, unforgettable, and conveying messages, as Madison Avenue would wish it, altogether seductive. How marvellous, that the hopes of mankind should be illustrated by an emblem so gloriously exuberant!

—Jan Morris, *Manhattan '45*

It's not mere nostalgia when 1945 is cited as the beginning of New York's greatest era. At that moment in history, the city was at its absolute zenith. More than any other place on earth, New York represented the promise of a new future, one that had been heralded by the World's Fair of 1939 and then withheld for six years while the world had blown itself apart. As Europe and Asia struggled to rebuild, America was booming. Its great gateway city was brimming with artistic, intellectual, and ideological possibilities and transforming its very fabric through wholesale architectural redesign. The city promised riches both financial and creative; it had become a massive magnet for talent of every stripe. And it would remain at this vibrant peak for the next twenty years—which coincided exactly with the time during which Pat Tanner made New York his home.

Pat wasted little time in Evanston when he came back to the States. He had already decided that New York was where he wanted to be. The decision did not sit well with his parents, but Pat was now twenty-four and determined to take charge of his life. "After the war," says his niece Sister Joanna Hastings, "there was a clash between him and my grandparents because he wanted to live in New York and they thought he should live in Chicago. They didn't understand some of the difficulties he was having adjusting to life after the war. I don't think they could have ever imagined what it had been like to be an ambulance driver through that kind of hell, which may have been worse than what many men experienced during combat."

Pat did not even contact many of his old friends in Evanston. Webster Jones was one of the few that Pat saw during his short stay before he moved to New York. "I met him at a restaurant called The Huddle," Jones says. "He was dressed in his AFS uniform, and he was looking around all the time to see if anyone was looking at him. We had a nice talk, but he was different—almost as if he had been shell-shocked. He just wasn't the same old Pat. He wasn't funny; he was very reserved. It was almost as though he were scared to face life."

One of the first things Pat did when he moved to New York was to seek out the noted Jungian psychotherapist Dr. Margaret Nordfeldt. He became a patient of hers for nine months. Their work together was so meaningful for Pat that he would remember her in his will twenty-five years later.

Meanwhile, he wrestled his demons well enough to build a new life for himself in the city where he had really always belonged. Pat's personality bloomed, fed by the sophistication, glamour, and creativity of New York at its peak. One of the many who flowed into the city to seek a fresh start as World War II drew to its close, Pat was the beneficiary of a magnificent confluence of America's cultures and classes: that brief moment before the country was overwhelmed by the TV, the automobile, and the tract home. This was the New York that Pat would chronicle and caricature for the next twenty years.

Pat's Atlanta cousin Ned Hitt, who had always been one of his closest friends, decided to try his luck in New York as well. He and Pat came to New York simultaneously and checked into the YMCA, but they soon found a small apartment together near Washington Square in Greenwich Village. Pat's drama-club buddy David Peterson came to the city on a visit and remembers fondly the weekend he spent with Pat and Ned. "On Saturday, Pat had just found out how you could break wine bottles in a pot of cold water and get goblets. We spent the whole day having fun doing that. The next morning I went back to their apartment, then Ned and Pat and I started from way down at Washington Square and began walking all the way up to midtown. We hit about six or seven places and had a drink at each one. One of the bars we went to was on the top floor of a building on Sutton Place. The place we had our dinner was the Burberry Room on Fifth Avenue in the fifties. Then we made another stop and we ended up with a nightcap at the Pierre Hotel. I don't think any of us really got drunk, but we walked every step of the way and just had a ball."

By this time Pat had given up his youthful dreams of becoming a set designer and realized that his most exploitable skill was his way with the English language. Shortly after arriving in the city, he found freelance work reading and reporting on manuscript submissions to the McIntosh & Otis literary agency. One of the first people to meet him socially in New York was Isabelle Holland, who became a friend and went on to write a great deal of successful young-adult fiction, including *The Man Without a Face*. Holland and her two roommates gave a party on a Sunday afternoon in the brownstone duplex they were renting on the south side of Stuyvesant Park. One of the roommates, a Chicago artist named Kaki Schwartz, had invited Pat to the party. Holland went downstairs to answer the doorbell, "and there was this dégagé young man in very long, British-type shorts. And he said, 'Patrick Tanner,' and he came in and joined the party. He didn't have his beard, not yet. He had recently come back from the American Field Service." In an interesting aside, she notes, "Pat invented himself. And he invented himself as the product of another era. An era in which elegance was terribly important. He wanted nothing to do with that Presbyterian Midwest background. He repudiated it all; he had already done it when I met him at the door of that apartment."

Pat made new friends quickly in New York and found himself invited to one party after another, where his brash wit and irreverent persona always shone. Charles Gurney, a friend of Forrest Williams's, remembers the one night he spent getting to know Pat in New York: "I was with some friends in a new Nash, and we picked him up for a bridge game. At the time, every new product was named a *master*— Mixmaster, Toastmaster—the term *master* was as overused as *awesome* today. And the new Nash models were advertised as having a backseat that could be made into a very comfortable double bed. When we stopped to pick up Pat, he got in and said, 'Oh! This must be the new Nash Fuckmaster!' That was one word that was *not* overused in those days. Nobody would get into a car full of strangers and say that!"

Pat's friend James Sherburne came from Chicago to live in New York, and Pat took him along on his party circuit. "Pat certainly had a wild streak," says Sherburne. "I remember one particular party on Central Park West where Pat disappeared into the bedroom with another man and a woman. They closed the door and were in there for about forty-five minutes. Nobody knew for certain what was going on, but they finally burst out half-undressed, arguing very loudly about cigarettes. Pat was accusing the woman of being a selfish bitch because she wouldn't share her last cigarette with him! He threw on the rest of his clothes and left, and that was the last I ever saw of Pat Tanner! For all I know, the whole episode may have been a gag that the three of them had planned." It probably was. That had been one of Pat and Anne Noggle's favorite party tricks back in Evanston.

Before long, Pat landed himself a full-time job writing copy for the Franklin Spier advertising agency, which specialized in servicing the publishing industry. Nobody who worked for Mr. Spier was ever paid very much; Pat's starting salary was less than $50 per week. However, Spier's employees found themselves in a creative environment where individualism and eccentricity were not only tolerated but prized, as long as you got your work done. Pat could not have landed a better first job in New York.

Spier himself was certainly an eccentric. At a time when all businessmen came to work in a jacket and tie, Spier dressed like a janitor in rolled-up shirtsleeves and suspenders. An amputee, he insisted on sporting an antediluvian wooden leg that had long been eclipsed by modern medical technology. The clumsy prosthesis would clank and clunk as Spier made his way around the office. Whenever the ancient elevator jammed—which was often—Spier would angrily kick a tattoo on it with his wooden leg. Although he could be gruff and formidable, Spier nonetheless encouraged an atmosphere in the office that was nearly as undisciplined as Ralph Devine's libertarian day school in *Auntie Mame*. Spier had a staff full of talented young writers, most of whom went on to have books published, and they were as intent on having a good time as they were on getting their work done. Dinners, parties, three-martini lunches—all were the norm among the employees, who bonded so closely that they became each other's best friends. Afternoon work was often accomplished in a tipsy haze, after which the next question was "Well, where are we all going drinking tonight?" or "So whose house are we going to?" Author Joy Singer (*My Mother, the Doctor*), a former Franklin Spier employee, says, "I had clients who said to me, 'Joy, please write this copy *after* lunch, because your style is so different then.' I'm sure I was much freer, although I don't think I was ever incapacitated. But some of us *were* some of the time. A few of us were *all* of the time. It was a group that accepted everybody's idiosyncracies. We all had *strong* idiosyncracies, and it was a place where you were welcomed for it. When you started there, people said, 'Oh, goody! Here's another one of us!' Spier changed the life of everybody who worked there. Your friends changed, your life changed, your attitude changed. I've never known another place like it. Everybody was young, eager, fond of each other. There was no politics because none of us really wanted to make our mark in advertising—we all wanted to be great writers."

Pat shared an office at Franklin Spier with Peggy Brooks, who went on to become a close friend and the editor of several of his novels. She recalls those days as the most enjoyable in her career. Pat would arrive in the morning, sit down, and immediately start typing up the previous night's dream for Dr. Margaret Nordfeldt to analyze. ("Whatever she did for him," says Brooks, "he seemed to be in very good shape.") After he'd finished with his dream, he would go to work on the reports he was still doing on the side for McIntosh & Otis. Then, with lunch hour just minutes away, he would roar through all of his copywriting for Franklin Spier, which included the prestigious Doubleday Books account. His unbelievable speed and facility left Brooks flabbergasted.

While at Franklin Spier, Pat got his first job as a ghostwriter. *There's a Fly in This Room!* was written by Pat and published by Rinehart and Company in 1946. The author was billed as Ralf Kircher, a newspaper columnist, and the book's illustrations were by Gluyas Williams, known for his unforgettable sketches that accompanied the writing of Robert Benchley. A series of brief, humorous vignettes about the petty annoyances of family life in the suburbs, the book was written in a waspish, cantankerous tone. Its humor doesn't hold up terribly well today, and it probably seemed a bit tired even then. The Gluyas Williams illustrations are the best part, and unfortunately they point up that these comic essays are similar to—but not as good as—Robert Benchley's. "The material is not very original," said the critic for the *New York Herald Tribune Weekly Book Review,* "and the laughs are scattered. Married people and bachelors will react quite differently, for reasons which even a fly could perceive."

Late in 1945, Pat's American Field Service buddy Kirk Browning returned from the war. Kirk's uncle had an apartment in a walk-up at 319 East Seventy-second Street that was owned by the famous Art Deco–era sculptor Paul Manship (best-known for his statue of Prometheus in Rockefeller Plaza), which he turned over to Kirk. Kirk had not yet found a job and was unable to meet the $92-a-month rent, but Pat got him work at the Doubleday bookstore in Pennsylvania Station. Meanwhile, Kirk invited Pat to move in and share the large apartment with him, as it was much bigger than the flat where Pat was staying downtown.

Kirk Browning remembers this period in his life with great fondness: "We had such fun! I just adored Pat, and we had the most wonderful time in New York. It must have been a year or so that we roomed together before I got married. We had so much fun buying stuff and furnishing the apartment. Pat did all the cooking. Oh, he was a *wonderful* cook! I'm sure everybody thought Pat and I were having an affair. But I don't think I even saw Pat naked! It was the most innocent sort of friendship you could possibly imagine. We respected each other's privacy. There was no talk between us about homosexuality; we didn't make jokes about it. I don't think we even knew many homosexuals." Another thing they didn't talk about was the war. "I knew Pat had gone through hell, and I just didn't want to bring it up."

Pat and Kirk were living on a shoestring, but it didn't seem to matter. At the time, Pat cared little for possessions. Although he had designed theater sets and then let others construct them back in his Evanston days, here in New York he made half of the furniture in his new apartment himself, including tables and credenzas. A fabulous cook, he created dazzling meals for himself and Kirk out of the scrappy ingredients they bought from a corner deli.

Soon there was an opening for a new copywriter at Franklin Spier, and Pat set up an interview for Kirk. At the interview, Spier gave Kirk a book and told him to go home, read it, then write copy for it as a test. "It was a book in which one of the characters was afflicted with syphilis," says Kirk. "I remember walking in the next morning after having read the book all that night, and I wrote one sentence that I put on the desk with the book. It said, 'Cupid shot a poisoned arrow.' " Kirk got the job.

While Kirk and Pat were both working at Franklin Spier, Pat began a romantic relationship with Frances "Frenchy" Martin, another young copywriter at the agency. Born and raised in the Midwest, Frances had had a long, on-again, off-again liaison with Thomas Heggen, who wrote the bestseller *Mister Roberts*. Those close to her knew that Heggen was the great love of her life. Heggen, however, was a deeply troubled man who was soon to become a suicide. At the time Pat knew Frances, she clearly had troubles of her own, which included a big drinking problem. Nonetheless, she was charming, and most people adored her. Pat grew to care for her deeply and tried to be protective. "He was trying to save her from herself, really," says his office mate Peggy Brooks, "but there was nothing anybody could do for her. Outside of Pat's writing ability, the most distinctive thing that I remember about him was his need to be generous, he couldn't help himself from generous impulses of all kinds, even if his better nature or his wisdom told him that it was a little foolish."

So it was during his impossible relationship with Frances. After his breakdown during the war, Pat had been diagnosed as impotent. Frances, meanwhile, was told by doctors that she was sterile. "They went to bed *one time,*" recalls Kirk, "and she got pregnant! One of the great ironies of all time!" Pat was terribly concerned for Frances and offered to marry her, but she refused him and instead decided to have an abortion. Her drinking was getting out of hand, and Pat eventually accepted that she was determined to destroy herself and that he could not save her. Before long, Frances left Franklin Spier and returned home to Minnesota, where, sadly, she drank herself to death in short order.

The entire incident affected Pat deeply. Kirk Browning retains a vivid memory of the night he passed by Pat's room and heard him sobbing. He knocked and asked Pat through the door if he was all right, but the sobbing just continued. Kirk opened the door and Pat, awash in tears, begged him, "Kirk, would you come and just hold me?"

Kirk went to Pat, sat down next to him on the bed, and held him as he cried and cried. Finally, exhausted, Pat went to sleep in Kirk's arms. When he became still, Kirk laid him out on the bed, turned off the light, and left him alone until morning. "And we never, never talked about it," Kirk says. "But we were close enough so that this kind of thing could be shared."

Soon Kirk met the woman whom he would eventually marry. "When Kirk introduced me to Pat," says Barbara Browning today, "I just loved him. From the very beginning. Soon after I met Kirk, he and I were in the country, where his family lived, and we were taking a walk and both of us picked up some kind of poison sumac or poison ivy. I was a model at the time, and I swelled up. In those days, they gave you heavy doses of calcium. You can imagine how much fun I had. But Pat called me up and said, 'Come on over for dinner! Kirk's miserable and you probably are too!' He cooked our dinner and then went out. He came back in much later, tiptoeing quietly so he wouldn't disturb us."

Pat loved entertaining, and Barbara Browning remembers some impressive dinner parties he and Kirk threw on their tiny budget. "When I started to sleep over there," she says, "they had a dinner party. To this day I remember the impression it made on me. They served artichokes as a first course, and I had never seen an artichoke. It was terribly sophisticated and ultra–New York for me. The two of them— Pat and Kirk—planned the party, and Pat did all the cooking." For his dinner parties, Pat would light the chandelier that hung in the hall with real candles—and the next morning, he, Kirk, and Barbara would always be on their hands and knees, picking wax out of the rug.

Before long, Kirk invited Barbara to move into the apartment. This odd situation might have led to all kinds of problems, but Barbara and Pat adored each other, and Pat was thrilled to see Kirk and Barbara becoming a couple. There was only a little awkwardness, and it was quite charming. Barbara worked on Saturdays, and Kirk would take the train Friday night to go upstate to his family's farm. It meant that Pat and Barbara would be spending Friday nights alone together. The first Friday night that Kirk left, Pat asked Barbara what she was planning to do that evening. She quickly invented a friend that she was going out with. Pat said he was doing something too and left, saying, "Well, good night—see you later." After Pat had gone, Barbara decided to go see a show at a movie theater across the street. The feature had already begun. She found her way to the smoking section in the dark, sat down, struck a match to light a cigarette—and there was Pat sitting next to her. They both burst out laughing. "It was the first and last time we ever made up a story about what we were doing on a Friday evening," says Barbara. "From then on, we *enjoyed* those Friday nights. He'd cook dinner, and we'd have long talks together. He was like a brother, I loved him like a brother. Oh, I just had *great* affection for him."

Somehow, nobody got on anybody else's nerves or felt intruded upon. Pat, Kirk, and Barbara would even leave the house together in the morning and ride downtown on the bus to work. Pat delighted in playing a nasty trick on Kirk and Barbara: On the crowded bus, he would bellow, "Oh, Barbara, you *snored* so last night! And Kirk, *you* were impossible!" People would stare, and both Kirk and Barbara would be thoroughly mortified.

But Barbara soon became grateful for Pat's friendship and solid brotherly support. Within a few months, she found herself carrying Kirk's child. "I was terrified of letting my family know," she says. "Pat was very supportive. I could talk to him about things I certainly couldn't have told anybody else, like my pregnancy. In that era, the way I was raised in that strict Protestant household, I wouldn't have dared let anyone know. There was only my friend Christine, who had had an abortion. And I was considering going to the same little dark back room to have mine. Since Kirk and I got married, I didn't go that route."

Pat, who always called himself "a devout atheist," refused on principle to attend the wedding, which was held in a church. "Pat at that point would *never* have gone to a wedding," says Barbara. "He thought the *idea* was great, but the fact that it was a religious ceremony was just too much. Pat was actually very funny about not coming. He would go around saying, 'Christ is *divine!* Oh, *divine!*'" Pat did bless the union in his own way, however: he made Kirk and Barbara a lavish prenuptial feast.

The Browning newlyweds didn't want to raise their child in the city, so they moved upstate to start a chicken farm. (Kirk's next career in the nascent television industry would bring them back to New York a few years later.) But Pat's old American Field Service buddy Bill Hooton had recently married Barbara Cattin; both had been friends of Pat's back in Evanston, and both were now in New York and looking for a place to live during the postwar housing shortage. In they moved with Pat, taking Kirk and Barbara Browning's old room.

It seemed that all of Pat's buddies were falling in love and getting married. Now it was his turn.

SEVEN

Social Register Rescue

One of Pat's accounts at the Franklin Spier agency was Creative Age Press, a small, offbeat publishing house owned by a heavyset Irish woman named Eileen Garrett. Garrett considered herself a psychic and edited and published a cult magazine called *Tomorrow*. Under the banner of Creative Age, she also published new literature, including work by Robert Graves and the Stuart Engstandt novel *Beyond the Forest*. The latter became a celebrated King Vidor-Bette Davis melodrama for Warner Bros. in which the star uttered the deathless line "What a dump!"

In 1948, Eileen Garrett lured Pat away from Franklin Spier to become the promotions director for Creative Age Press. The year before, Pat had ghostwritten a book for Creative Age called *The Doctor Has a Baby*. Signed by one Mrs. Evelyn (Werner) Barkins, it was a light, semifictional account of what a doctor and his wife went through during their first years of parenthood. Garrett had been happy with its critical and financial success.

Creative Age Press was another unusual, unorthodox working environment—"kind of a wacky place," according to Pat's secretary, Marilyn Amdur. "It was certainly *not* an insurance company." By now Pat had grown a full beard—which was quite uncommon at the time—and with his flamboyant personality and appearance, he fit right in among the psychics and bohemians who worked there.

Like the Franklin Spier office, Creative Age Press included a sizable contingent of heavy drinkers on its payroll. "There were editors who would come back from lunch," says Amdur, "and they'd have their pencil in their hand and the manuscript on the desk and you'd pass their office and they *looked* very busy. But they were really taking a little nap!" To Amdur, however, Pat's behavior seemed only a little stranger after lunch than before. "He'd come back from lunch and suddenly stand on his head in the doorway!" she says, laughing. "It was amazing! You know, there he was, tall and slim—on his head!"

Marilyn Amdur today is a petite, stylish lady with a sly sense of humor. But Pat may have had a different perception of her. Long before he got around to writing *Auntie Mame,* he was calling her Agnes Gooch—the name of Mame's dumpy secretary, immortalized in the stage and film versions by Peggy Cass. "When I worked for him, that's what he always called me!" she says. "He'd say, 'Agnes! Get in here! Sit down!' He was adorable. He had one of those large sketch pads, and he would draw Agnes Gooch in different poses doing different things. The one I really remember was 'Agnes Gooch, Birdwatcher.' He had her in the plaid shirt and the heavy skirt and the eyeglasses. It didn't look like me—I hope!"

Pat loved sharing his culinary expertise with his secretary. "He used to talk about making frogs' legs," says Amdur. "He'd say, 'Agnes, what you have to do is line them up and they look just like the Rockettes! Now, take your flour and powder the legs!' He also said, 'Now, Agnes, when you have company and you bring out a beautiful store-bought cake, make sure you put flour all over your apron, so they'll think you baked it yourself!' "

Pat and Amdur shared a small office, and Pat would chain-smoke all day. "If I'd known about secondhand smoke at the time!" Amdur laughs. "He'd be puffing and puffing. He would do his so-called work for the company—his releases and whatever else he had to do, and gave me my little work, and then he had his own typewriter, and he was always hammering away at it." Of course, it was his own work—ghostwriting and magazine articles—that Pat was pounding out.

Shortly after he began working at Creative Age Press, Pat was introduced by mutual friends at a party to a striking Social Register beauty named Louise Stickney. The electricity between them was instant.

Louise, a recent Vassar graduate, was pretty, popular, and possessed a sharp wit. She was also chafing under the constraints of being a Poor Little Rich Girl. The daughter of Henry Austin Stickney, a corporate attorney, and Helen Frith Stickney, a poet whose work was often published in the *New York Times* and the *New York Herald Tribune*, Louise had been given the kind of Upper East Side, Miss Chapin's School upbringing that left her searching for an escape route. Her every childhood afternoon had been programmed with some kind of socially productive activity: cotillions, skating classes, one sport after another—all of which she detested. The rest of the time, she always seemed to be sitting in pediatricians' waiting rooms opposite Gloria Vanderbilt. Both girls, of course, were perfectly healthy but were always being taken to the doctor and diagnosed with upper-class complaints.

Louise had been an only child, and both of her parents had grown up feeling neglected. "I would think, 'I wish someone would just neglect *me* for a while!'" said Louise many years later. "I *dreamed* of being a neglected child! The brides, the coming-out parties, the stuff that they did—this is what they wanted from me, and they had picked the wrong person. If they had been born at a different time, they would have been totally different. They just were creatures of a social system that I didn't want any part of. But they couldn't be *blamed*. They did it all from the goodness of their heart, and they were two of the most honest people I ever met. Their example was really very fine. If only they could have cut all the Social Register crap . . ."

Louise's stay at Vassar had been her first chance to get away and gain some perspective. She bloomed there, and when she returned to live in the city, she enjoyed a friendlier, more relaxed relationship with her parents. It was the first step in her liberation.

The second was Pat.

"I think if he hadn't come along, I would have been a very embittered ex-debutante," said Louise. Pat, with his flamboyantly eccentric manner and appearance, was considered something of a rebel. His beard alone qualified as shockingly bohemian at a time when 99 percent of American males had clean-shaven chins. But Pat reversed the norm: he sported a clean-shaven head. It was his answer to a hairline that was already beginning to recede at an alarming rate. The combined effect was striking and contributed to the arresting first impression he always made. At six feet two inches and 170 pounds, with his sky-blue eyes shining out between his chrome dome and furry jaw, he drew attention the minute he walked into a room. "When I first met Pat, I thought he was very handsome," said Louise. "And very funny. My mother and father thought it was so disgraceful that he had a beard; they said he grew it to cover his war wound."

Another source of kinship for Pat and Louise was their politics: both were extremely liberal, although each had come from conservative Republican families. And there was their sense of humor. Pat and Louise shared a droll, sardonic view of the world, and particularly of the social pretensions in which they had been steeped since childhood. The boy from Evanston, Illinois, and the girl from the Upper East Side had both seen plenty to laugh over, and they found each other at the moment when they were finally finding themselves as well. For them, it was a time of love, idealism, and excitement in a city where the opportunities seemed endless.

And as much as Pat had ridden to the rescue of Louise, Louise had done the same for him. While a psychiatric patient of Dr. Nordfeldt's, Pat wrestled with a growing inability to feel strong emotion. Nordfeldt noted, however, that once Pat met and fell in love with Louise, his "feeling function" returned to normal.

When Louise met Pat, he had just left Franklin Spier for Creative Age Press. Louise, meanwhile, was working at *Good Housekeeping* "for this maniac" and was looking for another job. She knew she could write—she had inherited her mother's talent and had already received *Vogue* magazine's prestigious Prix de Paris writing award. Pat put her in touch with Franklin Spier, who soon hired her to fill the writing position at the bottom of the pecking order that had opened up after Pat's departure. Louise stayed at Spier for eleven years. "It was a lovely place to work," she remembered. "I think that was the golden age of publishing—the fifties. Now publishers are afraid to take chances. Franklin Spier was a remarkable man, a kind of lovely man. Oh, God, he was very neurotic, but he was just a sweetheart, and he had this absolute knack of picking talented kids. Everyone was working for about forty-five dollars a week, which really did go a lot further in those days. We just had a great time. There were many three-hour lunches, although we all managed to get quite a lot of work done. At lunch, we'd often go to this place called Chappy's Television Bar, and I'd drink these huge Manhattans and then go back. . . . Well, our best work was often done in the morning!" Louise and the other Franklin Spier alumni remained close throughout their lives.

Pat and Louise became engaged and set December 30, 1948, as their wedding date. Pat was still sharing the Paul Manship apartment on East Seventy-second Street with Bill and Barbara Hooton. The rent was now $97.25 a month for four rooms—a bargain even back then—and neither couple wanted to lose it. The matter was resolved by a coin toss, and Pat won. The Hootons had to hit the pavement.

Earlier in December, Louise had given a party at her parents' apartment for her newly married Vassar chum Lydia Anderson, who was living in Connecticut. That day a major blizzard descended on the city, so Lydia, her husband, and everyone else coming in from Connecticut wore ski clothes to the party. "That was rather strange," relates Lydia, "since everyone else was dressed in cocktail gowns. I was talking to Louise, and I saw this bearded fellow sitting on the couch in the corner, and I said to Louise, 'Who on *earth* is that?' And indeed, it turned out to be the man she married!

"My tone of voice had *not* been complimentary," Lydia says, laughing. "He was tall, and his beard, of course, was formidable, and his head was shaved! The combination was indeed startling. And he had an unusual way of speaking. All in all, you tended to see him and then turn around and lift your eyebrows, as I'm sure *he* did to all of *us!* But in a good-natured way. He wasn't mean at all, but he could really poke fun at people. Telling stories the way he did, he could have you in absolute stitches. Just the way he'd say 'Oh my *God,* darling!' would have you rolling in the aisles."

The obvious question that arises is whether Pat ever spoke frankly with Louise about his sexual confusion. If not, did Louise suspect this problem when she agreed to marry him? When asked about this in 1998, her response was an annoyed "I don't see why it's any of your business." But she went on to say, "I don't think you realize that at the time there were a whole lot of people who were described as 'confirmed bachelors.' They were all gay, and it really wasn't the first thing you'd think of. Many people's jobs would have been endangered. I think I had the popular conception at the time that most people who were gay were either hairdressers or someone in the arts. I went to Acapulco once with Pat and I could not believe that there was a man who was an economist who was a homosexual; that there was a doctor who was a homosexual. I think his tendencies this way got more pronounced as he got older."

Louise's parents were not altogether pleased with her unconventional choice of a husband. A flamboyant, eccentric atheist was probably not what they had had in mind as a prospective son-in-law. But they were gracious enough to offer to have the wedding in their apartment at 215 East Seventy-second Street. It was preferable to City Hall, which was where Pat and Louise were originally planning to be married. "City Hall was kind of a specter in my family," said Louise. "They dreamed of me in yards and yards of white tulle. But we wanted a small wedding. There were only eight of us there." Isabelle Holland, who by now was also working at Creative Age Press with Pat, remembers him on the day of his wedding being shown out of the office by friends, dressed to the teeth and flourishing a walking stick.

Pat's parents came in from Chicago for the wedding. Louise had not met them before, and she was not impressed. "I don't think he cared for either of his parents, but particularly not his father. They didn't fight, but he was just a very insensitive man. Pat always said of him that he could do things like throw a peanut up into the air and catch it in his mouth, but that once you'd seen that trick performed, it was amusing until you were about ten years old. They were not very friendly. I didn't like him at all. He was very violently Midwestern, and I think he always thought of anybody who came to New York as sort of the Whore of Babylon. One time he came for the weekend. Up until that time he had never really struck me as being particularly a drunk; we all drank so much in those days. I guess he was trying to make a good impression, so he spent all Friday and most of Saturday cold sober. Then, I think, just before he was about to leave, he sat down and drank a large glass of straight gin. We practically had to pour him on the plane. He was really just babbling.

"My parents didn't like him very much either. Mrs. Tanner was okay, but her great conversational gambit was the price of lamb chops on the Twentieth Century Limited. She could go on about that. Once I met them, I really hoped they were never coming back, and I don't think they did. I don't think I saw them more than twice in my life."

The actual wedding took place amidst a flurry of pratfalls and insults and was worthy of a Preston Sturges comedy. Louise shocked everyone by wearing kelly green instead of the traditional white. Things went downhill from there. "My mother got off one of her witticisms on Mr. Tanner," said Louise, "and they took an immediate dislike to each other. That was enhanced by the fact that Mr. Tanner then managed to slip and fall and knock down a silver tray with about a dozen of my mother's best crystal glasses on it. My mother said, 'Well—at least he didn't break up the set. He took the whole thing.' "

The wedding was duly reported by the Social Register Association in the January 1949 issue of *Dilatory Domiciles*. Pat and Louise were already enjoying a honeymoon in Europe.

By all accounts, Pat and Louise made a dazzling pair at a dazzling time in a dazzling city. Sophisticated, elegant, and always ready with a *bon mot*, they typified a kind of idealized New York couple—a real-life version of William Powell and Myrna Loy in *The Thin Man* or Cary Grant and Constance Bennett in *Topper*. Louise was the rare mate who would be compatible with Pat's larger-than-life social persona. Although she was the more subdued of the two, she had the knack of allowing Pat to shine in the spotlight, and then—with a perfectly timed sardonic remark and the arch of an eyebrow—she could put him right in his place.

After Louise had been working at Franklin Spier for a year, Joy Singer joined the staff in the entry-level copywriter position. By this time Louise had been promoted. On her first day, Joy introduced herself to Louise, saying, "Mr. Spier told me that if I had any troubles, I should take them to you." Louise, surprised, shot back, "Take your troubles to *God*, dear child!" Then they both burst into laughter and instantly became friends.

"Long before Pat became famous," says Joy Singer, "he and Louise were the two most exotic people I had ever met. They gave wonderful parties; Pat was a gourmet cook; he made marvelous, elaborate things. Today this would not be extraordinary, but at that time, we went to spaghetti-and-wine dinners. The very elaborate dinners they had for me, for Isabelle Holland, for their buddies—were unusual. And Pat loved everything to be perfect. I remember him saying that he could not have somebody in a group that he wanted because he did not have enough matching chairs. Now, in my house, the folding chairs come out; that doesn't worry me. And at that time, most of us sat on the floor!

"I met Pat at a party," Joy continues, "and I was a little surprised when I met him, because, as you probably know, he was much more effeminate than was fashionable at the time. You probably wouldn't raise an eyebrow now. You know, you can't be around Louise very long without picking up her intonations. My children can always tell when I'm talking on the phone to Louise. That manner of speaking always led up to a punch line, plus he had a very dry delivery that was very unusual. But that was nothing like what Pat was like. He really went through life *wanting* to think that everyone was as nice as he was. And very few people were. This is going to sound corny, but it was pleasant to be in the world with Pat. You knew that the next time you saw him, something was going to happen that would make you laugh. It was just *fun*. I don't know if it was as much fun *being* him as it was being with him."

Pat remained at Creative Age Press until 1951, while continuing to ghostwrite and to freelance magazine pieces. Then, offered a job with a higher salary, he took it. He joined the staff of the Council on Foreign Relations as promotions director of *Foreign Affairs,* the Council's monthly magazine, a much stuffier place to work than Creative Age Press or Franklin Spier. In a rare bow to the social dictates of the era, Pat temporarily shaved off his beard before he began his new job.

The Council on Foreign Relations was and is a nonprofit foundation devoted to the study of international relations. Founded in 1921 by a consortium of businessmen, bankers, and lawyers, it was intended to fight isolationism and keep the United States engaged on the world political stage. According to its mission statement, the Council on Foreign Relations is "composed of men and women from all walks of international life and from all parts of America dedicated to the belief that the nation's peace and prosperity are firmly linked to that of the rest of the world. From this flows the Council's mission: to foster America's understanding of other nations near and far, their peoples, cultures, histories, hopes, quarrels, and ambitions, and thus to serve America's global interests through study and debate, private and public." Nonpartisan and nonideological, the Council also aims to serve "its members and the nation with ideas for a better and safer world." *Foreign Affairs,* with its circulation of over one hundred thousand, remains its major emissary; the magazine is a highly respected forum for articles on international relations.

When Pat began working there in 1951, the Council on Foreign Relations was still a relatively small organization and occupied the Harold Irving Pratt mansion on the southwest corner of Park Avenue and Sixty-eighth Street. The mansion's former ballroom served as a conference room; its servants' quarters became office space, with the old bell and buzzer systems still on the walls. Since then the Council has grown substantially, expanding far beyond the town house into four more adjacent buildings.

As usual, Pat's aptitude and intelligence made him an asset right from the start at the Council. Soon he was promoting not just *Foreign Affairs,* but also the various books that the Council published. He even began putting his artistic talents to use by designing the books' dust jackets. Then, because of his rapid-fire shorthand skills, he was also asked to act as what the Council called rapporteur. That meant being a glorified stenographer and taking notes during meetings with foreign diplomats. Pat abhorred the prospect and immediately grew back his beard. As beards were frowned upon at the time, it rendered him quite unacceptable to meet visiting dignitaries.

Although the Council was still a relatively small organization in the early 1950s, its employee roster was a blend of some distinct personalities. Pat fit right in, and of course, he relished the opportunity to do some amused observing. Hamilton Fish Armstrong, George Franklin, and Frank Carruthers, Pat's immediate superiors, were formidable bosses. The brusque, hyperefficient head librarian, Ruth Savoy, was referred to as "an ogre" by more than one employee, and her assistant was her exact opposite—an elegant gentleman who seemed a bit of a Milquetoast. To this mixture, Pat was considered by everyone a marvelous addition, a welcome touch of exoticism. Always friendly, always in a good mood, he was instantly embraced by his colleagues, who warmed to his eccentric persona. His elegant entrances each morning—in British tailored suits, pin-striped shirts, furled umbrella, and a homburg—are still fondly remembered by his colleagues.

While friendly with virtually everyone at the Council, Pat grew
particularly close to three individuals. One was Roger Ross, who was
in charge of corporate relations. A big man—even taller than Pat—
he had begun working at the Council as an awkward, uncertain
young fellow fresh out of Columbia University. Pat became his pal
and confidant, and the entire office noticed that Ross was soon loos-
ening up and becoming more secure and easygoing under Pat's
friendship and encouragement. Before long, Pat introduced him to
the fine art of the happy hour. Since the cocktails at the neighborhood
bar were awful, Pat and Ross began making their own in the office at
night, sitting and discussing such issues as whether the martinis needed
more or less gin.

The other employees to whom Pat grew especially close were Elaine
Adam and Vivian Weaver, who ran the offices. Now well into their seventies, they remain an engagingly vibrant pair of personalities, radiat-
ing copious amounts of warmth, wit, and clear thinking—qualities that
Pat adored and were reflected in his best-known creation. "They are
two of the coolest people I know," says Pat's daughter, Betsy, and they
remain two of the Tanner family's closest friends. Both retired from the
Council, Vivian and Elaine now divide their time between Manhattan
and a home upstate in Columbia County. The East Eighty-second
Street apartment that they have shared for decades has always been a
kind of after-hours salon for all of their neighbors. The door is literally
always open and the martinis mixed and ready every night for anyone
in the building who feels like dropping by after work.

"The best way I can describe this person to you," says Vivian
Weaver, "is to say that whatever he did, he made it fun. It was an
absolute delight, even if it was the most mundane thing. I remember
having to go through the stencils for our list of subscribers' labels, and
he even made *that* fun. He said, 'Look at this man's name—Joseph
Glasscock! What do you think of *that?*'"

"The mailroom would need a paint job," says Elaine Adam, "so Pat
would get a case of beer and say, 'Why don't we all go in on Saturday
and paint the mailroom?' And everybody loved it, because he made
everything fun. If he felt particularly put-upon or annoyed, he'd go from
office to office and say, 'Who am I?' and hold out his arms like he was
crucified, doing the Jesus Christ thing. He'd always keep us laughing."

One of Pat's favorite tricks was outsmarting the boss. He and Vivian had adjoining offices, and sometimes when Pat heard one of the directors coming down to see him from upstairs, he'd jump up on his desk, pull up the cuffs of his trousers, and start tap-dancing. Vivian would frantically be whispering to him, "Mr. Mallory's coming! Mr. Mallory's coming!" But Pat would nonchalantly keep tap-dancing and saying, "Don't worry," as the sound of the footsteps came closer and closer. Finally—just in the nick of time—he'd jump down and sit behind his desk, smile up at Mr. Mallory coming through the door, and say, "Good morning, Mr. Mallory. How are you?"

On one occasion, Pat hid in the closet while Vivian was talking to George Franklin, mimicking him from behind his back in full view of Vivian, who was trying desperately to keep a straight face. "He was always so much fun," she says. "I couldn't wait to get to work to see what he'd do next."

Pat hired a receptionist named Bita Dobo in 1953, who would stay at the Council for the next twenty-eight years. They became friends, and Pat quickly—perhaps inevitably—nicknamed her Bidet, which, he knew, would drive her crazy. Whenever she would call him on the intercom to let him know he had a visitor, he would say, "I'll be right down, Bidet!"

Pat had more responsibilities at the Council than he had had at Franklin Spier or Creative Age Press, but as usual, he astonished everyone by the amount of work he could take on and the rapidity with which he dispatched it. He could do something in a few days that would take someone else weeks. That left him plenty of time to do his own writing—and to enjoy long, five-martini lunches. He, Roger Ross, and others would usually go to their favorite lunch spot, Oscar's Salt of the Sea, on Third Avenue, and stay well into the afternoon. Bita Dobo often had to call there to try to get them out. Ross remembers the time they took one of Pat's former American Field Service buddies to lunch. After cocktails, lunch, and more cocktails, it had grown so late, and everyone was so plastered, there was no point in returning to work. Pat and Roger just headed home, and the AFS friend staggered up Third Avenue and simply disappeared, never to be heard from again. Apparently, he never even returned to his job. Heaven only knows what spiral of debauchery he was launched on that day.

During the afternoons when Pat did return from lunch, his behavior was often outrageous. He was even known to forgo the use of the Council men's room when he had to relieve himself after all those martinis. It was so much more fun to run up to the roof and shoot a sprinkle down onto East Sixty-eighth Street.

It's astonishing how much Pat was allowed to get away with, particularly under his demanding and rather straitlaced bosses. But his skills were such that he was considered a valuable asset to the Council, and his considerable personal charm helped smooth the way for his Peck's Bad Boy antics. Whenever it was necessary, he could be counted upon to do all the work that needed to be done. And he was willing to stand up for his colleagues if he felt they deserved better treatment. After repeatedly imploring George Franklin to grant the women who worked in the mailroom a raise, he finally said, "George, meet me tomorrow morning. We're going out to Coney Island and we're going to come in at rush hour on the train and I'll show you what their lives are all about." Franklin finally relented. The women got their raise.

"Even after he'd been gone from the Council for many, many years," Vivian Weaver stresses, "workmen would say, 'How's Mr. Tanner? How's Mr. Tanner?' He could get people to do anything. He was, to me, a true genius and a wonderful, wonderful person. I'm very indebted to him for everything I learned."

EIGHT

Noms de Plume

Pat's workload at the Council was heavy, but he could still devote large amounts of time to his own writing. With several pseudonymous magazine articles and two ghostwritten books behind him, he now embarked on a new project.

Dr. Nicholas Nyaradi, the former Hungarian minister of finance, had met Pat through the Council of Foreign Relations. Nyaradi was looking for someone to ghostwrite his memoirs, which would focus on his experiences as a foreign diplomat in the Soviet Union. He hired Pat for the job, and a publishing contract was signed with Thomas Y. Crowell and Company. Pat pounded out a three-hundred page manuscript based on lengthy interviews with Nyaradi. *My Ringside Seat in Moscow* was published in 1952, with a dust-jacket blurb that read, "New light on Communist tactics by one of the last diplomats to live behind the Curtain."

However, Nyaradi was, according to Louise Tanner, "a horrible man," and he and Pat soon had a falling-out of major proportions. Pat refused to ever write for him again, saddling Nyaradi with a marvelous literary style that he was quite incapable of reproducing on his own. Ironically, the flyleaf copy on *My Ringside Seat in Moscow* began, "Here is a book that could have been written by nobody else . . ."

The reviews were quite favorable. "It is astounding," wrote Marcus Duffield in the *New York Herald Tribune*, "that Mr. Nyaradi can write about his grisly ordeals with the Kremlin with so much poise, humor, and charm." *The New Yorker* said, "It is well written, it abounds in colorful detail about life on high and low levels in the USSR—the author's descriptions of upper-crust diversions in Moscow would make Kublai

Khan weak with envy—and it is also a handy guide to the labyrinthine ways of dirty politics."

Pat realized it was high time he did something more substantial and satisfying with his talent than ghostwriting and churning out magazine fluff. He was finally ready to write his first original comic novel. From start to finish, the job took him only about three months. Within a year it was published, also by Thomas Y. Crowell and Company, who probably felt they owed him one after his experience with Nyaradi. Entitled *Oh, What a Wonderful Wedding!*, it listed "Virginia Rowans" as the author. Pat had wanted to call his new literary alter ego Virginia Rounds, after his favorite brand of cigarette, but he was ultimately persuaded to make his new pseudonym just a bit less obvious.

Nobody was the wiser, least of all the critics. "Miss Rowans writes with a fine feminine realism," crowed Jane Cobb in the *New York Times*. "Few of the foibles of our competitive society escape her." A. F. Otis in the *Chicago Sunday Tribune* called the book "a riotous, hilariously devastating satire about marriage, with no punches pulled and no motives minced." Written entirely in the present tense, *Oh, What a Wonderful Wedding!* detailed the courtship and wedding of suburban Long Island's Mildred Boyd and suburban Los Angeles's Chester Field, from the night Chester asks Milly's father for her hand to the apocalyptic final moments of the wedding reception, when, simultaneously, a hurricane breaks out and Chester receives his draft notice. Like Pat's subsequent books, it is essentially light in tone but cutting in its social satire. For some, the humor was a bit too corrosive—in the *New York Herald Tribune Book Review*, Joanna Spencer called it "very funny and knowledgeable" but also found it at times "unpleasantly malicious."

Oh, What a Wonderful Wedding! is very much of a piece with Pat's fifteen subsequent novels, sharing a similar structure and tone. A sure sense of plot was never one of Pat's attributes as a writer; his greatest strength was the creation of characters. Although nearly all of his books come with a large cast, the best of them feature a central figure who dominates the action—Auntie Mame in *Auntie Mame*, Leander Starr in *Genius*, Tony in *Tony*. *Oh, What a Wonderful Wedding!*, on the other hand, is an ensemble piece in which both sets of families and their attendant friends, relatives, ushers, and bridesmaids are given

equal prominence. Although the novel is not overly long—242 pages—
the lack of a central focus ultimately makes it seem a bit stretched. In
an otherwise favorable review, J. H. Jackson of the *San Francisco
Chronicle* pointed out, "One thing, to be perfectly honest: There's too
much of it. The book, funny as it is, would have gained immeasurably
if someone had been tough enough to cut it down about one-third. You
can't carry a joke quite as far as the author here carries it and be funny
all that time. On the other hand, there is a kind of mad humor in it
that's like nothing I've ever seen."

Pat had a gift for creating characters who, while exaggerated for
comic effect, stopped short of being completely cartoonish. It gave his
waspish writing marvelous accuracy, which is in full evidence in the
scene where the future Los Angeles in-laws meet the future Long
Island in-laws for the first time:

> Just then the doorbell rings and they stand, paralyzed, for one full
> second.
>
> Suddenly there is a terrible thunder of feet on the stairs and
> Mrs. Boyd, Milly, Aunt Belle, Junior and Mr. Boyd, his face
> rather badly nicked, converge in the hall.
>
> "You answer, Milly," Mrs. Boyd whispers, although the Tudor
> door is a good three inches thick. "Murray," she adds, "button
> yourself up."
>
> Now the two families stand silently in the hallway facing each
> other.
>
> Mrs. Boyd arranges her face into a cordial smile and surveys
> cautiously every inch of Mrs. Field. She *does* have a certain style
> which Mrs. Boyd could never in a million years achieve, "But,"
> thinks Mrs. Boyd happily, "it's been *quite* a long time since she's
> been able to get into *my* dress size."
>
> Mrs. Field smiles benignly on her hostess. In a moment she's
> sized up the blue velvet as appropriate, though matronly, and
> pegged it at thirty-nine ninety-five, and she does wonder how
> Mrs. Boyd keeps so thin. "My dear," she says, "how can I ever
> thank you for those lovely flowers?"
>
> The ice is broken. Everybody talks at once.

A few moments later, the two women are having drinks in the living room, sniffing at each other like curs:

"Well, Peter and I were just captivated by Mildred the minute we saw her," Mrs. Field repeats, taking a big, bracing swallow of her drink. "Yes, Mrs. Boyd, I've always wished that Chester would settle down and write. I just know he could."

"Oh, so do I!" Mrs. Boyd exclaims. "Wouldn't it be thrilling to have a real, live author in the family! Chester tells me that *you're* very literary, too, Mrs. Field. Which reminds me that *I'm* right in the middle of a perfectly fascinating book."

"Oh, do you write?" Mrs. Field asks uneasily. She hadn't been prepared for an authoress as well as a social leader.

"Oh, no," Mrs. Boyd giggles. "I'm *reading* one. It's called *Dinner at Antoine's*. Have you read it?"

"Oh, *that*. Yes, ages ago." Mrs. Field hopes she hasn't sounded rude, but she does feel that she's scored something of a point.

"How I envy you, finding so much time to read," Mrs. Boyd says. She's on her guard now. "I'm just so busy running this house and what with the Garden Club and the Philharmonic and shopping in town and the League . . ."

She allows her voice to trail off, feeling that she's covered sufficient ground. In a few words she has established herself as a homemaker, a lover of nature and fine music, a free spender and a socialite, although the league she refers to is that of Women Voters and not the Junior.

Mrs. Field considers all this. She is impressed but not defeated. "Oh, don't I know! Men are always saying that we women have nothing to do all day. Well, I'd like to see them *try* it, just once. It's always a luncheon here, a meeting there—and especially in a place like New York. I just don't know how we got along before each of us had our own car."

Mrs. Boyd is slightly staggered, but she is game enough to appreciate a really good double play, even though it has put her out. Her adversary has neatly stated that New York is cramped and overcrowded and that the Field family's garage is slightly larger than the Boyds' house. Smarting, she changes the subject: "I believe you have a second son, Mrs. Field?"

"Yes, Bud," Mrs. Field says tenderly. "His real name is Cyril, after my father, Cyril Chester. He was an Englishman"—Mrs. Field likes to pronounce her father's name with its ring of empire, good tweed, burnished leather, and roast beef—"but of course Bud thinks the name Cyril is too silly."

"But how nice for you to have another son at home to replace Chester."

"Well, Bud's not really at home. He's in Stanford now and I'm afraid he'll be in the Army if he doesn't keep his marks up. He just barely got through last year."

Mrs. Boyd is not one to let a golden opportunity pass unheeded. "Now isn't that funny," she says. "With Junior it's just the other way round. I honestly have to *force* him to stop studying. 'All work and no play,' I keep telling him. . . . The mathematics master at Country Day says he has one of the most phenomenal minds for figures he's ever seen. Why, he assures me that Junior can have his pick of any scholarship in any top college in the *East*." Mrs. Boyd feels so pleased with herself that she takes a sizable sip of her drink.

A few days later the prospective fathers-in-law, who share their wives' pretension but not their vicious streak, meet for drinks at Mr. Boyd's midtown men's club.

"Say, speaking of California, I wish you and the missus would come out to see Lily and me sometime. It's great country out there, Boyd; you don't know what you're missing till you come out to our part of the world."

"Well, we'd certainly like to—just for a visit—but I'm too hidebound an Easterner to take to the life out there. Can't teach an old dog new tricks, you know." Hearty laughs.

"It's a funny thing, you know, that's just what *I* say. Now I like New York just fine, for a *visit*, but I wouldn't want to live here. Guess I'm just an old cowhand at heart."

Mr. Boyd is a native of Chicago; Mr. Field was born in St.

Louis, a matter of an afternoon's ride by slow train. Each becomes more expansive, more Eastern or more Western as the glasses are drained. At two o'clock the captain really must *insist* that the *gentlemen* order luncheon. The kitchen is about to close.

The dining room is exclusively theirs, just as the bar has been for the last hour. Respectable businessmen have long since returned to their desks. But Mr. Boyd and Mr. Field, once again "Murray" and "Pete," work their way gustily through lunch with occasional swigs of additional old fashioneds, while a knot of dour waiters examine their cuticles impatiently and wish the old lushes would drop dead.

Pat rarely went in for lengthy description, but when he did, he could use simile and metaphor mercilessly. Here is how he details the buffet table toward the end of the wedding reception:

Already the flowers, tortured by florist's wire, have swooned upon their green arches and bowers. The aspics quiver no more, but lie defeated and melting on their platters, flowing in canals and rivulets through the undergrowth of watercress. The dainty sandwiches, embellished with "M&C," have curled like Turkish slippers. The few devilled eggs which are left look up helplessly like blind and jaundiced eyes. The sweet bride and groom carved in pineapple ice decompose like snowmen in the sun. The wedding cake, once a proud monument of pillars and garlands and terraces, has crumbled like the ruins of Herculaneum. Only the champagne and the heartier guests endure.

The book was dedicated "to my mate," perhaps as a fond nod to the kind of wedding Pat and Louise had been lucky to escape. Like most of Pat's books, *Oh, What a Wonderful Wedding!* gives present-day readers a meticulous, detailed insight into a nearly vanished social world: that group that fell right into the crack between Old Money and the Nouveaux Riches; the Upper Crust of the Upper Middle Class, desperately clawing at the doorway to American royalty. This milieu was at its most aggressive during the first two-thirds of the twentieth century and was a rich mine of humor for Pat throughout his career as a writer.

Although he never wrote another novel in the present tense, *Oh, What a Wonderful Wedding!* served as a blueprint for Pat's future prose style: elegant, witty, and far more British in tone than American. *Vanity Fair* by William Makepeace Thackeray was always Pat's favorite book, and Thackeray's amused, somewhat Olympian view of human foibles maintained a marked influence on Pat throughout his writing career.

Despite the good reviews, sales figures on *Oh, What a Wonderful Wedding!* were not staggering. Undeterred, Virginia Rowans plowed into her second novel, *House Party,* which Crowell published the following year.

Like *Oh, What a Wonderful Wedding!,* *House Party* was set mostly on Long Island, in this case a dilapidated mansion sixty miles from New York City. Mrs. Lily Ames, of the old-money Pruitt family in the town of Pruitt's Landing, is hosting the Pruitts' annual Independence Day weekend party. What nobody but Lily realizes is that the Pruitt family's money has dwindled down virtually to pennies, and that the forty-room Shingle Style Pruitt mansion has become such a financial burden that it is on the verge of crumbling due to poor upkeep. Lily, the novel's central and most likable character, would be happy to just sell the place and have done with it, but she cannot even give it away. The noble Victorian structure flies in the face of fifties fashion, and its all-wood construction makes it a fire hazard and a termite trap. For years now, Lily has been living by the financial seat of her pants and has no idea how she's even going to pay for the weekend party.

There is once again a huge cast of characters, headed by Lily, her gauche, spendthrift sister Violet, and Lily's four grown children, Paul, Elly, Kathy, and Bryan. The list goes on—Lily and Violet's elderly gay uncle, Violet's bitchy, conniving daughter, Paul's social-climbing girl-friend, Kathy's gigolo boyfriend, and assorted guests, neighbors, and servants. By the novel's end, the good characters have been rewarded, the ill punished, and the house has gone up in a gigantic conflagration ignited by Fourth of July fireworks—much to Lily's blissful relief, as the house and everything in it are insured for twice their worth.

House Party depicts an era in American social history when old money was giving way to new. The upheavals of a depression and two world wars, not to mention the implementation of the income tax, had struck a blow at some of the nation's wealthiest families. It was becoming harder and harder for families to maintain their sprawling summer "cottages." Many of them were donated to nonprofit institutions as tax write-offs; many others were sold to developers and leveled, their sprawling grounds turned into cookie-cutter postwar housing tracts. Although Pat preferred the urban high life, he did not necessarily view these developments negatively. Here is the dialogue between Lily and her snobbish, pretentious son Bryan during the book's final pages, as the old mansion lies in embers and the family regroups to plan its future:

"This is what I plan to do. This tract of land is six square miles. It has driven me nearly into the poorhouse and virtually to drink. There are how many acres to a square mile?"

"Six hundred and forty," Paul said.

"Thank you, dear. Paul has an idea for a kind of housing development which would not be unattractive to anyone. In fact, I shouldn't mind living in a nice, efficient little house on a full acre of land myself."

"With a lot of riffraff?" Bryan said.

"It's nice to know, Bryan," Mrs. Ames said with a certain amount of irritation, "that our great liberal is still with us. In any case, Paul has this scheme which I think is a good one. I was planning to help him raise the money to get some land out here. But owing to the happy catastrophe brought on by Violet and the Aurora Borealis Gun Powder Company, I happen to have six square miles to give away. That's how many acres, Paul?"

"Three, nearly four thousand acres."

"Very well, then. The old Pruitt Place will shortly become a place for four thousand families to live. . . . For four hundred years this place has produced nothing but wood ticks and us. Now I intend to make it productive in a number of ways, by handing it over to Paul to fill with his nice cheap houses."

"For God's sake, Mother," Bryan shouted, "do you want to turn this place into a slum? If you wanted to sell off part of it to make into a *decent* subdivision, with houses in the thirty-to-forty-thousand-dollar bracket, for people who could appreciate the place, I might . . ."

"That is precisely what I do *not* intend to do. I have the feeling that Paul's people will be just as capable of appreciating this land as your people, Bryan, and more deserving of it."

Would Pat have considered living in a suburban tract home himself? Not bloody likely. But he was enough of a liberal Democrat to appreciate the postwar American dream idea of affordable, egalitarian middle-class housing. Today, of course, most of us would be horrified by the idea of a fabulous old mansion being sent up in flames and replaced with a housing development, but in 1954, that was interpreted by many as a sign of progress.

Although still overpopulated like *Oh, What a Wonderful Wedding!*, *House Party* is an improvement in that the character of Lily Ames provides a sympathetic focal point. Like Auntie Mame, Lily punctures the pretensions of those around her. She serves as an effective vehicle for Pat's own gentle but constant moral voice. Once again, Pat's work was greeted with rave reviews and scant sales. "The writing is polished and mature," wrote Rose Feld in the *New York Herald Tribune*, "and holds memorable moments of descriptions which are rich in subtle satire of a social scene." "A clever and entertaining novel," said *The New Yorker*. "The story runs on just a little too long, but up to a certain point, not far from the end, it is fast reading and often irresistibly funny."

In the *San Francisco Chronicle*, J. H. Jackson called it "a pretty funny book, and a nice satire too, sometimes gentle, and now and then sharp as a tack. I'd make one reservation: it all could have been a touch shorter and no harm done. One thing: With the right screen writer and director, *House Party* could make a wildly funny picture. Boxoffice, moreover." There would be no movie, but TV buffs may find that the basic plot of *House Party* seems familiar. That's because the story was eventually sold to television as the sitcom *The Pruitts of Southampton*, which had a one-year run on ABC during the 1966–67 season. *The Pruitts of Southampton* had only the bare bones of the *House Party* situation, tailored to fit the manic personality of star Phyllis Diller and second bananas Grady Sutton, Billy DeWolfe, Reginald Gardiner, and

John Astin. Halfway through the season, the program was slightly revamped and retitled *The Phyllis Diller Show,* but the public wasn't buying, and the show never made it to a second year.

By 1953, Pat and Louise were expecting their first child and needed larger quarters where they could raise a family. They said good-bye to the Paul Manship apartment and installed themselves eighteen blocks uptown at 1245 Madison Avenue. Located on the corner of Madison and Ninetieth Street, the six-story, brown-brick building was one of the oldest in the neighborhood and had once been owned by the Astors. Designed in what was known at the time as the Philadelphia style, it had thick walls, heavy French doors, and crenellated roofline ornamentation that made it look like a castle. Pat and Louise moved in on the sixth floor—"the literary floor," as it was known, because its other two apartments were occupied by a bookstore owner and by the Rabbi Henry M. Rosenthal and his family, all of whom were writers. A sense of community immediately began to thrive on the floor once the Tanners moved in. Most of the building's other tenants were conservative Republicans; the Tanners were proud Adlai Stevenson Democrats who warmed up instantly to their sixth-floor neighbors. To the Rosenthals especially, the Tanners' personalities swept through the place like fresh air. Lucy and Abigail—the teenage Rosenthal daughters—found Pat and Louise a terribly glamorous couple.

"They were wonderful neighbors," says Lucy, "irreverent and witty. They'd talk in aphorisms. They were a very interesting combination of old, traditional values of courtesy and generosity, and they were just so with it. Their irreverence, in the fifties especially, was extraordinary. They were doing things that weren't done in that stodgy, uptight time."

"They were a *team,*" agrees Abigail. "They worked very well together. They were so unconventional and they were so elegant. They were good neighbors, good friends, and they were attentive to all the decencies in life. I don't remember exactly when we started socializing, but I asked Pat once while we were waiting for the elevator, 'What do you do?' When he told me he worked for *Foreign Affairs* magazine, I said, 'Oh, how interesting!' And he said immediately, 'It's *not* interesting! I do absolutely nothing!' I think he said all he did was sit at this desk and write his novels. *Nobody* talked like that back in the fifties. You never heard that." Nonetheless, Pat and Louise were more than happy to introduce the Rosenthal sisters to the world of publishing, and both women went on to enjoy successful careers as authors and editors.

Nineteen fifty-four saw the birth of Pat and Louise's first child, Michael. Pat celebrated by painting charming, Rousseau-like murals of jungle animals all over the walls of the baby's room. Louise took a maternity leave from Franklin Spier, but would continue working there until 1959, long after the birth of their second child, Betsy. At Michael's christening, a beaming Pat greeted friends at the door of the apartment with a blanketed little bundle cradled in his arms. "Oh, you must see little Michael!" he would say— and then pull back the blanket to reveal a stuffed monkey.

Michael would not be the only Tanner production of 1954. That year also saw the completion of the novel that would change Pat Tanner's life once and for all.

NINE

"A Simple, Single Woman . . ."

Despite the disappointing performance of *House Party*, Pat got to work on a new book. Not really in the form of a novel, this interconnected set of short stories followed Mame Dennis, a glamorous New York madcap, through a series of comic misadventures over three decades. Narrated by Mame's orphaned Chicago nephew, Patrick, to whom she becomes legal guardian when the boy is ten, the book introduces Mame at the height of the Roaring Twenties. Mame then survives the Depression and World War II, marries a Southern millionaire, and saves Patrick from marrying the air-brained daughter of a pair of bigoted WASPs. Patrick gets sucked into every one of Mame's outlandish adventures, which makes him the ideal narrator for the story. The structure of *Auntie Mame* would serve as a paradigm for many of Pat's best novels: a basically average, basically decent fellow finds himself thrust into a bizarre situation amidst outrageous, often unscrupulous characters and attempts to restore some kind of balance. But Mame doesn't really need Patrick's help; every time she's nearly mired in a mess of her own making, she resorts to her wits and emerges triumphant.

Pat spent nearly a year working on the novel, not the ninety days that he would later claim. He enlisted the aid of his Council pals Vivian Weaver and Elaine Adam in typing the manuscript. "Typing up that manuscript was a wonderful experience," says Vivian Weaver. "Pat would come over to the house and say, 'I've got an idea; now, tell me if you like this.' And we'd tell him, very honestly, whether we thought it worked or not." Because Pat was narrating the story from the first-person point of view of Mame's nephew Patrick Dennis, that was the pseudonym he chose for this book. He would later claim that he had picked the surname Dennis out of the telephone book.

His agent, Elizabeth Otis, had a hard time selling the book and struck out with nineteen publishers, who rarely took chances on short stories at that time. In the early 1950s the short story was still largely regarded as the province of magazines. Moving down the list of possibilities, Otis came to Julian Muller at Vanguard Press. At that time, Vanguard was a small house with a small staff. Muller was its newest editor, having entered book publishing after seven years in the magazine world. Muller had told Otis that he was looking for something light, and Otis said she might have just the thing. The manuscript arrived on Muller's desk on a Friday; he took it home, read it over the weekend, and adored it. Monday morning, he asked Elizabeth Otis to set up a meeting for him and Pat Tanner.

During the meeting, Muller explained to Pat the difficulty of selling short stories and suggested Pat turn the book into a novel. "I'd be willing," said Pat, "but how?" Within the week, Muller had the solution: link each chapter with the thematic device of the *Reader's Digest*'s "My Most Unforgettable Character" series. Every month, the magazine featured a first-person story by a writer who focused on one memorable individual he or she had known. Pat considered the idea for two days, then called Muller and said, "It'll work. Easily." Over the next two weeks, Pat spent his free time with Elaine and Vivian, who produced a clean typescript of Pat's novel incorporating the new sections. Pat, who had nicknames for everyone, always called Vivian and Elaine "V V and Mme A"—V V as in Vivian Veaver—and those were the names that appeared on *Auntie Mame*'s dedication page: "To the worst manuscript typists in New York—V V and Mme A." Muller insisted that Pat draw up a release to be signed by Vivian and Elaine stipulating that they had no problems with the dedication and would not instigate any lawsuits over it. Pat was happy to comply and produced the following:

> We, Miss Vivian K. Weaver and Mrs. Elaine P. Adam, are fully conscious—and somewhat flattered—that Edward E. Tanner, 3rd, has dedicated his novel *Auntie Mame*, written under the pseudonym "Patrick Dennis" and published by the Vanguard Press of New York City, to us.

We have seen the dedication, which reads "To the worst manuscript typists in New York, V. V. and Mme A." We feel that this dedication is trustworthy, loyal, helpful, friendly, courteous, kind, obedient, cheerful, thrifty, brave, clean, reverent, and in no way libelous. For the above reasons, neither of us would *dream* of bringing suit against either the above mentioned author or the above mentioned publisher, or against any American or foreign publisher who might bring out further editions of *Auntie Mame* in reprint or translation.

Duly signed by Vivian and Elaine, and notarized by the State of New York, the release made its way to Julian Muller, who replied:

Dear Miss Weaver and Mrs. Adam:

Thank you so very much for the release you sent to me in connection with the dedication of the novel by Edward E. Tanner, 3rd, alias Patrick Tanner, alias Patrick Dennis, alias Virginia Rowans. The release is so far superior to the novel, both in content and style, that we would be in favor, personally, of publishing it instead of the book.

Unfortunately, last season proved a rather unsuccessful one for releases, and we do not believe, in all honesty, that the present market would be any more receptive to that form of literary endeavor. Consequently, the best we can do is give this magnificent writing a prominent place in our files.

I am, with much gratitude,
Most sincerely,

Julian P. Muller

Convincing Vanguard to accept *Auntie Mame* had not been easy for Muller, as the top editors there were disinclined to publish light comic novels. None of them had even read *The Egg and I* or *Cheaper by the Dozen*, two enormously popular humorous novels from a few years before. Muller basically insisted that Vanguard take on *Auntie Mame*. The move was risky for him, not only because Patrick Dennis was a name unknown to the book-buying public, but also because the publication date was set for late January—*after* the holiday gift season, the flattest part of the publishing year. Somebody had to come up with a decent marketing strategy, and it wasn't going to be the folks at Vanguard, who had little experience with or affinity for this kind of book. Pat and Julian Muller decided to take matters into their own hands. Their first salvo was to send out the review copies with a store-bought cocktail-party invitation reading, "It's high time for a high time," to which they added, "Here's the happiest way to start your New Year: Read *Auntie Mame*." No luck whatsoever. Undaunted, they turned their attention to the bookstores. With a virtually nonexistent marketing budget, they sent a letter on black, white, and pink stationery—the color of *Auntie Mame*'s dust jacket—to every bookseller. "Pat and I had a whale of a time composing that letter," says Muller. "It essentially read: 'Darling, my unscrupulous nephew Patrick Dennis has written a scurrilous book about me. It's full of lies. It says I was caught nude in the dormitories of Princeton. It's not so! It was Yale!' And it continued in this wacky way and concluded by saying, 'I'm going to sue Patrick, I'm going to sue Vanguard Press, and if you sell a single copy, I'm going to sue you! Love, love, love, Mame.' Apparently we caught the booksellers, because about that time the book moved well onto the bestseller list—it was the booksellers who did it." Without Pat and Julian's marketing instincts, and without the support of the nation's booksellers, *Auntie Mame* might have been as well-remembered today as *House Party* or *Oh, What a Wonderful Wedding!* Nearly all of the book's overwhelmingly favorable reviews appeared *after* it hit the bestseller list.

Those reviews helped turn a success into a phenomenon. "Here it is," crowed the *Chicago Sunday Tribune*, "the funniest story about the most unforgettable character you'll ever run across. If you want a good laugh, *Auntie Mame* is the surest bet in the bookstores today." The critic for *The Houston Press* wrote, "If there's a more rollicking, side-splitting story produced this season, I'll eat it chapter by chapter together with five pages of Norman Vincent Peale's *Guide to Confident Living*." The *Boston Herald* found it "gorgeously funny . . . enchanting—a very bright light in a dismal world." Pat and Julian capitalized on the reviews by offering booksellers a copy free with every ten copies ordered—a deal introduced by way of another outrageous letter from Auntie Mame.

"It was fascinating," remembers Muller, "going to the sales department at Vanguard and watching the demographics growing on this. In the early days, you could see it spreading out from New York, Boston, Chicago, ultimately Los Angeles, and moving into other areas of the country. That really was very exciting." With the book having proved itself a winner, Pat attempted one of his typical—some might say foolhardy—acts of generosity. He instructed his agent to give 10 percent of his *Auntie Mame* earnings to Muller. Muller was incredibly touched, but gently declined the offer.

What caused *Auntie Mame* to become so beloved by the American public? For one thing, unlike Pat's first two books, it centered on a single character. Certainly Mame is surrounded by Pat's usual cast of eccentrics, but she forms the core of the novel and provides an immensely likable focal point as the story spans the decades. Since character was Pat's strong suit, rather than plot, he was at his most successful when building a novel around a strong central figure who interacts with a variety of oddballs. And for all Mame's own capriciousness, she comes up a winner in every one of the novel's episodes, cheerfully thwarting all adversaries. That, coupled with her own beguiling lunacy, her determination to "Live! Live! Live!," made her an irresistibly attractive figure to socially straitjacketed 1950s America. Even if few readers of the time shared Mame's all-embracing outrageousness, they admired and adored her for it. Women, especially, loved that Mame was a dame who did as she pleased and had one hell of a fine time doing it. For the rest of his life, Pat would repeatedly be buttonholed by the matron from Portland or Peoria who would fawn over him and insist that *she* was such a madcap personality he simply *must* have based Auntie Mame on her.

Homosexuals immediately warmed to the character of Auntie Mame, and for good reason: she was the essence of camp, and this was the first time that elusive component was successfully distilled and introduced into mainstream American literature. While British wits such as E. F. Benson, Ronald Firbank, and Evelyn Waugh had already camped up their work, no American novelist had bothered or dared to until Pat. In *Auntie Mame,* gay men found exactly the kind of dialogue and the types of characters they had been affectionately spoofing all their lives. Auntie Mame was a delightful lady, but in her campiness she might just as easily have been your favorite gay uncle—the one who had left Buffalo and moved to New York City, become the most sophisticated of hosts, spoke, dressed, and lived with uncanny flair, and, flying in the face of society's disapproval, turned his world into one of utter fabulousness. It took Pat Tanner, whose comic sensibility straddled the gay and straight worlds, to show Middle America just what it had been missing. *Camp* would not become common parlance in American English until ten years later, and by then *Auntie Mame* could have served as a camp Bible. Without even trying, Pat Tanner had turned camp into accepted American literary currency. It's not surprising that now, a half century later, the role of Auntie Mame in the stage version is being assayed by popular female impersonators such as Charles Busch, who costarred in a memorable 1998 New York benefit performance with Peggy Cass re-creating the role of Agnes Gooch.

As playwright/screenwriter/novelist Paul Rudnick puts it, "Patrick Dennis was the first person to realize that American society is *automatically* camp; that American aspirations will always have an enormously campy edge to them because of their foolishness, their pretentiousness, and their passion." Pretentiousness—from the town houses of Manhattan to the plantations of the Deep South to the estates of Old Money Connecticut—is blown to bits whenever Hurricane Mame sweeps through. Pretension was Pat's favorite target, and it gets as thorough a drubbing here as in any of his other novels. His incredibly astute eye for fashion, decor, and possessions makes the japery even more pointed. In the chapter "Auntie Mame and the Call to Arms," he describes Peabody's Tavern, a pre-Revolutionary building in Southampton, and its owner:

> It absolutely stank with atmosphere. There were five plaques next to the front door proclaiming the treaties signed within, the remarkable age and state of preservation of the structure, and other notes of interest to the historian. . . . Miss Peabody herself,

who told us four times that she was the tenth generation to live there, greeted us at the double-hung door. She was a bony old piece and a crashing snob. She didn't allow a minute to pass before she told us that she was a Daughter of the American Revolution, a Colonial Dame, a Daughter of the Cincinnati, a Mayflower Descendant, and a number of other dreary things. She ran over the major historical events that had occurred in the tavern during the past two or three hundred years, described the annual pilgrimage which had appeared in *Antiques* and *House and Garden* and *Country Life* and a lot of other fancy places.

Miss Peabody served us a very light and very bad luncheon on Lowestoft and then took us on a little tour of the house, pointing out the authentic Revere wallpaper, the authentic Windsor Chairs, the authentic Copley portraits of bygone Peabodys, the authentic hewn beams and pegged floors. She touched each warming pan and pewter mug and hooked rug as though it were a bit of the True Cross. Auntie Mame, looking very much the country gentlewoman, all tweed and a shooting stick, stifled several yawns and expressed a counterfeit fascination with the whole place.

Pat captured New York's Bohemian scene of the 1920s equally well in the novel's opening chapter, where young Patrick gets his first glimpse of his Most Unforgettable Character. He and his nursemaid, Norah, have arrived at Mame's apartment while a party is in full swing, and Mame makes a grand entrance into the anteroom where Patrick and Norah are waiting:

A regular Japanese doll of a woman had strolled into the foyer. Her hair was bobbed very short with straight bangs above her slanting brows; a long robe of embroidered golden silk floated out behind her. Her feet were thrust into tiny gold slippers twinkling with jewels, and jade and ivory bracelets clattered on her arms. She had the longest fingernails I'd ever seen, each lacquered a delicate green. An almost endless bamboo cigarette holder hung languidly from her bright red mouth. Somehow, she looked strangely familiar . . .

In a famous exchange that was grafted virtually intact into every stage and screen version of the piece, Mame protests that she thought Norah and the boy were going to arrive twenty-four hours later:

"But why didn't you *tell* me you were coming today? I'd never have been giving this party."

"Mum, I *wired* you . . ."

"Yes, but you said July first. Tomorrow. This is the thirty-first of June."

Norah shook her head balefully. "No, mum, 'tis the first, God curse the evil day."

The tinselly laugh rang out, "But that's ridiculous! Everyone knows 'Thirty days hath September, April, June and . . .' My God!" There was a moment's silence. "But darling," she said dramatically, "*I'm* your Auntie Mame!" She put her arms around me and kissed me, and I knew I was safe.

When social historians of the twenty-first century are studying the decades of the midtwentieth, they will be able to use the novels of Pat Tanner as a road map for studying what people wore, how they decorated their homes, where they shopped, what they ate, and whose dinner party they felt they should have been invited to. Pat's skills as a social reporter shine throughout his work, particularly in *Auntie Mame* and in *Tony* (1966), both of which permit him to cover a span of thirty years. From Art Deco through Early American to Danish Modern; from Lanvin through Schiaparelli to Givenchy; from Woolworth to Macy's to Bergdorf, he deftly sketched and skewered public taste and the staunch dictates of fashion. All of that is vastly different now, but what remains the same is the greed, the coveting, the grasping social ambitions. Those will undoubtedly always be with us. For the social climber, each of Pat's books could be read as a "how *not* to," for he lovingly delineates the manner in which envious, ambitious snobs are usually slapped right back down to the bottom rung of the ladder.

"I found Pat to be tremendously acute," says Julian Muller. "He had a mind that was magnificently furnished. He was a marvelous observer of almost every element of the human comedy—and of serious things as well. As a writer, you would never find anyone as facile. He was able to pick up an idea and run with it; articulate it delightfully, and then set it down on the page in what were usually wonderfully crisp, precise, and very funny tones. The manuscripts he turned out were pretty polished. I would assume that most of the time they were essentially first drafts."

Muller found Pat enormous fun to work with and enjoyed the way he and Pat fed one another. Once in a while, when something seemed to present a block for Pat, Julian would throw out a couple of suggestions for him to run with. Since they lived just around the corner from each other, it was always easy for them to get together. Pat—and Virginia Rowans—would do many more books for Muller over the next fifteen years.

With *Auntie Mame* enjoying its extended stay on the *New York Times* bestseller list, and enthusiastic reviews beginning to pour in, the property was soon grabbed by a smart producer. Robert Fryer and Lawrence "Jimmy" Carr read the book the day after its Sunday *New York Times* review and bought the theatrical rights twenty-four hours later. Fryer and Carr were a hot young producing team who had just had a success with *The Desk Set* starring Shirley Booth, and Fryer had already produced the hit Broadway musical *Wonderful Town,* which was based on the popular novel *My Sister Eileen* and starred Rosalind Russell. Fryer and Carr originally had the book in mind as a vehicle for Shirley Booth, but soon realized that it was much better suited to the whip-sharp comic talents of Russell. (In her autobiography, *Life Is a Banquet,* Russell incorrectly insists that she bought the rights to the book and brought Fryer and Carr in as producers.) At that time, Russell was a middle-aged screen star whose film work seemed to be fading. *Wonderful Town* had proven to be the breakout stage role that jumpstarted her career, and she wanted to do everything possible to keep up that new momentum. She agreed to take on the part of Mame, but would insist on major input to the project from the very beginning before signing any contracts.

Despite Pat's great ear for dialogue, Fryer, Carr, and Russell felt that Australian novelist/playwright Sumner Locke Elliott (*John Murray Anderson's Almanac, Buy Me Blue Ribbons*) should be hired to turn *Auntie Mame* into a stage play. Elliott was represented by Annie Laurie Williams, the same agent who represented Pat on the theatrical and film rights for *Auntie Mame*. But when Elliott turned in his first draft of the script, it was rejected by all parties. Only then was Pat given a chance to adapt his novel for the stage. Unfortunately, his efforts too met with general dissatisfaction. His script was considered unsalvageable, and a search for yet another playwright began.

Pat never disclosed how he felt about this. Undoubtedly it was a painful experience. But when a new team of writers was signed— Jerome Lawrence and Robert E. Lee—Pat supported them, and when they turned in their finished product, Pat was so pleased with their work that he ultimately wrote them a tribute as a foreword to Vanguard's published edition of the play's script (see appendix). Janet Waldo Lee, the widow of Robert E. Lee, remembers Pat as "a wonderful man. A delightful, funny, endearing man. He was warm, witty, supportive, grateful to Bob and Jerry—he was so thrilled with what they did that he never stopped thanking them and telling them how grateful he was. And Bob and Jerry were genuinely, deeply fond of Patrick."

However, Lawrence and Lee, who could boast the hit *Inherit the Wind* among their credits, were not the only talents who worked on the stage version of *Auntie Mame*. In his exquisitely detailed account of the Auntie Mame phenomenon, *But Darling, I'm Your Auntie Mame,* Richard Tyler Jordan points out that Rosalind Russell was involved with script meetings right from the start, and producer Robert Fryer confirms that "when the play was adapted, Rosalind had her input too. Structure, scenes, the flaming drinks, were her idea. I know she did write some scenes. She did write a lot of stuff on pages from yellow legal pads and shoved them under the door at night [during tryouts on the road]." How much of the play is really Rosalind Russell's work will probably never be known. In *Life Is a Banquet,* Russell claimed vast amounts of credit for herself and director Morton Da Costa as script doctors. Da Costa, however, did not support her contention and refused to endorse her book with a jacket blurb "because of all the fantasies in it. There were, shall we say, a lot of *liberties* taken in that book."

Regardless of who was ultimately responsible for the script of *Auntie Mame,* the result was a finely crafted theatrical classic with an appeal as irresistible today as it was almost fifty years ago. In its transition to the stage, Pat's delightful book acquired a surefire emotional through-line: the ever-strengthening bond between Mame and Patrick.

In the novel, this area is never deeply explored. Patrick recounts the sequence of bizarre episodes in an acerbic, bemused, and relatively detached manner, as Mame entangles him in a series of events he'd just as soon not be part of. Lawrence and Lee's stage version emphasized Mame's increasing fondness for Patrick and her surprising—albeit unconventional—aptitude for parenthood. The playwrights pushed the plot into melodrama by building up the threats to that central relationship. In the first act, Patrick's financial trustee, Mr. Babcock, is the villain, determined to separate Patrick from Mame and keep him away from her influence. Mame is truly distraught at the prospect of losing the boy she has come to cherish. In the second act, Patrick's snooty fiancée, Gloria Upson, and her family are poised to derail Patrick into embracing everything Mame quite rightfully despises. Once again, Mame is in danger of losing her Patrick. She emerges triumphant, of course, but not before she, Patrick, and the audience have been wrenched through some strong emotional moments. In the novel, Pat glossed over those developments in favor of a more purely comic tone.

There were other changes between the page and the stage. Many of the book's episodes were jettisoned, including the home for British refugee children, the disastrous vacation on a New England resort island, and Mame's rather unsavory dalliance with a college student. In addition, the role of actress Vera Charles was expanded, providing Mame with a hilariously appropriate comic foil. All in all, this was a brilliant transference from novel to play, a profoundly satisfying enhancement of a property that already seemed pretty near perfect.

Pat had a ball spending week after week on the road with the *Auntie Mame* company during tryouts. Such luxuries of time were possible for him now, as he had been able to quit his job at the Council on Foreign Relations thanks to *Auntie Mame*'s success. In an interview shortly before her death, Peggy Cass—the original Agnes Gooch—exclaimed in her trademark squeaky-balloon voice, "He was *fun!* Nothing would please you more than to see him walk into your dressing room. He was a barrel of laughs. Not sitcom laughs. High-toned stuff. He really viewed the world from a kind of upper-class lookout, you know what I mean? He was very witty, but also a teeny bit Olympian. I loved the way Pat dressed. Slightly foppish, in very good taste. He looked more elegant than other people. And he was very good-looking, you know. Behind that beard were beautiful blue eyes. When he spoke, he had an upper-class sound, like he'd gone to the right schools. But you know, he wasn't a snob at all. Politically, he was the most proletarian person. Believe me, I'm a liberal, and it takes one to know one."

In the midst of his overwhelming success, Pat remained charmingly modest and unaffected. One would think that all the acclaim would have thrust Pat and Louise into a dazzling new social world peopled largely by celebrities. But oddly enough, this didn't seem to happen. Pat certainly met many illustrious people, but most of his close friends remained the old ones who had known him when he was a Franklin Spier copywriter. He and Louise were able to give bigger, more elaborate dinners and parties, but the guest lists were eclectic conglomerations of friends they had known for years, some successful, some not. Artists, actors, or accountants—all were welcome at the Tanner home, and Pat and Louise always knew how to put them together in just the right combinations to make a party hum. In spite of his newfound wealth and celebrity status, Pat seemed little different to his good friends. "His personality didn't really change," says Julian Muller. "His lifestyle did, because he was able to do a lot of things that he hadn't been able to before. But I didn't notice any ego change. Pat stayed the same complicated person that he always had been."

If anything, Pat's naturally generous tendencies increased. Not only did he naively expect Julian Muller to accept an enormous bonus, he also wanted to share the wealth with his accountant, Abe Badian. Badian had been doing Pat's tax returns for three years running and had been charging the going rate of around $40 per year. After the success of *Auntie Mame,* Pat tried unsuccessfully to get Badian to start accepting $2,500 for the job.

For Louise, Pat's transition to fame wasn't always easy. "The success of *Auntie Mame* changed things for us," she said, "and not always for the better. Being in the public eye is not all that pleasant. Being famous is not all it's cracked up to be. It's a very ambivalent thing. At first it's pleasant, but then you're on a sort of treadmill of social life that's hard to take." And the phone was always ringing with requests for Pat's time, money, and talent. "That was kind of tough, because Pat was such a warm person, he couldn't say no. People would call with every kind of business proposition. One woman even wanted Pat to collaborate with her on the life story of her *dog!*"

While *Auntie Mame* was climbing the bestseller list, Pat did say yes to one friend and found himself the wealthier for it. His old Evanston buddies Bill and Barbara Hooton, who had lost the Paul Manship apartment in the coin toss six years before, bought a dude ranch in New Mexico and poured every bit of their money into making it a successful tourist enterprise. When Barbara suggested to Pat that he write up the whole exasperatingly funny saga of Rancho del Monte in her voice, he came up with *"Guestward Ho!* by Barbara C. Hooton, as indiscreetly confided to Patrick Dennis, author of 'Auntie Mame.'" Vanguard published it in 1956, to enthusiastic reviews and skyrocketing sales figures. The *New York Times* called it "side-splitting"; *Time* magazine's book critic was correct in predicting, *"Guestward Ho!* will probably net double royalties: (1) at the bookstalls, as a highly readable romp with two innocents in pueblo-land; (2) at Rancho del Monte and vicinity, where soon a big traffic jam may set in." Today the book is a breezy, light read, and Pat assumes the feminine first-person voice with great charm and aptitude.

Like *House Party, Guestward Ho!* eventually became an ABC sitcom. Joanne Dru and Mark Miller starred as Barbara and Bill Hooton, J. Carrol Naish played Hawkeye, the Native American who runs the local trading post where he sells authentic Indian souvenirs that are made in Japan. The show had a one-year run during the 1960–61 season.

When the stage version of *Auntie Mame* finally opened at the Broadhurst Theatre the night of October 31, 1956, its production costs totaled $180,000. It was the most expensive nonmusical ever mounted on Broadway. Nobody need have worried. The play was an instant, enormous hit, and just as he had done at every performance on the road, Pat sat in his front-row aisle seat utterly enraptured, laughing at the comic high points and shedding copious real tears at all the sentimental moments. It would be thus each and every time Pat went to see it.

Ten-year-old Pat *(right)* and his best friend, Gordon Muchow, dress up as Margaret Dumont and Tom Mix in Pat's backyard, Evanston, Illinois, 1931.

Pat *(right)* and his father, Edward Everett Tanner, Jr., on a lakeside holiday circa 1929.

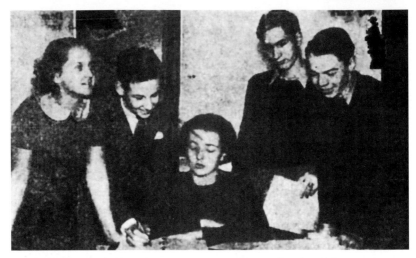

Pat *(second from left)* and Evanston Township High School drama class-mates go over the script for the school play. Pat was publicity chairman.

Pat strikes a match and lights a cigarette after finishing a makeover on his friend Barbara Harned Dorsett at a party circa 1940.

Moments later, Pat leads off a conga line that will wind out the door, around the backyard, and back in again.

Studio portrait, Chicago, circa 1940.

Pat *(front row at left)* and his buddies on overseas duty with the American Field Service during World War II.

Pat and Louise entertain editor Lois Cole *(seated on couch with Pat)* in their East 91st Street town house, which Pat redesigned to accommodate Louise's French tapestries. *(Steve Schapiro, Black Star)*

Pat and Louise on their flight to Moscow, 1959. *(Frank Dobo)*

A naked Pat meets a naked Jeri Archer, 1960. Pat would make Jeri his Belle Poitrine for *Little Me*. *(Cris Alexander)*

Pat with Cris Alexander's
portrait of Louise.
(Steve Schapiro, Black Star)

Pat and dinner guest, actress Jan Sterling, summon the spirits on East 91st
Street. *(Cris Alexander)*

Little Me: Belle Poitrine (Jeri Archer) and Mr. Musgrove (Shaun O'Brien) caught *in flagrante delicto* by her husband, Cedric (Pat), the tenth Earl of Baughdie, and Cedric's "Mum" (Cris Alexander), the Dowager Lady Baughdie. *(Cris Alexander)*

Louise as Belle's gal pal, Pixie Portnoy, in *Little Me*. *(Cris Alexander)*

Cris Alexander's photo of Pat with Betsy and Michael, ages 4 and 7. This appeared in the endpapers of *Little Me*, with Michael and Betsy sprouting cherubic wings. Pat soon got rid of his hairpiece. *(Cris Alexander)*

Patrick Dennis as God. *(Cris Alexander)*

Louise and Pat on Parents'
Day at Camp Winako, 1961.
(Frank Dobo)

Venice, Italy, 1962. Whether by accident or design, Guy Kent *(far right)*,
with whom Pat was having an affair, turned up in Venice during Pat and
Louise's vacation. *Left to right:* unidentified guest, Sisi Cahan, Pat,
unidentified guest, Dr. William G. Cahan, Louise, and Guy.

High times in 1962. Shaun O'Brien, Louise, Cris Alexander, composer Harry Percer, Pat, and Walter Pistole raise a glass. By the end of the year, Pat would attempt suicide and be committed to a mental institution.

Cris Alexander and Pat dress up Corry Salley, the Tanners' beloved household employee, for her role in *First Lady*. *(Steve Schapiro, Black Star)*

Pat tarts up Peggy Cass during a photo session for *First Lady*. *(Steve Schapiro, Black Star)*

Pat with his pal Dody Goodman, 1964.

Pat in his Fifth Avenue apartment, inspired by the Muses, Mrs. John D. Crimmins III and Sylvia Josa Wild, both former Margaret Morris dancers.

Betsy and Michael with their grandfather, Edward Everett Tanner, Jr., 1963.

Pat, comedienne Alice Pearce, and novelist/playwright James Kirkwood (*A Chorus Line*). In lieu of underwear, which he destested, Pat wore specially made shirts with long tails which could be pulled up between the legs and buttoned at crotch level. *(Cris Alexander)*

Pat and his good friend Nina Quirós, photographed in Mexico City in 1968.

Pat and Nina Quirós posed for gag photos in Mexico as a dance team named Nina and Nudnick. Pat had this picture blown up to poster size and placed outside his favorite Mexico City restaurant, the Rivoli.

The last days: Cris Alexander's final portrait of Pat, taken shortly before Pat died of pancreatic cancer in 1976.

TEN

"Will the Real Auntie Mame Please Stand Up?"

Rosalind Russell played *Auntie Mame* to SRO audiences for fifteen straight months, then left for Hollywood to star in the Warner Bros. film adaptation of the play. She was replaced by Greer Garson, who—although she drew out the dialogue to such an extent that the final curtain fell much later every night—was, by all accounts, quite good in the role. Garson was followed by Beatrice Lillie, who also went on to play Mame in the London production. And a gaggle of Mames toured the show all over the United States, including such former film stars as Constance Bennett, Sylvia Sidney, and Eve Arden.

The *Auntie Mame* cash cow continued with the 1958 Warner Bros. film version, which, with a $9-million box-office take, became the highest-grossing movie of the year. In addition to critical raves, it also received six Academy Award nominations, including Best Actress (Russell), Best Supporting Actress (Peggy Cass), and Best Picture. "The contract with Warners," Pat joked, "was longer than the book. Took me almost two hours to initial all the pages in one copy. After that I gave up. They can keep their filthy money."

Auntie Mame made Pat a millionaire, but it proved a perverse blessing. He now had a staggering standard of critical and financial success to live up to, and he had also unwittingly created a subtle trap for himself. By making Patrick Dennis the first-person narrator of the novel, and by basing a few elements of the character of Auntie Mame on his own eccentric aunt Marion, he had inevitably led his readers to think that *Auntie Mame* was, more or less, a true story. In a *Life* magazine interview, he stressed, "I write in the first person, but it is all fictional. The public assumes that what seems fictional is fact; so the way for me to be inventive is to seem factual but be fictional." Fans of the novel, however, seemed determined to believe what was essentially a fairy tale.

But Pat insisted that the only similarity between Auntie Mame and his aunt Marion was that they were both crazy. "Anyone with any sense would know who Auntie Mame really is," he once said, then pointed to himself. The truth probably lies somewhere between Pat's claim and his aunt Marion's repeated insistence that she served as the Auntie Mame model.

Pat did indeed have an unusual aunt, Marion Tanner, who lived in a Greenwich Village town house. When Pat was growing up in Evanston, Illinois, Aunt Marion's somewhat bohemian existence in New York City must have seemed terribly glamorous and appealing. Marion, however, would play a far larger role in Pat's life after the publication of *Auntie Mame* than before.

Marion Tanner was born in Buffalo—like Auntie Mame—on March 6, 1889. She and her brother, Pat's father, Edward, were not close. Marion's free-spirited manner was neither appreciated nor understood by the straitlaced Edward. Marion—again like Mame—attended Smith College, graduated, and came to New York. There she promptly got a job as an ice-hockey instructor, certainly an unusual profession for a young woman in the 1910s. She continued her education by studying psychiatry and psychiatric methodology with Erich Fromm and Karen Horney and received a master's degree in sociology from New York University.

Just as Auntie Mame did, Marion worked at Macy's and had a fling at the stage, appearing in small parts in several plays. In *The Fires of Spring* (1929), she supported the young Judith Anderson. She was also in a 1935 revival of the old-dark-house chestnut *The Cat and the Canary,* and the original 1938 production of Kurt Weill and Maxwell Anderson's *Knickerbocker Holiday.* During the 1930s, she was also active in the National Labor Relations Board, for which she mediated and conducted elections. She was married and divorced twice, first to a writer, then to an English engineer. Never terribly practical when it came to finances, she went through her own money and her husbands' money quickly.

In 1927, Marion took possession of the redbrick town house at 72 Bank Street, and it rapidly became known as a gathering place for artists, writers, and intellectuals, who were flooding the Village. Marion made a name for herself as a sophisticated hostess whose parties attracted a diverse, eccentric group of characters. She and Pat would see each other on her occasional visits to Chicago. He also saw her during his brief stay in New York prior to his departure for the European battlefields of World War II. His American Field Service buddy C. B. Squire remembers a small farewell dinner Marion gave Pat and his friends in her town house shortly before they left.

Louise Tanner always insisted that Marion served only as a point of departure for the character of Mame, not a prototype. Louise found Marion entertaining—at first—and enjoyed getting to know her during the early years of the marriage: "She *was* very interesting, and she could be very amusing, and she did know all these famous people. Her father was very stolid, a businessman, and Pat had more in common with her than he did with his parents, I think. He always referred to her as his favorite relative, up until the time of their great falling-out. She was a lot of fun in her eccentricity, but a very bossy woman. I sort of gave her a wide berth, because when Michael was born, she immediately decided that she was going to take over Michael's feeding habits. And she said, 'Well, now, I've taken a lifetime membership for him in a goat farm.' It was the most repulsive thing—you were supposed to pour goat's milk into this awful-looking piece of latex shaped like a breast and feed the child with it, which was supposed to give him some kind of security. I think it caused me to have a bit of a break with her when I said, 'No, thank you.' She didn't have any children of her own, which I find kind of a mercy."

Following her marriages, Marion turned 72 Bank Street into a kind of bohemian boardinghouse for struggling artists, writers, and performers. Will Geer, Billie Holiday, and *A Walk in the Sun* author Harry Brown are said to have been residents early in their careers. Writer Dachine Rainer lived there for some time; she based her novel *The Uncomfortable Inn* (1960) on her experiences. "I remember there was

one couple living there that had a calendar called Birthdays of Anar-
chy," Louise Tanner said with a laugh. "I thought that was kind of wonderful. They were probably grinding out pamphlets in the basement!"

Frank Andrews, who became a close friend of Marion's, met her in
1960 when he came to live in her house. He remembers her as being
supportive and encouraging: "She certainly encouraged me to go into
the work I do now, which is psychic readings. I've been doing a combination of tarot, astrology, and numerology for nearly forty years. And
Marion was really the one who triggered the whole thing." A member of
the Theosophical Society, Marion was always open to matters of the
spiritual and the occult. "She palled around with a woman by the name
of Genevieve Camlian," says Andrews, "who was like an Irish witch. A
very colorful character. Genevieve was always running around doing
everybody's I Ching. She was a bit like Marion's Vera Charles, except she
wasn't an actress. Those two ladies seemed to go together. Eventually
they both wound up at the Village Nursing Home."

Andrews was made welcome at 72 Bank Street, but by that time, so
was everyone else. Marion's keen interest in social work was now
beginning to dominate her life. She had always shown concern about
the needy and the homeless decades before such problems became
widespread issues; it was practically inevitable that she would open the
doors of 72 Bank Street to the dispossessed. "Marian took the lock off
the door on Bank Street; it was open and anyone could go in and stay
there," Andrews continues. "People took advantage of her. The place
was a shambles; it reeked of urine. Little kids were running around and
they would just pee on the walls. She was into yoga, and she'd be off in
a corner doing her meditation, and people would be in and out eating
from the kitchen; it was like she was running a soup kitchen. There
were bums off the Bowery living there. And it was a very fine house,
but she'd let it run down." The kids who lived at the house—and there
were many of them—had been more or less abandoned to Marion's
care as infants by their mothers. According to Andrews, Marion named
each one of the boys Patrick.

"She was very angry with Patrick at the time, and she told me that
he was not her real nephew," says Andrews. "But I suspected that she
was lying, because she was so mad at him. She was very upset with him
because she wanted him to give her more money. You couldn't reason

with her. One guy was fighting with her and pushed her down a flight of stairs and broke her leg. The other guys rushed to beat him up, and she said, 'No, no! don't hurt him!' One time I said, 'Marion, what happened to all of the silverware?' And she said, 'Oh, somebody probably needed the money and they sold it.' She was just letting go of all material possessions; she was getting into what she thought was Zen; she wanted to be like Buddha, but she had her head completely in the clouds. At one point I wanted to buy the house from her, fix it up, and live on the first two floors and let her and her friends live on the lower floors. But the plan was too practical; she didn't want to do it. I was trying to find a way to make it work for her, but she wouldn't have any part of that."

When *Auntie Mame* became a hit with readers, Marion began publicly insisting that she was the inspiration. No sooner had Rosalind Russell begun rehearsals for the stage version than Marion, billed as "the real Auntie Mame," turned up as a special guest contestant (and won $20,000) on the TV quiz show *The Big Surprise*. Marion was indeed a surprise to Ms. Russell, who, like Pat, was quite perturbed. "Patrick did not want Marion going on television," says Andrews, "because she spoiled it a bit. She was not Rosalind Russell, you see."

Indeed, the dowdy, straggly-haired Marion was more evocative of a bag lady than anyone's idea of the elegant Auntie Mame. "Pat said that the real Mame was a combination of his mother and his grandmother," says Pat's close friend singer-songwriter Murray Grand. "He certainly didn't base the character on that dykey-lookin' number in the Village, that's for sure. She was practically snapping at his heels."

Marion did take advantage of Pat's generous nature. "There was a very compassionate element in him," explains his friend the prominent surgeon Dr. William G. Cahan. "Pat was good, noble. His field service was a result of that; he wanted to help the wounded. And I think this compassion extended to that aunt of his—who was the bloody bore of all time. She was a dowdy old girl, with a soft touch for any tramp that wanted to come in and camp out at her house. Of course we looked at her with a certain degree of curiosity when *Auntie Mame* came out, but Pat kept saying, 'No, no, this is not based on her.' In a funny way, you thought that there *was* some influence, with his having this zany aunt, but with Pat's sense of snobbism and his arch ways he made her into a glamourpuss. We met her just once; that was it. She was the bane of his existence for a long time. Pat kept trying to pay for all these old derelicts and support her too."

Auntie Mame's editor Julian Muller felt that the extent of Marion's influence over the character of Auntie Mame was simply that she had generated the idea of an eccentric aunt. Pat had never made any mention of Marion to Muller; when she entered the picture claiming to be the real Auntie Mame, it came as a surprise to him. Only after the book hit the bestseller list did Marion begin taking credit. Pat assured Muller that Marion's assertions were nonsense.

As early as January 1956, shortly after the publication of *Auntie Mame,* Pat was bailing Marion out. At that time he took her officially out of debt by completely paying off all of her accumulated bills. Later, she asked him to cover all of her legal costs from a series of a dozen lawsuits in which she had been involved. Peter Swords, who was her lawyer at the time, says, "I never saw anything of this kind of happy-go-lucky character that Pat wrote. She had become a kind of guru type. I would characterize her as a highly spiritual person, very quiet and almost mystical."

"She was a first-class pain in the ass," snaps Pat's financial manager, Abe Badian. "Her house on Bank Street became a flophouse for itinerants and other people. She could not afford to run this as a flophouse, and she started giving out false information to newspapers about her nephew who wrote *Auntie Mame* and how he had based it on her life. Totally not true. Pat was really on the spot."

Marion lost the house twice through foreclosure. The first time Pat saved it, on condition that she stop using the house as a shelter, that she sell the house and use the interest from the principal as a source of regular income, and that she stop referring to herself as the real Auntie Mame. He also agreed to send her a monthly stipend of $300 for the rest of her life. Marion promised that she was going to move to Connecticut. In a withering letter to Marion dated September 19, 1958, Pat writes:

> You are now being paid $3600 annually as a reward for nothing but your seventy years of fecklessness and improvidence. You can expect no more from me. Not only am I totally disinclined to give

it to you, I am unable to. I live on a very small allowance, and all of my income goes directly to Badian and Barouch, who endeavor to keep me afloat with the Internal Revenue people and put aside what little remains for the years when I am out of fashion and forgotten.

It's probably useless to remind you once more that I am thoroughly finished with you and that your constant nagging for money wastes only your time and mine.

The stipend was sent every month to the address in Connecticut. But a year and a half later, Pat saw the following item in Robert Sylvester's "Dream Street" column in the *New York Daily News:*

A woman named Marian [*sic*] Tanner may be the original of "Auntie Mame." At least, she has a four-story house in Bank St. in Greenwich Village and has given over two floors of it to various indigent artists, sculptors, poets and writers. The landlady feeds her flock and generally sees to it that they have the proper creative atmosphere, but lately she's been getting some complaints. Miss Tanner is a vegetarian and some of her free boarders are complaining about the cuisine.

Pat, who by this time was no longer communicating with Marion directly, had Abe Badian write her regarding the matter. In a long reply to Badian, Marion wrote:

The house on Bank *was* sold at the time Pat engaged you to handle his communications with me, to Mrs. Rita Terrell, who owns and operates a profitably-remodeled house on West Eleventh Street. My "activities" were almost entirely transferred to Roxbury Road, Stamford, for the next two years, at which time the house and property I occupied there was sold over my head for a great deal more money than I could have paid for it. I had retained an apartment at 72 Bank Street (as Pat had suggested my doing when he had proposed buying the house himself, for the amount of the mortgage and a dollar cash) and Mrs. Terrell became so much interested in my plan to incorporate an organization called "Foster Aunts and Uncles" for active assistance to children in inadequate family situations, that after I lost the Stamford place she offered to arrange a resale of the Bank Street house for the benefit of the project, and she and I are still engaged in negotiations for a very good sale just as soon as I locate appropriate quarters for the work.

Meantime there are six small children living in the house, with parents in serious economic, housing or health situations, living on a temporary basis and quite a lot of others receiving help on the outside; I feel sure that if Pat were really aware of what is being accomplished with the aid of his $300 a month, he would regard it as a very sound investment in human nature and American civilization . . . and might even want to increase what he sends me rather than suggesting stopping it.

During the next month, Badian investigated Marion's situation and discovered ample evidence that the 1958 sale of 72 Bank Street had indeed been a sham. In a "paper" sale, Marion had sold it to a friend for one dollar. At Pat's insistence, Badian notified Marion that her monthly stipend would be discontinued.

He received the following reply:

Dear Mr. Badian,

Whatever may have been your surprise at my answers to your questionnaire, my surprise was probably greater at the conclusion you seem to have drawn from those facts, namely that I have been trying to *cheat* my nephew.

If Patrick doesn't *want* to share any part of his large income with me, I don't want him to *have* to do it, and if he does not want me to have some part of it for my own personal use; I can't understand why he doesn't make it available to me without making even so honorable and intelligent and devoted a steward as you, the judge of my fitness to receive it.

You speak of the "spirit" *and* the "letter" of an agreement between Patrick and me. When as articulate (and experienced in the use of words) a person as Patrick employs *two* people to communicate his wishes regarding a gift to as loving and cooperative an aunt as I am, she doesn't have much except the "letter" of the operation to guide her. The "spirit" has become pretty vague and evanescent, and about all I have been able to sense of it since Pat stopped communicating directly with me is that the less he sees of me or hears of my interests or "activities" the better pleased he is; and that "spirit," painful as it is to me, I have consistently tried to observe.

I have written him close to a hundred letters, keeping him informed of my thoughts, feelings and deeds, the great majority of which I have never mailed because I knew he didn't want to know *anything* about me or give any thoughts to my ideas or desires.

Nothing that he does or doesn't do with his money now is ever going to make me stop loving him or wishing for his good. I am glad he wanted me to share some of his blessings for awhile, and sorry he wants now to have me appear unworthy of any consideration, but it would be pointless for me to say more to you than that I have never lapsed in *love* for my nephew, nor in execution of any comprehensible "spirit" of any "agreement" he has asked me for.

Sincerely,
Marion Tanner

When Badian forwarded this letter to Pat, Pat's reply to Abe was succinct:

Alternately bad-tempered and self-pitying, this letter can be construed as the last feeble fart before the toilet is flushed and need not be answered.

Somehow Marion was able to keep things going at 72 Bank Street for another three years. By now the house was a run-down, garbage-strewn eyesore filled with addicts, alcoholics, and newly released inmates of state prisons and asylums. Neither Marion nor her guests were fondly regarded by the neighbors.

Elizabeth Bishop, a student at Sarah Lawrence, was doing a study on housing and landlords in New York at the time and met with Marion at 72 Bank Street. The two became close, and Elizabeth rallied the interest of several of her Sarah Lawrence classmates when Marion's house was going to be lost through foreclosure. The girls all came down to paint the house and make an attempt to tidy it up a bit. They also organized a benefit poetry reading at the house featuring such celebrated Greenwich Village residents as W. H. Auden and Muriel Rukeyser. The reading included a skit in which Marion was thrown out by an evil, mustache-twirling landlord. "The place was packed," Ms. Bishop says, "and we were on every newscast. We raised a lot of money for Marion, but it wasn't enough, because she had made a faulty mortgage with loan sharks. It was a triple mortgage, with no way out."

One of Marion's neighbors, Nancy Hoffman, lived around the corner on West Eleventh Street. She would see all the denizens of 72 Bank Street gathered around neighborhood garbage bins, filling up shopping carts, and taking them into the house. She also frequently spotted Marion around the village, usually buying rotten vegetables at the back doors of local grocers. It was her nightly routine: bargaining for produce so putrid that it was about to be discarded. "Marion was probably one of the most brilliant, articulate women I've ever met," says Hoffman. "She could really turn a sentence. Wonderful vocabulary; she was beautifully spoken. The trouble with her was that she had one major screw loose, and it manifested itself time and again. We offered to buy the house from her, and she'd say, 'Oh, someday, maybe . . .' She wouldn't allow us to buy. We finally had to get the house at auction. She was successful in delaying the auction four times; the fifth time we were there and bought it."

Seated in the cool basement study of the house today, Ms. Hoffman explains what the place was like when Marion lived there thirty-five years ago. "I had to prepare my husband to come and see this house. I said, 'Listen, I found a house, but you're not allowed to look around. It needs a paint job, but don't pay too much attention to how it looks. Look at the dimensions of the house and undress it with your eyes.' So we walked in with our lawyer and Tessa was there in the living room bent over a pillow, tearing out handfuls of feathers and throwing them into the air, making them into a snowstorm. And Marion said, 'Oh, don't mind Tessa, she's a wonderful little ripper-upper!' And this lawyer walks in on this scene in the middle of the living room! And Ben's eyes went absolutely white and rolled around about six times! There were, I guess, about thirty-seven denizens living all over this house when we bought it. They were all in different stages of depravity. She herself lived in a black sleeping bag in a corner of the top floor of this house, which was riddled with roaches. She had a woman here who had three children, each one from a different man. I don't think she was ever married. She had people living in every corner. One room was for the drunks. Then she had three men living in the cellar; she had to make *tunnels* through the debris in the cellar, and they sat at a three-legged table with a bottle of ketchup on it. The living-room areas were, I think, inhabited by a couple of people who were *really* insane. It was the period of the closing of the insane asylums, and there were people on the streets who needed more care than they got, and needed medication; they really couldn't make it on their own. She would take the welfare checks of the people who were receiving them who lived here and give them to the drug addicts and the alcoholics. Then the alcoholics would make a repair or two. When the electricians came in to fix this house up, they said it was like a spider's web; you couldn't possibly undo what had been done. And it was the same with the plumbing. The kitchen was barely essential. *Barely* essential. Everything was in disarray; this was not recognizable as a place to live. The smell of the place was absolutely fierce; I thought we'd never get rid of it.

"We ultimately had to move her out. When we told her what we were going to have to do, she said, 'You have to! I want the publicity!' We decided to hire people from the sheriff's office who were used to doing this. She was entitled to have two vansful taken off and stored for sixty days. The people who did it for us said that this was worse than the Collier brothers. They were here with the biggest vans I'd ever seen in my life parked in front of this door for two solid days."

True to her word, Marion alerted the press. Reporters flocked to cover the eviction. Patrick, of course, was nowhere to be found, and the press and the public could easily infer that he was utterly heartless and ungrateful. "So many people would say, 'How could he abandon her, after she brought him up?'" said Louise Tanner. "I'd get absolutely blue in the face saying that she had absolutely *nothing* to do with bringing him up. And the money he gave her went right through her hands and into the hands of the derelicts." To make matters worse, Marion's broken leg was still healing at the time of the eviction, and she was in a cast and on crutches. One of the deputy sheriffs who was evicting her remarked to a reporter, "She's an amazing woman. There's no place left in our society for a person like her. It's too bad. In an earlier time she might have been a saint."

After the eviction was finally complete, the house had to be thoroughly cleaned, and a crew of four men spent a week of twelve-hour days on the job. Next came fumigation. The house was thoroughly sprayed and then sealed for twenty-four hours. When Nancy Hoffman and her husband finally entered the house, it was to the crunch of a carpet of dead cockroaches under their feet.

Thirty-five years later, 72 Bank Street is fully restored, a classic New York town house on one of the most charming blocks in Greenwich Village.

The publicity Marion received during her eviction brought her to the attention of Elizabeth "Libby" Lyon, a social worker who was also running her own homeless shelter called Bierer House. Bierer House was similar to 72 Bank Street, but more professionally run, and its tenants had to pay a small amount on a sliding scale to live there. Ms. Lyon, who held a full-time job, offered to let Marion stay if Marion would look after the house and the tenants while Ms. Lyon was away at work each day. "As I remember," says Ms. Lyon today, "she didn't jump with joy. But I got a bedroom ready for her. She waited until her things were being thrown out on the street. We salvaged what we could."

Now living in a Chelsea nursing home, Lyon carries only the fondest memories of Marion. "Marion was unique," she stresses. "Nobody could ever be like her. Living with Marion changed my life. And everybody in the house loved her. Who couldn't get along with this wonderful woman? There was only her nephew who threw up his hands and walked out, but I understand that. What else could he do? She was giving everything away to everyone else and running that home. It was a very productive period for her, and exactly what was needed, but he was getting sick and tired of it. For me, she was heaven-sent. She could be there, on duty, so to speak, and it worked out magnificently. I would not have missed this wonderful experience for anything else in the world.

Nothing else could match it. When it's over, you realize you've absorbed a lot of Marion. You're always more aware of people on the edge. Once with Marion, you have to think twice before you turn people away."

Marion stayed at Bierer House for the next thirteen years. But as her mental and physical health declined, she became a frequent patient at St. Vincent's Hospital. Marilyn Rogers, one of the hospital's social workers, was assigned to her. In 1977, Marion was admitted for phlebitis. She had become incontinent and was deteriorating into senility. Libby Lyon could no longer take care of her at Bierer House and told Marilyn Rogers that it was time to find a more closely supervised situation for Marion. Marion, however, was full of denial and refused to accept that fact. "I was really put in the middle," says Rogers, "because Libby didn't want to hurt her feelings and confront her day in and day out with the reality of the situation. She didn't want to push it home to Marion that she couldn't go back there. That was falling into *my* lap, because I had to make a plan for where she went afterwards."

Marion's senility accentuated the most difficult aspects of her personality. "To be honest," says Rogers, "having seen the movie, I thought that if in fact this was Auntie Mame, she would be wonderful. I went in there planning to love her, and it took me a long time to realize that this lady wasn't anything at all like Rosalind Russell. She was superior and haughty and had an arrogance about her you could cut with a knife. She was one of the most difficult people I ever dealt with, and I was there at the hospital sixteen years, I can tell you. And I've always worked with the elderly. That's a lot of people in all those years. I saw nothing in that woman that showed any joie de vivre, except her own haughty, imperious sense of self. I say that not because I'm a very critical person, but I did have to deal with her day in and day out for months, and I was so predisposed that the Rosalind Russell character was underneath there somewhere, and I kept looking hard. But I couldn't find anything about her that I could call lovable. I always say Marion Tanner gave me my first gray hairs.

"She was very canny and very wary," Rogers continues. "This is typical of people with memory loss and senility: she chose the agenda. She would talk about what *she* could remember and *she* wanted to talk about. And if you asked her questions, you didn't know whether she didn't remember or she didn't want to tell you. Because her manner could be so severe and off-putting, she implied, 'Well, who are *you* and why should I answer that question?' But after you got enough of that day in and day out, you realized that was part of her defense. Because she really *didn't* know."

Rogers was finally able to convince Marion to move into a limited-care facility nearby, but within two days Marion had so disrupted the home's normal routine that her stay was terminated and she was sent back to St. Vincent's. Rogers tried again to find a suitable group home for Marion and finally placed her at the Village Nursing Home, only a few doors down from 72 Bank Street.

"It was like the Second Coming when she went to the Nursing Home," Rogers says. "They gave her her own room. She had charmed a male nurse, and she had found her lofty pedestal again. That nurse was quite smitten with her in her elegant, superior phoniness. I thought, 'Well, that's good, *he* likes her!' I had felt a little guilty, because I had come to almost dislike her, which was unprofessional. I just hated that haughty, superior attitude of hers."

The Village Nursing Home became Marion's final domicile, and she was definitely one of its stars. "She was a totally consistent personality," says Ann Wyatt, the Home's assistant administrator. "When she came to us, she basically couldn't take care of herself. She was not cognitively altogether intact. But she had a regal quality, as if she were always holding court. By which I do not mean unfriendly; I just mean that you felt you were in a definitive presence."

Marion's old friend Genevieve Camlian was already a tenant of the Nursing Home, but by this point the two ladies detested each other and were no longer speaking. "They were two of the most pronounced personalities we ever had," says Wyatt. "Genevieve was Irish, and she used to quote long passages from Yeats. She used to go over to a nearby bar every day for a cigarette and a sandwich." Both ladies proved helpful in saving the Nursing Home, which was constantly threatened with closure due to lack of funds. The media loved them, and their photographs and quotes frequently accompanied articles and TV news spots about the Nursing Home's looming demise. Enough contributions soon poured in to save the Nursing Home, and it is still thriving.

During Marion's stay, the Nursing Home had to be renovated to meet state requirements. That meant moving everybody twice—first off the floor that was to be renovated, then back on. Every effort was made to discuss the details of this procedure with residents ahead of time, so that it would not prove traumatizing. But when moving day came, Marion would not budge. With workmen breaking through the walls, she held firm and refused to leave her room. "Finally," says Ann Wyatt, "it reached the point where I told her, 'We're gonna have to do it.' I finally had to wheel her into the elevator myself. She spat in my face!" With a chuckle, Wyatt adds, "So I totally understand what Patrick may have been facing!" When the time came to move Marion back into her new room, she was simply taken down to an activity in the morning and wheeled up to her new room in the afternoon. She never knew the difference.

"My guess," says Wyatt, "is that the cognitive difficulties had been around for a long time. It's not hard to imagine that, if you had direct responsibility for her, it made your life difficult. Nobody there blamed Patrick for anything. You work in a nursing home and you realize that, without exception, family relations are more complicated than they appear on the surface."

During the eight years Marion spent at the Nursing Home, she received a constant stream of visitors, the most prominent of whom was First Lady Rosalynn Carter, who had lunch seated next to her while on an official visit. Libby Lyon continued to remain a deeply caring, involved presence in Marion's life. Michael Tanner also came to visit his great-aunt several times and taped an interview with her. Michael disagrees with his mother about the Aunt Marion question; he has always felt strongly that Marion Tanner *was* the inspiration for Auntie Mame. "Unquestionably," he insists. "That first scene in the book—when Nora and Patrick arrive at Mame's party in the house on Beekman Place—that's obviously Aunt Marion in the twenties; there's no question about it. Absolutely. Knowing everybody, being very gay and sophisticated and having wonderful parties—that's totally her; I know it was her. She *was* a big pain in the ass; when I told my uncle Jack she was dead, he said, 'Good,' and he was one of the sweetest men who ever lived. She pissed so many people off. But she did know everybody and she was flamboyant, just like the character. Anyone who says that she wasn't the inspiration for the character just isn't right."

Perhaps this is where the kernel of truth can be found. Pat may well have been inspired by Marion's early years and her eccentricity, just as he was also inspired by his stylish, vivacious mother and his grandmother Samantha, whom he actually used to call Mame when he was a child. There was also his mother's best friend, Eileen Barrows, a stylish, entertainingly offbeat woman he called Aunt Eileen. Added to the mixture was a strong dose of Pat's own bawdy, campy persona, as well as his considerable creative imagination. The result was one of the most memorable ladies in American popular literature. But no matter how many women in Pat's life served as inspiration—ingredients in the cocktail—the only person who could fully lay claim to the creation was Pat himself. It was Pat who knew how to emphasize the most charming aspects of these maddening women; Pat who blended them into a cohesive whole; Pat who spiked the mixture with so much of his own wit and inspiration that the character became beloved by millions.

Marion died on October 30, 1985, two months after a severe stroke. On November 16, a memorial service was held for her in the St. James Chapel of the Cathedral of Saint John the Divine. Graham McKeen, a composer who lived in Montreal, came to New York to attend. "I met her in February thirty years ago," he told the New York Times, "in the basement of Seventy-two Bank Street. I was sick, drunk. She got me to St. Vincent's Hospital. She saved my life. She never preached to me. She just kept saying, 'Keep composing! Keep composing!'" The Reverend Al Carmine of the Judson Memorial Church in Greenwich Village gave the eulogy. "In her presence, things glittered," he said. "One was no longer just a painter, but Caravaggio. Or just a teacher, but Socrates. Or just a singer, but Caruso. She lived in capital letters."

At the end of the service, everyone exited to the sound of a tape deck filling the chapel with Jerry Herman's song "Mame."

PART THREE

Pat in the mid-
1960s (*Cris
Alexander*)

ELEVEN

Bosom Buddies

Auntie Mame not only allowed Pat to quit his job at the Council, it also bought him a showplace of an Upper East Side town house. The house that Mame built was located at 101 East Ninety-first Street between Park and Lexington, close by the Madison Avenue apartment. Pat indulged his set-designing fantasies to the hilt, and he spent the better part of a year knocking out floors and walls, extending the ground floor, and generally doing an outrageous redecoration job worthy of Auntie Mame herself.

He started by combining the first and second stories to create a living room of striking height. The impetus for this was a pair of ten-foot-high medieval tapestries Louise had inherited: this was the only way they could be properly displayed. By adding a chandelier and a spiral staircase, Pat gave the space an even stronger effect of verticality. (And he created a base for the chandelier by finding a huge salad bowl, painting it black, and hanging it on the bottom.) Throughout the house were elaborately wrought items ranging from French Empire pieces to a huge eighteenth-century porcelain Viennese water heater to Pat's growing collection of antique clocks. There was even a garish old piano from a New Orleans whorehouse, an ebony upright with candelabra permanently attached to each side. But in spite of the mixture of styles, Pat's liberal use of black—plus copious amounts of gilt, marble, and ormolu—created an effect that was somehow both flamboyant and harmonious. "Club Ormolu," in fact, was what his friends called the place.

"The more gilt and ormolu, the better he liked it," said Louise. "He was *not* a disciple of Shaker furniture. I would say I gave him full rein when it came to decorating. I loved my office, which was the one sort of modern area, but then one day I came in and found him dismantling it all, and the next thing I knew, it was filled with Regency furniture from then on. I would say he had very flamboyant taste, but it all worked." Little Michael and his newly arrived sister, Betsy, had the top floor, which Pat rather acerbically dubbed Toyland.

As a final luxurious touch, Pat installed an elevator. That elevator provided a memorable afternoon for Pat and Louise's friend Dr. William G. Cahan. Cahan and his family, including his seven-year-old son, Anthony, were guests for Sunday brunch. Shortly after the meal, Anthony decided to start playing elevator operator and promptly got himself stuck between floors. Pat frantically called the elevator company and asked them to send over a technician right away. After a tense wait of several hours—it was, after all, Sunday afternoon—the technician arrived and got the elevator back down to the ground floor and the door open. Anthony rushed into his parents' open arms, leaving a large puddle behind.

With *Auntie Mame,* and with the move to the town house, came a new addition to the Tanner household. With Louise still working at Franklin Spier, extra hands were needed at 101 East Ninety-first Street, and the Tanners hired Corry Salley, a Harlem domestic servant of Hattie McDaniel proportions and personality, to help them run their home. Forthright but friendly, Corry quickly made herself an indispensable part of the family. She was treated by the Tanners with respect and real adoration. "Corry started out as our cleaning woman," said Louise. "We had had a perfectly appalling woman taking care of the children. Corry had been sick, and she said, 'Wait till I get well. I want to take care of those two kids.' Corry was very, very funny. One time she was watching the St. Patrick's Day parade, and a group of people who were black as the ace of spades walked by, and she said, 'Well, that's black Irish!' Once she discovered that Michael had swallowed a little bell, and—I never would have thought of this—she took him by his feet and shook him until the bell finally tumbled out. Another time Betsy was on a sled going down a hill and was just about to crash into a rock when Corry interposed herself. She really was a noble creature."

"Corry was very much a part of the household," says Joy Singer. "If they had left the children alone with her for ten years, the kids would have gone to the right schools, gotten into Harvard, worn the right clothes. She felt there were certain things that were right for 'her children,' and that she wanted for them." Corry was even happy to assume some of the more masculine child-rearing activities that would have been anathema to Pat. A rabid sports fan, she took Michael to ball games and led him on fishing expeditions to Sheepshead Bay. She also taught him to play poker and sip beer by the time he was eight. "All this stuff I consider to be quite innocent," says Michael today. "She was a doll; she was very funny; and we adored her."

In her midfifties when the Tanners hired her, Corry had already lost most of her teeth. Pat insisted on buying her a set of dentures, but she was just as happy to leave them out as wear them, and Pat repeatedly pleaded with her in mock exasperation to PUT THE DAMN DENTURES IN!

"That was *not* a servant relationship," said Peggy Cass. "She was like a relative. She was the head of the house!"

Auntie Mame provided Pat with wealth, celebrity status, a stunning town house, and a highly valued employee. It also brought him a friendship that would change his life.

When rehearsals for *Auntie Mame* began at the Broadhurst Theatre on August 27, 1956, one of the cast members present was Cris Alexander. A good friend of Rosalind Russell's, Alexander was playing several small roles including the snide floorwalker Mr. Loomis, who fires Mame from Macy's. (Alexander would repeat the role two years later in the film version.) Alexander had last worked with Russell in *Wonderful Town* and had initially made his mark on Broadway as the original Chip, one of the three young sailors in the classic 1944 Leonard Bernstein/Jerome Robbins/Comden and Green musical *On the Town*. He was also known as a prominent photographer, particularly of performers, which helped keep him afloat during the lean periods between shows. Tall, aristocratic-looking, yet possessed of a campy sense of mischief, Alexander found himself delighted by *Auntie Mame's* idiosyncratic author. "We met at that first read-through," he explains. "The author of the novel, uninvited, showed up with his beard and umbrella and actually gave a speech to the cast. And he was so divinely nutty, and nobody knew what to make of him. He had a wonderful kind of self-constructed accent; I could never imitate him. It was sort of long and drawn out; more of a speech pattern or cadence. He was most entertaining." After his impromptu address that morning to Rosalind Russell and the entire *Auntie Mame* cast, Pat left everyone speechless. They simply had no idea what to make of him. Nobody had been primed for his witty speech and outlandish image, and he was perceived by most of those assembled to be a bit pompous. Alexander, however, was one of the first to realize that Pat was himself playing a part—the role of the Great Author. When the play went on the road for tryouts and Pat came along with the company, everyone began to appreciate him.

In Cris, Pat found the perfect camp soulmate. Wildly inventive, Cris was a Renaissance man, a jack-of-all-arts who could sing, dance, act, paint, and photograph. He and his life partner, New York City Ballet dancer Shaun O'Brien, were the unofficial center of a kind of camp circle that also included their friends Katherine Walch, Hervey Jolin, and Jolin's now-deceased lover, Carl Reynolds. Jolin and Reynolds boasted camp credentials going all the way back to their youth in the 1920s. When it is suggested to Jolin, now in his midnineties and residing in rural Pennsylvania, that he qualifies as the Queen of Camp, he corrects, "I am the *Dowager Empress* of camp. At fifteen I corresponded with the great female impersonator Julian Eltinge, and I knew Carl Norman, the Creole Fashion Plate, so I started pretty early. To my mind, the birth of camp was during the Depression, when there were no jobs, and no WPA yet. Everybody hung together, and we made fantastic groups and called each other by strange names. Carl and I lived with a group and we all went Russian—we became Pushkins. We had no money, and we played around New York that way, making our own entertainment. We went to watch the *Bremen* departing, played charades, took the Staten Island ferry—it was a period when imagination emerged as a real accessory in getting along. I took camp as playfulness, and also as a retort to smugness, and to the straight people that were a bore." When Cris and Shaun entered the circle in the early 1950s, they were an infusion of young blood that roused the camp shenanigans to even greater heights of fabulous excess. The group would get together and restage whatever display artist Gene Moore had created for Bonwit Teller's windows that week—if Moore used Renaissance backgrounds, they'd all go Renaissance; if the theme was Victorian, they'd pull out the ruffles and parasols. Before long, Cris was directing twenty-minute eight-millimeter extravaganzas with the whole gang as stars. "We had two film companies," says Jolin. "The first was called Hygenic Productions; the second, after we met Dody Goodman, was called Cooz-a-Rama. And we made many films. I wrote all the scenarios. One of our most famous was called 'Clap Over Cairo.' In that one I played a brothel mistress. I also played a leper. Cris went out and bought skirt steaks and applied them all over my legs. Gene Moore was in several of our films. We made one on Sutton Place called 'The Webfoot of Destiny.' We even went on location to the Bronx Botanical Gardens when we were doing a Viennese thing."

Before long, Cris unofficially adopted Hervey Jolin as his spiritual mother, dubbing her Mrs. Rhoda Fleming and himself Florence Fleming. (And he still sends him a Mother's Day card every year.) Cris always created new names for his friends; one of them, the nationally syndicated columnist Liz Smith, he christened Chester. For a while, the gang became a solidarity known as the Pig Women of America. "Our creed," says Hervey Jolin, "was just to snuffle around and find truffles, and the good things in life. So I became Rowena Razorback. And Carl was Eunice Headcheese. And Katherine was Blanche Silversides. Oh, she was a lovely sow!"

Pat stumbled into this mad circle, and once he did, he was changed for life. For him, it began a kind of liberation. Cris and the gang recognized a kindred camp spirit in Pat and got him to blossom as he never had before. There had always been a wild campy beast struggling to burst out of Pat, even when he had been a kid growing up in Evanston; now he had finally found a group of friends who not only encouraged but nurtured that aspect of his persona. "We all just had a high old time," says Cris. "With us, he never pretended to be straight. But you know, he let his hair down with Louise, too. We had the best time with him and Louise socially, as a pair, that we had in all of our days in New York." And indeed, although Louise didn't always take part in the group's flagrant flamboyant antics, she thoroughly enjoyed observing them from the sidelines. In Louise, Pat was fortunate to have a partner who could appreciate his burgeoning ultracampy personality. Smack in the mid-1950s—an era when most of America was aping Ozzie and

Harriet—Pat was emerging from a kind of chrysalis and spreading his wings as a creature of sheer fabulousness. That might not have been welcomed in any kind of average American household, but Louise was perfectly keyed into Pat's sense of humor and larger-than-life theatricality. It's all summed up by a moment she recalled fondly: during a drive out to Long Island, she and Pat passed a sign that read Protestant Camp. Pat grandly intoned, "I am he."

Louise at one point became an unwitting accomplice to one of Cris Alexander's greatest masquerades. She and Pat were going to give a magnificent dinner party in their town house, and the guests were to include Rosalind Russell, the designer Orry-Kelly, Anita Loos, and director Carmen Capalbo, who had made a big off-Broadway splash with his acclaimed production of *The Threepenny Opera*. A photographer from *Look* magazine was to be present to document the night for an upcoming profile on Pat. Cris and Pat got the idea that the Tanners should decide to hire an extra servant for the occasion, and that servant should be Cris—or, more correctly, Cris in a new alter ego as Loyola, a friend of Corry's from Harlem. Pat immediately took Cris and Corry down to Bloomingdale's and bought them matching maid's outfits— rented ones would *never* do.

"I was terribly Stanislavsky-proud of myself," says Cris. "I was in the kitchen with Corry, going over the guest list and the menu, while the guests were arriving downstairs. And Corry kept saying, 'I just can't believe it's you!' I had spent two hours doing myself up in Louise's downstairs bathroom. First I stuffed my cheeks with Kleenex. I wore rimless glasses, and I squinted, so that you couldn't see any blue in my eyes. Pat had taken me down to a place that specialized in wigs for black people. He had me try on all kinds of different wigs to see what they looked like. Finally he chose the wig that was called First Lady. It was very close-cropped, and I wore a net. For makeup, there was something available at the time—from Max Factor, I think—called Negro Number Two. To make it realistic, on top of the Negro Number Two, I put a nice coating of *light* makeup."

Louise, meanwhile, had gotten into a beautiful gray satin gown— her Modess Regal, as she called it—and retrieved her diamonds from the vault. "There I was down in the kitchen," says Cris, "and there was my pal Louise, who didn't have the vaguest idea who I really was, talking to me and giving me the basic instructions for the night. She was very nice, very ladylike, and she must have talked to me for a good five minutes or more under the fluorescent lights in that kitchen, and she never had a clue. But what really got me worried was when little Michael came in, because children *always* know. Well, Michael did *not* know. I fooled him, absolutely. Corry had the best time in the kitchen with me. She'd keep a straight face whenever anyone walked in, and then as soon as we were alone, she'd just crumple with laughter."

Cris served the entire meal, appetizer to demitasse. He knew nearly everyone at the table, and they knew him, but only Carmen Capalbo caught on. When Loyola served him his coffee, Capalbo whispered in her ear, "May I see your Equity card?" But he didn't give Cris away.

Finally everyone left the table, and Rosalind Russell was sitting on a couch. Loyola just plopped herself down beside her and said, "Whooo! My feet are killing me!" and kicked off her shoes and put her feet up on the coffee table. Ever the grande dame, Russell did her best to ignore the entire display. Finally, Cris and Pat both decided the joke had gone on long enough. Cris leaned over into Russell's ear and emitted a basso profundo belch. He did this as a gag every night in *Auntie Mame* from behind the curtain, and its unmistakable timbre left no doubt as to Loyola's true identity. Russell jumped up and shrieked, utterly flabbergasted. "I knew you were a good actor," she told Cris, "but this!" Fortunately, the entire sequence was caught on camera by the *Look* photographer.

Louise was still laughing years later when she remembered the evening and the way she was hoodwinked along with Russell and everyone else. "I should have known there was something strange about Loyola," she says, "by the way she had of *breathing* down the back of your neck!"

Pat rarely attempted any such drag masquerades of his own—the beard would have proven a slight hindrance—but his flamboyance quotient certainly flared under the influence of his new pals. It soon found its way into the most mundane corners of his daily life. Regular trips down to Gimbel's to get Louise's diamond necklace cleaned, for example, turned into triumphs of mise-en-scène. Pat would wear the jewels around his own neck under one of his impeccably tailored Savile Row suits, and at the jewelry counter, he would nonchalantly unbutton his shirt down to his hairy chest, take off the necklace, and with a flourish, hand it over to the astonished shopgirl.

Pat even came up with a campy new name for himself: Miss Modessa Priddy. "Patrick was just *fun,*" says Cris. "The only man I can think of who came close to Patrick was Clifton Webb, with whom I'd done a show on Broadway. He liked to be just as outrageous as Patrick, but he just wasn't as much fun naturally. And Patrick was kind. Not to compare the two, but Clifton was just pure acid. But so good at it. I don't know anyone who didn't love Patrick. My father, who was a real square—a Rotarian who played the trombone—was a darling man and was funny although he didn't know it. We almost strangled several times trying not to laugh at him. He had never met *anyone* like Patrick. He was crazy about him."

Nineteen fifty-six saw the publication of not one but two books by Pat. *Guestward Ho!* came first; it was followed by Virginia Rowans's latest opus, *The Loving Couple.* The latter is one of Pat's best books, although few critics liked it at the time. Nonetheless, it enjoyed a long stay on the bestseller list. *The Loving Couple* had a highly effective gimmick: it was two books in one. "His Story" and "Her Story" were printed back-to-back with the covers reversed, so that the reader would have to turn the book over and upside down to switch from one to the other. Both stories detail a single day in the life of a pair of young married New York suburban-ites named, naturally, John and Mary. A silly spat in the morning leads to both of them swearing they never want to see each other again. John storms off alone to Manhattan, as does Mary, where both spend the day confronted with some of the worst the city has to offer in terms of clubs, restaurants, gigolos, whores, sexual predators, and two-faced friends. In the happy ending—de rigueur in a Pat Tanner book—both John and Mary improbably find themselves in front of the old walk-up they shared when they were first married. Falling into each other's arms, they swear to sell their suburban nest and move back into the decrepit little flat, which just happens to have a "To Let" sign hanging on it.

The ending may be contrived, but what precedes it is masterfully acrid social farce. Except for John and Mary, the dramatis personae is a gallery of grotesques, including John's lecherous boss, the boss's equally predatory daughter, a weaselly buddy of John's from his men's club, Mary's conniving, fashion-obsessed sister, and a slew of snobbish neighbors from the suburbs. As usual, Pat clothed a slim plot with plenty of wickedly memorable personalities. Not only does he slam the smug, sterile complacency of upper-middle-class suburbia, he pulverizes Manhattan's social climbers and tawdry decadents and clearly has a marvelous time doing so. Here is how he describes life at Riveredge, the exclusive real-estate development where John and Mary reside:

> You didn't just buy a little plot and put up a little house at Riveredge, you *joined* Riveredge. And you joined Riveredge only after the board of governors had put you to a number of soul-searching questions as to the education, occupation, race, religion, political affiliations and financial and social standings of you and your spouse, your parents and their parents. This was also followed up by private investigation and all references were carefully checked. . . . Once you had been admitted to the charmed circle of Riveredge, there were other restrictions as well. No plot could be smaller than an acre and no house less expensive than thirty thousand dollars. If you commanded a view of the Hudson, the land cost more. No two houses were alike and they were so far apart that you saw your neighbors only through binoculars—a popular pastime at Riveredge. . . . Not everybody could live at Riveredge—just a hundred lucky families. But it was *so* worth it.

Spoofing suburbia was not new at that point—Mr. Blandings had already built his dream house ten years before—but nobody had truly laid waste to suburban conformity and narrow-mindedness the way Pat did with *The Loving Couple*. That's not to say that Manhattan fared much better under his pen. The nightclub where everyone ends up, Chandelier, certainly squelches any nostalgia one might feel today for the nightclub era:

> As nightclubs went, Chandelier was as firmly established as the Metropolitan Museum. Housed in a large, lofty old building which had once served as a showroom for tombstones and rather elaborate funerary statuary, it had been Chandelier for twenty-

five years. Through long endurance and careful press agentry, the Chandelier had become synonymous with Elegance, Money and Taste, although the Chandelier management lacked all three attributes. The place had become an institution. (Happily the unfortunate shooting that took place there in 1936 had been largely forgotten.) . . .

A number of tables were occupied by May-and-December couplings. There were fun-loving old gentlemen in their sixties boyishly cavorting with chemical blondes who could easily have been their daughters. The girls with their soft curves and hard eyes all looked enough alike to be sisters and they were of a genre usually described by the tabloids as Starlets or Models. . . . There were far fewer older women with young men, but they, too, were at Chandelier this evening, grateful for the concealment of flesh and hair in the dim light, eager—but not obviously so—to return to their rose-lit parlors for ". . . one last drink and a bit of mood music . . ." with their polite, resigned and rather bored youthful escorts. ("You're so lean and muscular, Jimmy, I'd love to paint you sometime.") Haughty with nice old cab drivers and doormen, vicious to their maids, these women were like aspic in the long, lean hands of the handsome boys who offered their services in exchange for a tailor-made suit, a silk brocade robe, half a dozen ghastly ties, or, possibly, a two-week trip to the warmer climes before the Big Scene—the tears, the accusations, the renunciation or denunciation—that took place.

The extended section of the two stories that takes place at Chandelier is a prime example of one of Pat's great skills—the ability to place a large number of distinctly different characters within the same scene, and to keep the scene going for pages and pages (in this case thirty-five), building it in comic intensity without ever wearying or confusing the reader. With *The Loving Couple* Pat posed himself the added challenge of narrating this scene—in which all the major characters converge—from two totally different perspectives, and he did it brilliantly. Like a juggler who keeps adding more and more balls to toss up in the air, he achieved this feat with an apparent effortlessness. The sequence is a skillful, sharply written tour de force.

The Loving Couple did receive positive reviews from *Kirkus*, the *Chicago Sunday Tribune*, and the *New York Herald Tribune*, but *The New Yorker* referred to its characters as "2-D stereotypes," and *The Saturday Review* climaxed its negative review with "a more grievous fault is the fact that the author, in an all-out effort to be devastating, bears down much too heavily on the victims of her satire." Pat's bile *does* flow freely throughout the book, right up until the unconvincing happy ending. At times it almost seems *too* nasty—especially for readers of the mid-1950s—yet Pat's audience devoured it and it became a bestseller. Undoubtedly the suburbanites and New York socialites who adored the book assumed that Pat couldn't possibly be writing about *them*. Today *The Loving Couple* remains one of Pat's fiercest, funniest books.

Did the writing styles of Virginia Rowans and Patrick Dennis differ? Pat liked to say that they did, that each author had a distinctive voice. "The strangest thing," he told *The Saturday Review*, "is that each of the two pseudonyms writes in a different style. Don't ask me why. Virginia is more thoughtful. Patrick is more slapdash. I guess that's why he wrote *Auntie Mame*." It made for good interview copy, but it wasn't exactly true. The books of Patrick Dennis and Virginia Rowans share the same prose style, the same sense of humor, and the same comically bitter view of mid–twentieth century America and its ridiculous social pretensions. Under both pseudonyms, all of Pat's strengths are evident—the wit, the vivid characterizations, the knack for rendering accents in dialect—as are his weaknesses: thin plotting, occasional repetitiveness, obligatory happy endings. The question that remains is why Pat felt the need for any pseudonyms at all. An answer may be gleaned from an interview he gave the *New York Post* in 1958. In a quote that seems devoid of his usual levity, he stresses how much he cherished his privacy: "I always wanted to and did keep my identity private. I have my own life . . . and nobody cared who I was until that fine publication, *Time* magazine, decided the world couldn't live another hour without knowing."

The success of *The Loving Couple* gave Pat the distinction of being the first author ever to have three books on the *New York Times* bestseller list simultaneously. *The Loving Couple* moved in next door to its neighbors *Auntie Mame* and *Guestward Ho!*—which had already been on the list for months. At thirty-five, Pat was now one of the most widely read contemporary authors in America. He was well on his way to being a millionaire, but it wasn't easy for him to hold on to his money. The IRS was taking a huge bite—"After taxes, I have an incrumb of fifteen cents on the dollar," he claimed—and he still spent copiously. The house, the family, his aunt Marion, trips to Europe, charitable donations, his expensive tastes—all were responsible for heavy cash hemorrhages. He also liked to take large parties of friends out to dine with him at his favorite top-of-the-line French restaurants—Voisin, Passy, the Colony—and he never let anyone else grab the check. Pat Tanner was rapidly getting a reputation as a notorious soft touch. "He would be the last person to say so," says Cris Alexander, "but he really was genuinely a Christian."

Pat continued to spend, even though he had a suspicion that his huge success might not last. "I can tell you," he often said to Cris Alexander and Shaun O'Brien, "that I'm soon going to be old-fashioned."

TWELVE

The Children's Hour

Pat collaborated with his friend Dorothy Erskine on his next book, *The Pink Hotel*. Erskine, like Pat, was a writer who specialized in light comic fiction and adored skewering snobs and social climbers. All but forgotten now, she enjoyed a reasonably successful career in the 1950s with such novels as *The Crystal Boat, Miss Pettinger's Niece,* and *Dr. Smith and the Antic Assembly*.

She and Pat had been friendly for many years; Pat had even dedicated the "Her Story" half of *The Loving Couple* to her. ("His Story" was dedicated to his editor, Julian Muller: "To J. M., another dedicated book from an undedicated author.") Little is known about Dorothy Erskine today, but Louise Tanner remembered, "She was great fun; a *wild* drinker. One time, I think, she collapsed face-first with a straw hat on into a pizza. But she was always very ladylike, very elegant, and very well-dressed. And very funny." Erskine's photograph on the dust jacket of *The Pink Hotel* shows a conservatively attired, middle-aged woman in pearls with an oddly wicked glint in her eye.

Although Dorothy Erskine and Pat were great pals who shared certain sensibilities, that did not make them perfect collaborators. *The Pink Hotel* definitely reads like the work of two writers; it's an uncomfortable hybrid. Set in a large Florida resort, the novel features Pat's usual broad range of characters—half of them employees of the hotel, the other half guests. Most are snobbish and egomaniacal; a handful are decent sorts who manage to escape with their dignity and principles intact before the hotel burns to the ground at the end. Clearly intended to be another light comic potboiler, the novel suffers from serious problems of tone that were undoubtedly the result of the collaborators' differing styles. Unlike Pat's other novels, *The Pink Hotel* features some unsavory and disturbing characters and situations. The hotel's new cook is an asylum escapee with typhoid who has criss-crossed the country under various aliases while intentionally spreading her disease through the food she prepares. A thirty-six-year-old guest falls victim to panic attacks and nymphomania. Another guest, neglected by her oedipally inclined husband, commits suicide by throwing herself out a high window. A young chambermaid, pregnant following a rape, undergoes an abortion at the hands of a sympathetic retired female doctor who is staying at the hotel. The doctor buries the fetus at midnight on the beach.

None of these perverse elements—which are probably Erskine's contribution—are well integrated with the novel's lighter characters, among them a hair-fetishist elevator operator who snips locks from the scalps of unwary women, a parsimonious wealthy couple, and the hotel's owner, a Pat Tanner specialty: a nasty old queen with an eye for the hunkiest male employees. "To a great degree," wrote critic Rose Feld in the *New York Herald Tribune,* "this concentration on distortions of human nature and character mars the quality of the book. The highly sophisticated will prefer to read their Krafft-Ebing straight; the less sophisticated will not find the deviations from normal behavior a prod to laughter in spite of the authors' sprightly lines." The *Kirkus* review chided, "A shoddy piece of fustian this one turns out to be, with scarcely a moment of relief from tedium . . . I should think it would take more than Auntie Mame to rescue this." But other publications greeted the book with raves. Richard Blakesley in the *Chicago Sunday Tribune* called it "a realistic, mature novel which is outstanding not only for its depiction of characters but also for its craftsmanship." And the *New York Times* summed it up as "pretty funny indeed."

Some of Pat's contributions *were* pretty funny indeed, especially the sequences depicting the hotel's self-serving staff members planning the annual Christmas party. The conference-room rivalry of the social hostess, Peggy Furman, and the public relations director, Edythe St. Clair Conyngham, is memorable for its bitchy Southern-accented bigotry and pretension:

"Charming," Mrs. Conyngham said, "rilly charming."

"*Chowmin'*, Edie?" Peggy Furman said in her thick, fake Southern accent. "Why, it's dowlin', that's what it is, honeh. *Dowlin'!*"

"Quite so dear," Mrs. Conyngham said. "Rilly charming."

Edythe Conyngham and Peggy Furman, the Social Hostess, hated one another so intensely that they always made a point of conversing a great deal in public, their repartee salted with endearments, peppered with slightly upstaging corrections. Purcell couldn't for the life of him understand why they disliked one another so much. Conyngham and Furman had many things in common—poverty, pretense, loneliness, frustration and a tendency toward alcoholism that should have made them inseparable. They were both on the make, although the disparity in their ages had rendered them non-competitive in the matrimonial sweepstakes. But hate they did and in their loathing of one another they became even more nauseatingly gracious and false under public scrutiny.

"Dowlin'," Furman added, determined to have the last word. . . .

"Oh, but it's so charming, Mr. Wenton," Mrs. Conyngham said, coming suddenly, vivaciously to life. "Like the Christmases at home when I was just a tiny little girl. I remember how the help used to come up to our big veranda and serenade us. And then we always had this rilly enormous Christmas tree lighted only by candles with our footmen—these two lovable old darkies—stationed beside the tree with—*hahahaha*—big, wet sponges tied to the poles in case anything caught on. . . ."

Peggy Furman rolled her eyes dangerously in Mrs. Conyngham's direction. It was tacitly understood that while their backgrounds were supposed to be equally aristocratic, Mrs. Conyngham's territory was to be *above* the Mason-Dixon line, Furman's below.

"Did yoah darkies really do that 'way up in New Yoke City, Edie honeh?" Furman asked dangerously. "Ah'd always thought yew came from *Yankee* stock."

"Of course, Peggy darling," Mrs. Conyngham said velvetly.

"But we always spent *Christmas* down on the Eastern Shore of Maryland with the—"

"Yes, yes," Mr. Wenton said, interrupting Edythe's girlhood reveries.

Pat learned his lesson after *The Pink Hotel:* no more collaborations. It was the last time that Patrick Dennis or Virginia Rowans would coauthor a book.

Nineteen fifty-seven marked the birth of Pat and Louise's second child, Elizabeth. Michael was three years old. Being a kid and having Pat for a father was an eccentric situation, but not quite as permissive and Auntie Mame–ish as one might imagine. Pat had certainly not known much affection from his own father; although he was able to be affectionate with his kids, he could also be strict, stern, and somewhat distant. "His sheer force of personality was very great," says Elizabeth, now known to everyone as Betsy. "He was a very authoritative person; an incredibly strong personality. When he told you to do something, you jumped. Someone else could ask you to do something eighteen times over, but he just had to *think* it and it got done. He wasn't a tyrant at all; it was just that he had amazing command. He didn't need to be a disciplinarian; he'd say something in a normal tone and it was done."

"He was very strict in a way, and we were very frightened of him," Michael admits. "But he was also very laissez-faire and would say, 'Oh, let them do it.' So it was very paradoxical. He was not overprotective, but he certainly demanded total politeness and good behavior. We were impeccably well-behaved."

In a sense, Pat raised the kids in the rather cool and somewhat distant manner of a father from the Edwardian era. It was very much in keeping with his mode of dress (British, circa 1913), his rejection of such emblems of the twentieth century as modern art, and his general longing to have lived in the past. ("I'd like to have been killed in the First World War," he once told *Life* magazine. "Just before that would have been my era and I'd have died happy.") Basically, Pat treated his children like grown-ups. He refused to talk down to them, and he expected them to comport themselves in the manner of little adults. Just like Young Patrick in *Auntie Mame,* both Michael and Betsy were taught to mix a martini for houseguests at a young age. "You'd be four years old," says Betsy, "and offering to make cocktails." In the midst of all this decorum, Pat rarely held back his language in front of the kids. "He had a terrible mouth," says Michael, "and would use obscenity almost like Richard Pryor to get laughs. He talked worse in front of us than I think any parent would now. He used to call me 'Mr. Bastard' and Betsy 'Miss Bitch' in front of the company. That wouldn't go over now. He was very foulmouthed—but usually in a good-natured way."

"The children *loved* him," says Pat's longtime friend Katherine Walch. "They *adored* him. But they would be brought down like exhibits and then sent back upstairs to the fourth floor. That's no way to treat children. And Louise tried *so hard* to give them a life, to take them places."

"It's not like he was an iceberg," Michael stresses, "or that he couldn't express affection. He couldn't really mete it out in an appropriate way; he was kind of stiff and formal." One of the ways in which Pat showed affection was through merciless tickling. "He overtickled," says Michael. "He tickled almost to the point of torture. There was no question about it. He would not quit. It was sadistic tickling, and he took it a little too far."

In spite of the problems, however, Pat couldn't help but be fun for the kids, as he was so effortlessly funny himself. And Michael and Betsy's friends always warmed to him immediately, as he never seemed like a serious grown-up to them. "One of the important things for us in our family," says Betsy, "was a sense of humor. You always wanted to put forth something that was going to be humorous; you always wanted to make somebody laugh. That was a very strong guideline. And it's like that in my life today. My father and mother and their friends were some of the funniest people I ever met in my life. I aspire to be one-tenth as funny as they are on the day I die, and I'll be happy."

Louise was from a Catholic family and felt strongly that Michael and Betsy should be sent to a Catholic grade school. Since Pat was irreverent to the point of blasphemy and pretty much detested the Catholic Church, it must have been something that he agreed to only grudgingly. He referred to Catholics as "bead fumblers." (When

Michelangelo's *Pietà* was displayed in New York, Pat shocked young Michael by stage-whispering to the naked Jesus, "Put on your clothes, honey, he's coming home any moment.") Once Michael was given an assignment to write an essay for a school event entitled "February's Parade of Famous People." When he asked Pat to help him, Pat sat down at the dining room table and instantly turned out a twenty-verse poem about Abraham Lincoln that was far too bawdily disrespectful for little Michael to ever get up and read before his class. Written to a barn-dance, foot-stomping hoedown beat, the epic included such rhymes as "Married too long to a mighty mean wife / Mighty damn happy when he lost his life." Yee-hah!

When Parents' Day came around at St. David's school, Michael was quietly terrified that his daddy would say something to embarrass him. "But of course he didn't," says Michael, "and he was very charming to everyone. He *did* show up in a mink pillbox hat. . . ."

In addition to being a parent, Pat was also playing Favorite Uncle to his nieces, Patty and Susan. Both were still living in Chicago, but they frequently visited Pat and Louise in New York. "I thought it was marvelous," says Sister Joanna (Susan) today. "Louise and Pat were the ideal couple as far as I was concerned; I always had a marvelous time with them. They really had quite a profound influence on my life. Pat introduced me to a lot. He introduced me to opera, and I've been an opera buff ever since. He introduced me to exotic foods and wine and antiques; he made me more aware of culture in general. My parents had introduced me to the symphony and the ballet and the Art Institute of Chicago. But things Pat said had a particular impact on me, and what he liked I also tended to like. Partially that was because I knew that he knew what he was talking about, and his taste was erudite, impeccable."

Susan came to New York more frequently than her sister and often stayed with Pat and Louise. Pat treated her like the young adult she was, allowing her to stay out late, smoke, and enjoy the city's nightlife. He also took her on a trip to Europe when he went to meet with the various European translators and publishers of *Auntie Mame*. World War II and its Nazi atrocities were still fresh in his memory, and he refused to set foot on German soil. Sister Joanna remembers that on their flight from Vienna to Paris, their plane had to touch down in

Munich. All passengers were to temporarily disembark and wait inside the Munich terminal, but Pat refused to enter the building and would not allow Susan to do so either. Instead, the two of them waited outside alone as he furiously paced and chain-smoked until it was time to get back on the plane.

While in Paris, Pat was briefly reunited with his old high school chum Anne Noggle, his favorite dancing partner, whom he had not seen for nearly fifteen years. Since her Evanston days, Anne had gone on to become one of the first female fliers in the U.S. Air Force. Although she and Pat only spent two or three days together in Paris, it was as if they picked up their adolescent friendship right where they had left it off. "Oh, Jesus, it was fun!" she says today. "First we talked about everybody we'd ever known. Then he told me he was well into his second million, and he said, 'I'll tell you what let's do. Let's go out and see how much we can spend for lunch.' It lasted for hours! We had one course here and one course there and champagne everywhere. We had so much to drink we couldn't find my car. We had to hire a taxi and go circling around one block and then another until we found it!"

Pat once said in an interview, "I always start writing with a clean piece of paper and a dirty mind." Paris was just the place to nourish that dirty mind. He took Anne to a live sex show that was raunchier than anything to be found at the usual Pigalle strip-club tourist traps. "I never really knew there *were* such things. This just about shocked me," says Anne, who is not particularly easy to shock. "There were women and horses and just all kinds of—*stuff* going on on that stage. Then, you only had to walk a couple of feet and there was a whorehouse connected to the theater. The madam was absolutely gorgeous; very attractive; very nice. And Pat was just talking away with her. We all went upstairs to this room, and in came a guy with two girls. The room was so small, we were right by the bed! After a while I got so *bored* with their *fucking,* and here's Pat on the other side of the bed conversing with the madam while they're—*doing* this! Pat may have occasionally been casting an eye over at them, but he was more interested in interviewing the madam!"

The next night, Pat gave a huge party in his hotel suite—and the madam was one of the guests. As the party wound down into the wee hours, Pat told Anne she was welcome to stay over. The two of them innocently climbed into Pat's bed like kids on a sleepover and stayed up the rest of the night talking and catching each other up on their lives. "It was wonderful," says Noggle. "We talked about everybody and everything. We had been so close when we were young and had so many things to talk about and laugh about, it just seemed perfectly natural. It was amazing how we fell right back into our old relationship." The next morning, when Pat got up and got dressed, Noggle noticed something strange: "Not only did he still not wear underwear, but he had a special shirt on. The shirt went down in back, and there was this flap that came up and buttoned up front, and that was his underpants, holding his peepee in. This was obviously custom-made. He said it kept his shirttails down. I'd never seen anything like it."

That was the last time Anne and Pat would see each other. Some twenty years later, Anne would be shocked and saddened to read Pat's obituary in *Time* magazine. "It wasn't very often that you broke through Pat's sophistication into something else," she remembers today. "I think he wasn't as sure of himself as he pretended to be. There must have been things about himself that he kept inside. The most comfortable, delightful times we had when we were kids were not when we were shocking people, but when we would sit and read those plays together."

Pat got his fill of the theater from 1957 to 1958 when, for one season, he became the drama critic for *The New Republic* under his Patrick Dennis pseudonym. He saw plenty of bad plays and bad productions, and every negative review seemed to take something out of him, until he realized that he was not cut out to be a critic and quit. His January 13, 1958, review of Tennessee Williams's *Garden District* displays his diffidence: after listing ten good reasons not to go to the play, ranging from "it is an evening of unrelenting horror" to "the dialogue often tends to be arty, abstruse and highfalutin'," he turns around and praises the evening as "vintage Williams, exquisitely directed and performed." He also manages to take a hypocritical, poorly justified potshot at the play's enthusiastic gay audiences (see appendix). Referring to his drama-critic stint some years later in an interview, he said,

"I had it up to here. Most of the time the snow outside looked better than what was going on inside."

Auntie Mame had by now become such a phenomenon that its fans were clamoring for a sequel. Pat obliged with *Around the World with Auntie Mame*, published by Harcourt, Brace and Company in 1958 and dedicated "to the one and only Rosalind Russell." Auntie Mame mania was nowhere near diminishing—the week before its publication, *Around the World* had already racked up fifty-five thousand advance sales to the nation's bookstores. Another loosely connected series of episodes, the book had the framing device of Patrick Dennis picking up the story two and a half years after the original left off, with him and Pegeen worried about their son, Michael, who has still not returned from his trip to India with Auntie Mame. Patrick begins telling Pegeen the saga of his own lengthy around-the-world trip with Auntie Mame during the late 1930s. Each chapter delineates a specific adventure as they roam through London, Paris, Biarritz, Venice, Austria, Lebanon, and the China Seas during the stormy years just before the onset of World War II. A chapter that placed Mame and Patrick on a collective farm in the Soviet Union was suppressed by the publisher for fear of raising McCarthy-era disapproval; that innocuous episode, "Auntie Mame and Mother Russia," was restored for the book's 1983 reissue.

While lacking the freshness of the original, *Around the World with Auntie Mame* was an enjoyable romp that gave Pat plenty of wide-open opportunities to skewer the hubris and pomposity of Americans abroad—Auntie Mame included. When Mame buys an Austrian *Schloss* and makes her first appearance in the town square of the village of Stinkenbach-am-Tirol, Patrick dryly notes that she has dolled herself up in quaint native garb to the point of "looking like the natural child of William Tell out of Heidi." Upon arrival in Venice, Mame is distressed to see that all gondolas are painted black, including the private one that she hires. She makes up for it by designing for her gondoliers black-and-pink costumes with long, fluttering pink streamers on the hats. "They caused," remarks Patrick, "a distressing number of low, lewd whistles when Auntie Mame's men rowed past the other gondoliers. In fact, they got into so many fist fights proving their masculinity to less spectacularly-dressed oarsmen that Auntie Mame's gondola often looked more like the emergency ward at Bellevue than the regal barge it was supposed to be."

Pat took a cue from Lawrence and Lee and wisely included large doses of Mame's pal Vera Charles, who keeps turning up at different points in the journey. Through Vera, Mame ends up thwarting Nazis, sharing the services of a sleazy South American lounge lizard, and making a half-naked debut onstage at the Folies-Bergère. Pat also added some memorable new characters to the cocktail, including Bella Shuttleworth, another wealthy widow from Buffalo; Elmore Burnside, a thoroughly obnoxious Ugly American who is a cousin of Mame's late husband Beauregard Pickett Burnside; and most memorably, Sarita Mont D'or, the supremely affected social leader of an American expatriate community in Lebanon, who is shamefully attempting to camouflage her true identity—Sadie Goldberg, Bronx housewife.

It's to Pat's credit that he was able to keep *Around the World with Auntie Mame* bubbling, because he had not undertaken the project with much enthusiasm. "I don't like to bite the hand that feeds me," he whined to *Newsweek*, "but I'm tired of Auntie Mame. . . . Some of these characters, like Wodehouse's Jeeves, that have been feeding people for years are just too much. By now Auntie Mame would be funny with leukemia." He went on to say, "I just can't think of new situations anymore. I wish I had one of those plot wheels that mixes characters and situations. You know, you just spin it and you get a dethroned queen in a lumberjack camp."

Pat's depressive tendencies were a frequent impediment to his work, never more so than in a situation such as this, where he was under pressure to live up to the original *Auntie Mame*. The initiative and industriousness he had shown during his early days as a writer were now inhibited by his having to feed a hungry public, and to maintain his new level of fame and financial success. According to Louise, Pat's modus operandi for each book was now weeks or months of procrastination, followed by a sudden outpouring of creative energy that produced an entire novel within about ninety days. "I remember that each year he seemed to have a different enthusiasm," Louise said. "One year it was soap operas, another wrestling. He loved to watch wrestling on television, especially when the six-hundred-pound guy crashed to the mat just in time for the commercial. He'd watch this, and I thought, 'He's going mad!' Because it was all he would do, for weeks. And people kept saying, 'Should we talk to Louise about this?' And all of a sudden one day he got out of this thing. Without a shift of gears, he was working around the clock on another book. He turned around and showed such incredible discipline." Once a novel had burst out of him, it was fully formed—Pat rarely did any rewriting, nor was he asked to do much by his editors. "I write fast or not at all," he told *Life* magazine.

But writing *Around the World with Auntie Mame* taxed Pat so, he was unable to finish the book. He couldn't—or didn't want to—come up with the final chapter. Not for the first time, nor the last, he had stopped short of writing an ending. One year before, his editor, Julian Muller, had had to write the final scene of *The Loving Couple*. For *Around the World with Auntie Mame*, Muller had already met with his sales forces (by now he had moved to Harcourt, Brace and Company), written the catalog copy, and set up a production schedule, but Pat still wasn't making the deadline. Muller's repeated calls were met with assurances from Pat that he was coming along fine with the work and would have the novel finished and ready shortly. Meanwhile, Pat and Louise were only days away from a scheduled trip to Europe. "I said something to him," says Muller, "probably in a vulgar way, about how he needed to deliver a manuscript to me—that the gestation period had passed. He said, 'I told you not to worry about it.' I said, 'You're leaving tomorrow! Where the hell's the manuscript?' Pat answered, 'Stop by the house for a drink on your way home, and the manuscript will be waiting for you at the front door.'"

Arriving at 101 East Ninety-first Street, Muller found that Pat and Louise were throwing themselves "a small cocktail party of about seventy people. It took me about twenty minutes to find him. I asked him where the manuscript was, and he said, 'It's at the front door!' I said, 'Okay, have a marvelous time.'"

Muller went back to the front door and found the manuscript, beautifully gift-wrapped for him in a box. He carried it home, had dinner with his wife, then opened the package. To his horror, he saw a note from Pat where the final chapter should have been. "Dear Julian," it read. "Haven't started packing, haven't finished the manuscript. If I don't pack, I'm not going to go. So here's the manuscript. YOU finish it."

Muller had no choice but to jump in. "I knew pretty well how to wing it," he says, laughing. "In short bursts, I could imitate Pat's style. So I wrote the last chapter. I had it set by the time Pat came back, and he gave me a B-plus."

Around the World with Auntie Mame would have been critic-proof under any circumstances—within a matter of months 130,000 copies had been sold—but it received a high number of good reviews, particularly from the New York critics. "As extravagantly full of gags, slapstick comedy and general hilarious confusion as its predecessor," wrote Rose Feld in the *New York Herald Tribune.* Ben Crisler in the *New York Times* said that Pat "shows no signs of flagging invention. . . . Mr. Tanner is a most entertaining writer." Charles A. Wagner in the *New York Mirror* found it better than the original. Not so William Hogan, the critic for the *San Francisco Chronicle.* "I found the new adventures of Mame Dennis Burnside, ninth richest widow in New York, not only less crisp than the original, but a somewhat vulgar and insular book," he sniffed. "It is, I think, a classic example of the middlebrow brand of humor that generates canned laughter on the *I Love Lucy* show. It has no subtlety, grace or imagination." Pat undoubtedly had a memorable rejoinder to that.

A year after the publication of *Around the World with Auntie Mame,* Pat got to take his own trip to the Soviet Union. He and Louise went as part of a group of Americans on a guided tour led by Norman Dorsen, who is now a law professor at New York University. Dorsen remembers Pat and Louise as the stars of the group and says that they exuded a kind of glamour and elegance that must have been similar to that of Gerald and Sara Murphy, the famous American couple whose Mediterranean beach house was a locus for expatriate artists and writers during the 1920s. A photo taken of Pat and Louise during the Paris-Moscow leg of the flight shows Pat smiling but looking as if he'd rather be elsewhere—for all his globe-trotting, he was forever nervous about air travel.

When Pat and Louise were in Russia, they both realized their smallpox vaccinations had run out. Louise immediately had herself vaccinated in Moscow, but Pat refused, assuming he could get it done at Idlewild International Airport when he returned to New York. He was wrong: at Idlewild, Pat found himself hustled off to a government quarantine hospital on Staten Island for two weeks. Instead of raising a fuss, Pat made light of his situation. "It's very pleasant here," he told a *New York Herald Tribune* reporter who called him in the hospital. "Private room, fine food, good service, restful atmosphere. Even the trip here was nice. I had a chauffeur. Why, I don't think I've ever been to Staten Island before. Very nice country, really."

THIRTEEN

The Birth of Belle Poitrine

By now Louise had finally left Franklin Spier and was devoting more of her time to her own writing. In 1959, Crowell published her first book, a collection of fourteen biographical essays on famous Americans of the twentieth century entitled *Here Today*. Louise would follow this with four more books, three of them novels, plus an overview of 1930s pop culture entitled *All the Things We Were*. "I certainly never produced much," Louise said modestly in 1998, "but Pat was always very encouraging to me as a writer. Very encouraging. He would always read my work and make suggestions. And it really didn't go the other way." Pat was, in fact, hugely and humbly admiring of Louise's writing talent and often said so to their friends.

Following the success of *Auntie Mame* onstage, Rosalind Russell's husband, producer Frederick Brisson, optioned *The Loving Couple* for development as a Broadway musical. The hot young stage talent at that time was producer-director Carmen Capalbo, who had burst onto the New York theater scene with the enormous success of his landmark 1954 revival of *The Threepenny Opera* starring Lotte Lenya. He had gone on to produce and direct three important American premieres on Broadway: Graham Greene's *The Potting Shed* with Dame Sybil Thorndike; Eugene O'Neill's *A Moon for the Misbegotten* with Wendy Hiller, Franchot Tone, and Cyril Cusack; and William Saroyan's *The Cave Dwellers* with Wayne Morris and Eugenie Leontovitch. Rosalind Russell knew Capalbo and arranged a meeting for him and her husband to discuss possible projects.

When Brisson suggested *The Loving Couple,* Capalbo was more than open to the idea. "Pat had already given me two or three rave reviews in the past," Capalbo says. "So I read the book and was intrigued by the way it was written—you could start it from either end. It created a lot of problems in terms of how to dramatize it, but that was part of the challenge." Capalbo thought Pat should collaborate with him on the project and arranged to meet him.

The two instantly became great friends. "We had a great deal in common," explains Capalbo, "and we had the same kind of slightly sardonic view of life. Basically, he and I both disliked pretentiousness; I guess that was the basis for it." They signed with Brisson as collaborators and got started on *The Loving Couple*. Capalbo enjoyed Pat's eccentricities, which, at one point in the collaboration, included Pat's sudden decision to have all of his teeth removed. Spending too much time in the dentist's chair, Pat decided to have done with his troublesome teeth altogether. Having lost quite a few already, he figured it would save him time and money. But instead of replacing them with a well-made set of dentures, he got a set of "clackers," as Capalbo refers to them. "That's the only word for them," he says. "They looked like the kind you'd buy in a magic shop. He got the cheapest, most obvious-looking teeth you could imagine, upper and lower. Many times in the middle of a dinner party, he'd say, 'I can't bear these things!' and he'd pull them out and put them right down on the table." (The dentures also came in handy every Halloween, when Pat would insert them upside down, answer the door, and send the neighborhood trick-or-treaters screaming in every direction.)

"In addition," Capalbo goes on, "he was losing his hair. He wasn't bald, but his hairline was receding a bit. So he said he wanted to get a hairpiece. I said, 'You don't need a hairpiece,' but he wanted to get one. So he went and literally paid fifteen dollars. It looked like a dead bird sitting on his head. It was strictly amateurville. And he wasn't a tightwad—he just said, 'Look, why should I spend three hundred bucks when this one is perfectly good?' There again, he'd take it off and put it down in front of everyone. He didn't wear it all the time; it was like a hat. It would flap in the breeze! He wouldn't even apply it with whatever you use. And he was a great-looking guy! People used to confuse him with Commander Whitehead in the Schweppes ads!"

By early autumn of 1958, Capalbo and Pat had finished Act I of *The Loving Couple*. While working together, they had often discussed how

Hollywood writing teams of the 1930s and 1940s would take off to Catalina or Palm Springs for a few days to make some solid progress on a project far from the city's distractions. The two decided to try the New York equivalent, and to get started on Act II at Gurney's Inn, an old seaside resort in Montauk, Long Island. "At that time of the year, the season was basically over," says Capalbo, "but the weather was still pleasant. So we went out there and spent about ten days working together. We just pissed ourselves laughing, because there were still people staying there, and right next door to us there was a crazy couple. Every night you could hear the walls shake as their bed banged up against our wall. But in addition, you heard the woman moaning over and over, "Ahhhhhhhhh, ahhhhhhhhhhh!" And she did it so loudly, we would both collapse. And then we'd go and watch them in the dining room!"

That dining room was another endless source of entertainment for Pat and Capalbo. During dinner they would hardly speak to each other because Pat would have his head tilted back in one direction and Capalbo's would be tilted in another, as both were eavesdropping on their neighbors' conversations and gleefully making mental notes.

"So we knocked off the first draft of the show," Capalbo goes on. "We never took it seriously; that's the only way I can put it; it was very unprofessional of both of us. We worked hard on it; but it just was not . . . well, anyway, we showed it to Freddie Brisson and he just didn't know what hit him." Once they had read Brisson's extensive notes, the collaborators decided it was time for another little escape—this time to Cuba. By now it was early 1959, and the revolution had just taken place.

When the two stepped off the plane into Havana's chaotic airport, suddenly the crowd seemed to part for them. A group of young soldiers pointed at Pat almost reverently with awe.

It was the beard. Beards, popularized by the new national hero Fidel Castro, had become a symbol of the revolution. Immediately Pat and Capalbo gained a police escort through the airport, where they were allowed to bypass customs and were driven right to their hotel in Veradero Beach. For the entire ten days in Cuba, men and boys kowtowed to Pat. "They wouldn't even take our money in the restaurants," Capalbo says, laughing.

"Of course, he was a great social critic," he continues. "I once said to him, 'The difference between you and Bertolt Brecht is the jokes.' I think they were both railing against the same things in society. And he was a very, very sentimental person. In terms of human suffering, and poverty-stricken people, he was amazingly concerned about that. And it was not bullshit. When we were in Cuba, Pat could be brought to tears."

Once back in New York, Pat and Capalbo gave the new script to Frederick Brisson and waited while Brisson showed it to every unlikely prospect from Milton Berle to Tony Martin and Cyd Charisse. Like so many projects, the musical of *The Loving Couple* simply sank into oblivion, never to be heard of again.

Nonetheless, Pat came up with another idea for a play for Frederick Brisson to produce that would be a perfect Rosalind Russell vehicle. Virginia Rowans would write a play titled *All About Love,* concerning a woman who tries to run everyone's life but her own. The project was announced in the press on February 24, 1959.

But what Virginia Rowans started as a play eventually turned into her fourth and final novel, *Love and Mrs. Sargent,* published by Farrar, Straus and Cudahy in 1961. A bit of a change of pace for Pat, it relied on a smaller cast of characters than his other novels. It also was the only one to have a basically downbeat ending. Sheila Sargent is a nationally syndicated advice columnist living in the posh Chicago suburb of Lake Forest, Illinois, with her two troubled grown children and her frumpy secretary. When Peter Johnson, a left-leaning young journalist, is sent to interview her, sparks start flying and the two plunge headlong into an affair. Within a matter of days, however, Sheila loses all the love in her life— Peter's, and that of her two children, which she has actually lost long before due to her excessive attempts at control.

"Momism" was a popular target at that time. After decades of being stereotyped as a self-sacrificing martyr, the American Mom was now getting a new image as a misguided, manipulative bitch in such films as *The Manchurian Candidate* and such plays as *Oh Dad, Poor Dad, Mama's Hung You in the Closet and I'm Feelin' So Sad. Love and Mrs. Sargent* falls squarely into this mom-bashing genre, but of course its predominant tone is satirical. Pat pulls a neat reversal on his readers by introducing Sheila as a strong, sympathetic, accomplished figure—the image her fans perceive—only to peel that away and reveal the Monster

Mom underneath. Not until the final paragraphs, when she is left abandoned in her beautiful home by all her loved ones, does she determine to change her ways. By Pat Tanner standards, this is fairly bleak stuff. Interestingly, Pat dedicated the book to his parents, but that may have had more to do with its suburban Chicago setting than with any subliminal messages he was trying to send them. Its leading character, after all, is a native of Pat's hometown of Evanston, and Pat takes obvious delight in skewering everything in town from the clubwomen who meet at the Orrington Hotel to Miss Jessie Pocock's dancing school.

But the *New York Times* review by Martin Levin was correct when it stated, "Having set the stage for what could be a slick bit of popular fiction, the author neglects to hatch either enough plot to keep the reader curious or enough comic interludes to keep him amused." Moreover, Pat resorted to the hoary, contrived device of The Other Sheila: her conscience, a tough-talking alter ego with whom Sheila has clumsily drawn-out expository conversations. Unfortunately, none of the book's central characters are as interesting or as much fun as the subsidiary ones. Even Rose Feld of the *New York Herald Tribune,* who had given raves to Pat's previous work, had to concede that *Love and Mrs. Sargent* was "pretty much of a bore."

But the novel had no trouble attracting readers, thanks largely to an inspired marketing strategy that, for the first time, emphasized that Patrick Dennis and Virginia Rowans were one and the same. In one ad, Virginia Rowans even penned her own letter to Sheila Sargent:

> Everyone keeps calling me "Patrick Dennis." . . . Although I may be America's only bearded lady of letters, my books aren't in the least like Patrick Dennis's silly novels, and I'm getting pretty sick and tired of this confusion. . . . I could tell you a lot more about it, but I'm late for my analyst. Help me, Sheila Sargent, help me, help me—before I lose my sanity!

Love and Mrs. Sargent was the first of Pat's books to be produced through his own corporation, a playful but legitimate entity called Lancelot Leopard, Ltd. Lancelot Leopard was like an independent film production company that releases its movies through a big studio. Most of Pat's books after *Around the World with Auntie Mame* were produced by Lancelot Leopard. A contract would be signed with a major publisher stipulating publication terms and profit details. Then the books would be printed and distributed under the publisher's aegis. Lancelot Leopard was created because of the tax laws at that time. It enabled Pat to keep more of his income because he was considered an employee of the corporation, to be hired for the purpose of writing books. The law stipulated that in such a corporation, 51 percent of the profits were to be distributed amongst people other than the literary personnel. Pat had no trouble convincing a group of close friends, including Julian Muller, Cris Alexander, and Shaun O'Brien, to each put up a small amount of money and get the corporation started. Cris even designed stock certificates for the corporation members emblazoned with a coat of arms showing Pat naked on a leopard skin.

Meetings were held annually at Pat and Louise's town house, and they were basically excuses for a party. Here are Pat's minutes for the meeting of Thursday, December 15, 1960:

The second annual meeting of the stockholders of Lancelot Leopard, Ltd. was held at 101 East 91st Street, New York, New York at nine o'clock on the evening of Thursday, December 15, 1960.

Because of the unseasonable snows, attendance was down. Drinking was up.

The business meeting was mercifully short. It was called to order by former President Muller. The Secretary, Mr. Tanner, read the minutes and social notes. Happily, none of the Officers and Board Members had anything to say.

Mrs. Otis Kiser, Vice President in Charge of Literature, was more than an hour late and it had nothing to do with the snow.

Dividends of twenty per cent (20%) were paid and there was a good bit of undignified and unnecessary scuffling to get at the checks.

Mr. Cris Alexander wore leopard shoes and Mr. Shaun O'Brien was radiant in leopard necktie.

Delicious refreshments were served in the Employees' Lunchroom. And will the smart cookie who threw up in Mrs. Hollister's sable muff please not do it again this year.

Pat turned forty in 1961, and to mark the occasion, Louise threw him a huge party aboard the *Manhattan II* yacht. "Sailing punctually at seven o'clock," read the engraved invitation. "Dress sensibly." "Dress warmly" might have been more appropriate, as unseasonable gale-force winds howled around the city that night. Nonetheless, the ship set sail and the party went on as promised, although most of the guests fled the weather on deck and crammed into the yacht's cabin space, where a huge roast beef was being carved and served and New York's most famous omelette maker was artfully flipping and folding his creations. Cris Alexander, Shaun O'Brien, Hervey Jolin, and Carl Reynolds had bought marine hats on Forty-second Street and arrived looking like German submarine officers. Pat had outfitted himself jauntily with a skipper's cap, and he distributed long Auntie Mame–style cigarette holders as party favors. His *Pink Hotel* collaborator, Dorothy Erskine, managed to overimbibe, as usual, and had to be carried home after nearly falling overboard into the East River. Transsexual pioneer Christine Jorgensen somehow succeeded in crashing the party. She stalked the yacht relentlessly, asking everyone, "Where's Patrick Dennis? The only reason I'm here is because I want to play Auntie Mame!" When she entered the ladies' room, a beeline of women immediately followed. Upon exiting, many were heard to whisper, "You know, she has very large feet!" Shaun O'Brien's mother came out and said, "Well, that's the first time I've been in a ladies' room and had an ex-GI in the stall next to me!"

Nineteen sixty-one would be another two-novel year for Pat. If the first book has largely been forgotten, the second has rightfully been accorded a place in the Pantheon of classic camp fiction. *Little Me* sprang from an idea Pat had when he saw the stills Cris Alexander had shot during the production of his latest 8mm Cooz-a-Rama camp extravaganza. This film purported to expose the shocking conditions in private nursing homes, and Cris, Shaun, Hervey Jolin, and the gang were all tarted up as some of the ugliest nurses in creation. When Pat saw the photos, which Cris had just put up all over the bathroom wall, he was so struck by them that he could hardly tear himself away. The next time he saw Cris, a few days later, Pat proposed a new adventure for them. "What would you think," he asked Cris, "of doing pictures just like you have in the bathroom to document a phony autobiography of a rotten movie star?" Cris didn't have to think twice.

The result was an audacious, irreverent illustrated novel—featuring over 150 photos by Cris—that was unlike anything ever seen in America. (Its only antecedent may have been Cecil Beaton's *My Royal Past,* a mock autobiography of a decidedly lesser and wholly fictitious member of the British royal family that was published in England in 1936. Pat adored that book, but his own creation was far funnier and more ambitious.) *Little Me* is narrated in the first person in an unbelievably self-important tone by Belle Poitrine, née Belle Schlumpfert, of Venezuela, Illinois. Belle's rise to notoriety as a movie star, followed by her fall from grace and eventual redemption (Chapter 20: "I Find God in Southampton"), is recounted in her own fatuous, affected prose, which is always sprinkled with bad French when it's not slipping into cheap slang. A grasping, conniving, white-trash Lady Macbeth, Belle stops at nothing, including larceny, blackmail, and murder, in her efforts to scramble to the top of the Hollywood heap. Of course, she takes great pains to portray herself to her readers as a sweet young thing, guileless, trusting, and innocent. Pat perfectly skewered the inflated, pompous tone of the Great Female Star autobiographies that had been turning up at the time from the likes of Pola Negri, Mae Murray, and Zsa Zsa Gabor.

Belle's first-person narrative voice was a campy progenitor to the self-infatuated Miss Piggy from the Muppets. Typical was the section in which Belle describes the results of her overreaching Hollywood ambitions during 1933:

> Because Baby-dear was in an Episcopal boarding school, I had a natural interest in religion. I offered my services as star of *The White Sister,* but for some reason that was never made quite clear to me, the role was given to Helen Hayes, a competent performer. At Paramount my desire to play a nun in *Cradle Song* was somehow ignored.
>
> However, the same studio was planning an all-star production and everyone said that I would be absolutely fantastic as the star of *Alice in Wonderland* and staunch, reliable old Dudley du Pont and Carstairs Bagley even telephoned to encourage me to take a

screen test as Alice. "Belle, darling, it would be *the* camp of the year," Dudley said. "*You* be Alice and *we'll* be the queens. Do it with us, for laughs." Those darling boys were so gay, how could I refuse? Just thinking of myself as the star of a huge cast that included Gary Cooper, Cary Grant, W. C. Fields, Edward Everett Horton, "Jack" Oakie, "Ned" Sparks, May Robson, Polly Moran, "Skeets" Gallagher, "Dick" Arlen, Roscoe Ates and Mae Marsh (who had thrilled me so in *Birth of a Nation*) sent chills up and down my spine. We rehearsed together for weeks and, while it didn't seem to me that Dudley and Carstairs were exactly right as the Red Queen and the White Queen, I appreciated their faith in me. Over drinks, Travis Banton designed the simple dress I was to wear in my test. (He said that it brought out all my most girlish qualities.) On the day of our test the studio was mobbed with famous faces. I had been nervous about playing comedy, considering myself more of a dramatic actress, but any fears of mine were quickly quelled. The visiting stars and other "top" names shouted with laughter at my performance with Carstairs and Dudley. There was thunderous applause at the end of each "take." When it was all over, I was mobbed with admirers. Adorable Carole Lombard was laughing so hard that Clark Gable and Leslie Howard had to help her out. "*Alice?*" Carole gasped through tears of merriment. "Have you ever thought of co-starring with Shirley Temple?" No idle compliment when one recalls that sweet little Shirley was America's biggest box-office attraction during the thirties.

Flushed with triumph, I returned immediately to Casa Torquemada to await the call from Paramount. Can you imagine my shock when the choice role of Alice went to an unknown *child* named Charlotte Henry! As for poor Carstairs and Dudley, the parts of Red Queen and White Queen were given to Edna May Oliver and Louise Fazenda. The boys were very philosophical about it. "You can't fight sex," they said. Studio politics again!

Accompanying the above excerpt was Cris Alexander's photo of Belle in her screen test as an Amazonian Alice, replete with coy *moue*, garish lipstick, and plunging neckline.

Throughout the book, Pat displayed an encyclopedic knowledge of screen stars and American film history that was remarkable in those days before film schools, VCRs, and laser discs. No less astonishing were the photos by Cris Alexander. Cris too had a camp aficionado's love of old movies, and he demonstrated it in shot after shot, creating set stills from imaginary epics that were so spot-on accurate they looked like the real thing. Belle Poitrine was shown starring in such unknown silent dramas as *Thou Shalt Not, Gay Husbands,* and *Plutarch's Wives,* early talkies such as *Tarzan's Other Wife* and *The Broadway Barcarolle of 1930,* and the high point of her career, *The Scarlet Letter,* which Belle produced herself and decided to revamp into a college-football romance. There was also page after page of photos from Belle's private life, domestic scenes with her many husbands, and family portraits including her mother, daughter, and granddaughter. "I didn't contribute one thing to the story," Cris swears. "I thought up some of the ideas for the pictures, but always to fit what Pat had wrought. It was absolutely all Pat, and it all came from the whole spirit of those foolish pictures in the bathroom, mixed with something that was supposed to be real but never possibly could have been."

Belle and all of the generations of women in her family were portrayed by a sometime actress and "model" named Jeri Archer, a six-foot stunner who could always be counted upon to appear nude each year in The Illustrator's Show. A good friend of Cris's, she was obviously not dumb. She gave an incomparable performance, perfectly entering the tone and period of each of Cris's elaborate photo setups. Cris had first met her in an elevator, where she was introduced to him by the camp name of Herman Buelefeld. They became friends instantly. "She had a number of—clients, shall we say," Cris delicately explains. "One was a producer who was very important shortly before that; he was much older and heavier by then. He had asked Herman Buelefeld to pose for a nude, and Herman, who was always a businesswoman, came to me with the project. She had a wonderful background; she was Turkish; her parents were both Turkish; her real name was Gladys Tinfawichee. She had a wonderful nose, which of course she had done, which made her much more usable. But when I met her in the elevator as Herman Buelefeld for the first time, she was a real stunner. Dark hair and dark

eyes." For the role of Belle, she became a blonde and gave the performance of her career.

Cris also recruited plenty of other friends of his to play key roles in
the photos. Comic actress Alice Pearce was Belle's reform-school pal,
Winnie; Dody Goodman and Kaye Ballard played film stars Helen
Highwater and Vivienne Vixen. Cris's partner Shaun O'Brien was Mr.
Musgrove; Hervey Jolin, Cris's "mother," played the dual roles of Mrs.
Palmer Potter and Belle's third husband, Hollywood producer Morris
Buchsbaum. Most memorable to a certain contingent of the book's
audience was actor Kurt Bieber, who, as Belle's frequent costar and
fourth husband, Letch Feeley, displayed plenty of muscular flesh in
nearly all of his photos.

Pat got Louise to play Belle's dykey pal, Pixie Portnoy. Elaine Adam
and Vivian Weaver, Pat's old friends from the Council on Foreign Relations, turned up—Elaine as Belle's archrival Magdalena Montezuma,
Vivian as a pair of legs jutting into one of the photos. Even Corry Salley got into the act as Belle's no-nonsense, Hattie McDaniel–esque
housemaid. Pat cast himself, dentures inserted upside down, as Belle's
second husband, Cedric Roulstoune-Farjeon, and Cris, in grim grande-
dame drag, was splendid as Cedric's mother, Lady Baughdie. Cris also
played Belle's first husband, World War I army private Fred Poitrine,
as well as the magnificently homely nurse who announces the birth of
Belle's baby girl.

The photo shoots took place on weekends and were so elaborately
lit, costumed, and decorated that only one or two per day could be
done. Although the project stretched out for nine months, it was like
one long party. "The whole thing was marvelous fun for all of us," says
Shaun O'Brien. "There was always a bottle of Scotch or something
around, and Pat would be carrying on, and we'd all come up with ideas
and start laughing. Pat would say, 'Get me a cute blonde!' and I'd go to
some girl at New York City Ballet and say, 'Do you want to be in this
book, just for fun?' We did all the casting like that. My mother was in
it; my father was in it. People were pleased to do it, and to have their
photo taken by Cris and to meet Pat." Everyone in the cast was
promised a signed copy of the book, one silver dollar, and all the liquid
refreshment he or she could hold. That included *Auntie Mame* stars

Rosalind Russell and Peggy Cass, each of whom was delighted to appear in a photo.

In the book's endpaper collage is an adorable shot of Pat writing on a scroll with a quill, while Betsy and Michael, ages four and seven, hover lovingly over him as cherubs. "We all had a great time when he was doing *Little Me*," says Michael today. "I'd come home from school to find a naked lady posing in my bedroom! It was all a lot of fun; there was a big, exciting ensemble feeling in the way he used us and all his friends in the book."

Unfortunately, one nasty episode besmirched the *Little Me* experience for Pat. As the "star" of the book, Jeri Archer had a verbal agreement with Pat that she would be paid a good amount of money for her efforts. Being a generous fellow, Pat naturally offered her a large sum. He also promised her a percentage if the book was sold to Broadway or Hollywood. "She would have had to have done a thousand blow jobs to make that amount of money," says Cris Alexander. But about halfway through, Archer told Pat that she would not pose for another photo unless Pat increased her salary—to about ten times more than the price they had originally agreed upon. Pat was forced into an impossible situation—pay Jeri Archer the ransom, or start all over again with a new Belle Poitrine. He had no choice but to capitulate to her demand.

"She apologized severely later," says Cris. "She said that somebody had gotten to her and given her the wrong advice. I said, 'They sure did, honey.' We were never good friends again after that, unfortunately. Many times she said, 'I certainly made the wrong decision; I never should have said that.' Had I known her better at the time, I would have said to Pat, 'Look, you better get this in writing.' But I never anticipated that. Jeri and I had always had the jolliest, easiest time. But it turned out that she really didn't behave very well with anyone she knew. She was an operator."

Pat's contract for *Little Me*—or, more specifically, Lancelot Leopard, Ltd's contract—was with Dutton, where his old Franklin Spier office mate Peggy Brooks was now ensconced in a low-level editorial position. "Pat came to me with the idea," says Peggy. "I really think he did it to help me. I was scouting around to get books to bring to the company. It was 1959 and I'd only been doing it a couple of years. The only smarts I had to have was to get it past the rather stuffy editorial board, but they were very pleased to have this rather stellar name on their list."

After Pat's copy was written and Cris had finished all the photography, Pat allowed Cris to take complete charge of the book's layout, including where the pictures would appear in the text and what size they would be. "I appreciated that a great deal," says Cris, "because I daresay that's unusual. He was absolutely sweet, and said, 'Whatever you want.' Who could ask for anything nicer?"

As publication time drew near, Pat and Cris concocted a remarkable publicity ploy: the two of them went on the booksellers' convention circuit and actually performed an original cabaret act to promote *Little Me.* Pat wrote it; his friend Harry Percer composed most of the music, with the exception of Harold Rome's "The Money Song" from the flop musical *That's the Ticket.* It ran about twenty minutes and featured Pat and Cris both armed with umbrellas and bowler hats; Pat played himself and Cris a hayseed reporter. Cris would sing to Pat, "Won't yew tell me, Mr. Dennis, how yew author fellas do it?" and Pat would answer in suave, elegant contrast. The two of them also jumped up on the piano and sang a duet. "Pat loved to sing," says Cris. "He was very musical, although I wouldn't call his singing voice pleasant. But he was always on pitch! He knew what he was doing, so he could sing without having much of a voice. Pat was really *wonderful* in the act. He was such a ham, and he just loved doing it." The act actually had little to do with *Little Me,* other than to poke fun at the publishing business. But Pat and Cris were so well received everywhere they performed that the act made it to the Waldorf-Astoria Hotel's monthly booksellers' luncheon, where it was broadcast live over WNYC radio. Pat and Cris shared the dais with Jane Jacobs, author of *The Death and Life of Great American Cities,* and Frederic Morton, who wrote *The Rothschilds.*

Sitting in the front row that day was eight-year-old Michael Tanner, who remembers it as one of the proudest days of his life. He sat quietly and patiently through Jacobs and Morton reading excerpts from their books. But when it came Pat and Cris's turn, and they jumped onstage and did their entire act, little Michael was utterly dazzled. "They just brought down the house," Michael says today. "They were *so* tremendous. I thought it was just great, and it made me so proud of my father."

Naturally, Pat and Cris were next approached by agents dying to book the act on television. Cris would have loved to do it, but unfortunately for everyone involved, Pat adamantly refused to go on TV. "It may have occurred to him," says Cris, "that, as I was an actor, I hoped it would further my own career, but this was not the case. He was very blunt about saying, 'I'm not going to do this, even for you.' I felt gently reprimanded, and thought that maybe that *was* how it looked to him. I never thought that he wouldn't just love doing it. It wasn't really any kind of argument; that was really the only time he just firmly said no. He didn't want to do it, and that was that." Pat's constant refusal to go on television or radio, even to promote his books, is a loss to posterity. He would undoubtedly have been a telegenic personality; one might even imagine him as a regular constant on such game shows as *What's My Line?*, *Password*, or *To Tell the Truth*, where his wit would have registered with a national audience. It's easy to guess how masterfully he must have inflected this quote from a *New York Times* interview he gave regarding *Little Me*: "It's a broad spoof of the typical actress's typical ghost-written autobiography, capturing—I hope—the ignorance, arrogance and egotism of a no-talent nitwit. Done for pleasure and profit, it may perform the service of discouraging other stars from inflicting their memoirs on the reading public." But radio and TV appearances were never to be. "I have an unpleasant voice, I think," he once said in an interview in *The Saturday Review*. "In any case, there are writing authors, and there are talking authors. I'd rather be a writing author."

Audacious, uproarious, and original, *Little Me* was published in the fall of 1961, got rave reviews, and hit the bestseller list almost immediately. "Patrick Dennis has finally done it," wrote Joe Hyams in the *New York Herald Tribune*. "The prolific and pseudonymic author of *Auntie Mame* has written a book that may discourage all future actresses from writing their memoirs. If ever there was a typical star's ghost-written autobiography capturing all the ignorance and arrogance of an egotistic no-talent nitwit it's his *Little Me*. . . . The wonder of the book is Mr. Dennis's ability to make it all seem perfectly plausible and real." Frank Gatlein in *The New Republic* called it "a masterpiece of parody of a sub-form that has needed this treatment for some time. . . . Literary burlesque is a tricky thing in any size; but to create it and maintain it for a full book is something of a minor miracle." Gerold Frank, who already bore "as told to" credits on the autobiographies of Lillian Roth, Diana Barrymore, and Zsa Zsa Gabor, was assigned to review the book for the *New York Times*. He found it "enormously funny. If anything, Mr. Dennis lays about him with such prodigality, his dialogue is so hilarious, his pages such a riot of magnificent absurdities, interlarded with sly puns, quips, malapropisms, inside jokes and other verbal buffoonery, that the reader may have to pause to take breath—and then plunge in again." In every review, Cris Alexander's unique contribution was also singled out for equal praise.

It took Pat and Cris and their gleefully wicked synergy to spring such pure, unadulterated camp on the American public. Perhaps the biggest surprise is that it was such a success. Readers got the joke, even if some of the finer points of the book's flamboyant humor may have escaped them. *Little Me* could have been a flop that appealed only to a handful of homosexuals in the big cities; instead it was embraced by a far wider public. Pat built on the foundation he had laid with *Auntie Mame* and pushed the camp element to the forefront of *Little Me*. In many ways, *Little Me* virtually defines camp. Its pretentious narrative tone, its fascination with Hollywood glamour and outrageous, self-invented personalities, and its daring, go-for-broke humor brought camp out of the closet and into the face of an unsuspecting America. It was subversive; it was an ambush, but one clothed in comic drag.

A generation of gay men, and even young gay boys, came to cherish *Little Me*. In it, they found the crystallization of a brand of humor they knew they shared but could not quite name or describe. They were especially smitten by the beefcake photos of Kurt Bieber. ("After *Little Me* came out," says Bieber, "I couldn't walk down Fifth Avenue without a dozen people saying, 'Hey! It's Letch Feeley!' and asking for my autograph. I got loads of fan mail, especially from members of the military! Even today, I'll sometimes walk into a store and someone will say, 'Wow! Letch Feeley!' How they recognize me after all these years, with my white hair, I'll never know.")

Although *Little Me* has long been out of print, it has proved a source of inspiration for many contemporary writers. Robert Plunket, the author of such blackly comic novels as *Love Junkie* and *My Search for Warren Harding*, claims that the influence of *Little Me* can be seen throughout his work. In a 1996 issue of San Francisco's leading gay paper, *The Bay Area Reporter*, journalist Daniel Harris pointed out that Belle Poitrine is "everything Mame isn't, a sort of anti-*Auntie Mame*," and went on to say: "Although *Auntie Mame* and *Little Me* were written quite independently of each other, they constitute two contrasting panels of the same portrait of American snobbery, and it is a shame that, now that *Little Me* is out of print, we can only read what is in fact the lesser of the two books by a neglected satirist whose work cries out for a full-scale revival."

Little Me made such a hit that the Broadway musical rights were immediately bought by the producing team of Feuer and Martin. And when that happened, Pat basically lost all control over the material. Instead of bringing Pat in to write the musical's book, the producers hired Neil Simon, at the time New York's hottest young playwright. The focus of the musical was completely shifted to its male star, Sid Caesar, who played eight different roles as the many men in Belle's life. Beyond the names of the characters, the show had almost nothing to do with Pat's book. Belle became little more than a device to link up various episodes and to act as a glorified straight man for Caesar and his antic shtick. The book's camp quotient was completely expunged in favor of Caesar and Simon's broader, burlesque-house style of humor.

On its own terms, the show worked well: Simon's script was fresh and funny, as was the memorable score by Cy Coleman and Carolyn Leigh; Bob Fosse contributed the inspired choreography and codirection (with Cy Feuer); Sid Caesar was seen to his best advantage. But the result was something far closer to Caesar's popular television program *Your Show of Shows*—a series of sketches and vaudeville turns—than to anything that Pat and Cris had created. Neil Simon never even actually met Pat. The closest they came was during one of the rehearsals, when Simon noticed a tall, bearded man standing in the shadows at the rear of the theater. Someone whispered to him that it was Patrick Dennis. But before any kind of introduction could be made, Pat walked out of the theater, shaking his head sadly.

The musical version of *Little Me* opened in 1962, one year after the book's publication. In spite of good reviews and initially good box office, it never seemed to find its audience. The city's history-making newspaper strike, which lasted 114 days, took a huge toll on Broadway box offices. *Little Me* played out the season and closed after 257 performances. But the show remains fondly regarded by many. Since its initial run, it has had two major Broadway revivals, one in 1981 with the male roles divided between James Coco and Victor Garber; the other in 1998, with Martin Short as all of Belle's unfortunate husbands and lovers.

Pat was too much of a gentleman to ever publicly disparage the musical version. "I think he had a pretty healthy attitude," says Carmen Capalbo. "He was not that judgmental. He was a good critic; but I think he would have preferred to say something good rather than to say something negative about another artist's work. He never said, 'God, they wrecked my work!' Instead, he tended to slough it off." But Pat admitted privately that he felt absolutely rotten about what had been done to *Little Me*. "And so did we," says Cris Alexander. "He was totally crestfallen. He felt it was a huge mistake. I think it was somewhat of a shock to him."

Twenty years after its first publication, *Little Me* was reissued as a trade paperback, complete with a funny new foreword written by Michael Tanner in dead-on imitation of the narrative voice his father had created for Belle Poitrine (see appendix). Unfortunately, this time Cris Alexander's photos were badly reproduced. In many instances they appeared so soft and smudgy that the fine comic details were completely lost. Now, forty years after Belle Poitrine made her literary bow, she has become a collector's item.

FOURTEEN

The Fat, Hairy Old Thing

Long before there was ever a Stonewall Uprising, there was the Luxor Baths.

Located on West Forty-sixth Street, the Luxor was commonly known as a Turkish bath. Men could go in to relax, get a steam bath or rubdown, and socialize with their buddies in a clubhouse kind of atmosphere. But the Luxor served a dual purpose. It also allowed men to meet other men and to do more with each other than just chat. The general public was unaware of the Luxor's reputation among homosexuals; it's probably safe to say that most of the establishment's straight clients had no idea what was going on right under their noses. Thus, the Luxor provided a relatively safe haven for closeted gays and married men who led double lives. To be spotted entering a specifically gay bathhouse—such as the notorious Everard on Twenty-eighth Street—would have been asking for trouble.

Pat became a frequent visitor to the Luxor. In this era, when appearances had to be kept up at all costs, no straight friend or acquaintance seeing Pat inside the Luxor steam room would suspect him.

Outwardly, Pat appeared to be enjoying his life, his family, and his career. But his natural tendency toward depression was intensifying. Like many successful individuals, he was plagued by the knowledge that the ride couldn't possibly last forever. Compounding this was the sense of guilt he felt about his clandestine activities, and the toll he knew they were taking on his life at home. His drinking—a legacy from both his parents—was becoming excessive, and he would sometimes go off on a bender and stay out all night.

It was getting harder and harder for Edward Everett Tanner III to be the famous author Patrick Dennis. It was also hard for him to say no to social invitations, for fear of appearing selfish or rude. "For several years, it seemed, we were having breakfast, lunch, and dinner with people we didn't know and basically didn't care about," said Louise. "Pat always had to be onstage, and I think that took a lot out of him. He frequently then would go into a terrible sort of—not speaking. I think that it must have been a manic-depressive cycle. Difficult as he was when he was drinking, this other thing would be a total repudiation of life. I would see him go and do something where everybody was cheering him; he was so funny and entertaining; and then he would come home and just collapse, because it had been such an effort. It takes a lot out of you. My son once said, with great wisdom, 'It's very tiring to be nice.' And I think it was very tiring for *him*. Pat was really, basically shy. That's something people don't realize about him."

Like most of the married men who frequented the Luxor Baths, Pat was in search of brief, anonymous encounters. His feelings for Louise remained strong; he was not consciously seeking love. But love sneaked up on him at the Luxor in the unlikely form of a short, simian-looking costume designer by the name of Guy Kent.

To this day, Guy Kent remains a shadowy figure, one of the millions who came to New York, achieved some success or failure, and moved on. The facts of his life remain murky. Most of the information available on him—if it can be believed—comes from his official résumé and biography as released by the publicity department at NBC, where he was under contract at the time he met Pat. An army brat, Kent was born May 4, 1922, at Fort Leavenworth, Kansas, where his father, a colonel, was stationed. His mother was a painter, and he claimed that his aunt was the patrician silent-film star Irene Rich, who starred in the classic Ernst Lubitsch film *Lady Windermere's Fan* opposite Ronald Colman. Guy attended private grade schools and prep schools all over the Northeast—in Pennsylvania, Massachusetts, and Washington— and eventually received a presidential appointment to West Point. One can guess that his father pushed him in this direction. Regardless, at some time Kent broke free and accepted that he took after his mother rather than his father, resigned from West Point, and enrolled in classes at the Boston Museum of Fine Arts. But World War II intervened, and he spent four years in the army in Europe. Once returned to the United States, he continued his art studies in New York at Parsons and the Art Students League. Soon he was at work as a window dresser at Lord and Taylor. NBC then hired him as one of its first two costume designers during the early days of television, and at the same time, he began designing costumes for Broadway. Starting as an assistant on *Kiss Me, Kate* and *Summer and Smoke,* he received his first full credit on *Magnolia Alley* (1949), with Julie Harris. He went on to design the costumes for seven other shows, including *Season in the Sun, The Inn Keepers, Wake Up, Darling,* and *Everybody Loves Me.* His long list of NBC-TV credits was more impressive: he designed costumes for everything from *The Jack Paar Show* to the NBC Opera to *Hallmark Hall of Fame.*

Guy Kent was stocky and short—about five feet eight inches—with reddish brown hair and a ruddy complexion. His penetrating eyes were surmounted by heavy, arched eyebrows that curled up in the center, and he had a deep speaking voice with a ready, infectious laugh. By most accounts, he was witty, as much of an entertainer as Pat, and he certainly shared Pat's interests, including alcohol. But unlike Pat, who remained gentle and charming while under the influence, Kent could be a mean drunk. Once he'd had too much, his wit could sour and turn evil.

A composite portrait of Kent, who is now deceased, can be gleaned from the recollections of those who knew him. The picture is not always pretty. People initially found him charming and fun, especially at a party, but often changed their minds after spending too much time with him. Costume designer John Boxer (*Presumed Innocent, Orphans*), who worked with him at NBC and became chummy with him for a while, eventually had to call a halt to the friendship. "Guy and I were quite friendly," says Boxer. "We saw a lot of each other, but we were never intimates. He was quite a lot of fun; my wife liked him and we used to go out a lot. Guy was not what one would consider a scrious person; you would not discuss politics or what have you with him. He didn't seem to have a lot of friends, if you know what I mean. He zeroed in on one person at a time. And at a certain point, that would become more trouble than it was worth. For what you had to put up with, you were getting less and less. And so at a certain point you shrugged and discontinued.

"Until it went too far, he was very nice company," Boxer stresses.

"He was funny, and he had a sort of malicious wit, not unlike Pat. But Guy didn't have Pat's kind of charm. His wit was mean; it had a mean edge to it. Pat's didn't. But you know, people like that can be very amusing, as long as their wit isn't turned on *you*. My wife and I both had the feeling that, when Guy was telling funny, malicious stories about somebody else, when he was with somebody else, he would be telling very funny, malicious stories about *us*."

Boxer and his wife also got tired of the impromptu 3 A.M. visits from Guy and his drunken pals. It all finally came to an end the night that Guy showed up unannounced during the wee hours with an equally tipsy female friend. By the time the two left, dawn was about to break. With Guy and his drinking buddy finally out of the apartment, Boxer and his wife began to clean up, and they noticed that the girl had left a cocktail napkin on the couch. When they picked it up, they saw that it had been concealing a fresh, wet pee stain. "I think it was around that time," says Boxer, "that my wife said, 'Look, it's just not worth the effort.' "

"I don't know why I love the fat, hairy old thing," Pat said of Guy Kent to his pal Cris Alexander. "Guy Kent was neither old nor fat," says Cris today. "But he *was* hairy! Pat was absolutely captivated by him. To me, he seemed totally unacceptable from every viewpoint. But that's a different matter. I do think Guy Kent was some kind of strange, unaccountable obsession for Pat. The first couple of times I was in his company, he was such a blowhard, I remember thinking, 'Oh, he's a bit interesting.' But by about the third time, I thought, 'Oh, no. No, you ain't.' "

"He seemed like a really *dreary* personality," adds Alexander's partner, Shaun O'Brien. "I think he was seldom entirely sober. As I remember him, he never contributed anything positive to a conversation. If it was a joke, it was negative. If he was talking to you, it was about who had dirty underwear. You'd see him and he'd say, 'Oh, I've had such a *horrible* day with Jeanne Moreau and her mother and those *filthy* white kid shoes she wears! And then I had to fit Nureyev, and my God, I've never *seen* such filthy underwear!' And I thought, 'What is the point of this? It's only to downgrade and diminish others.' "

Regardless of how much Guy Kent alienated people, for Pat he was a romantic lightning rod. Pat's feelings for Guy were instant and overwhelming, emotions that by all accounts were far stronger than what

Guy felt for Pat. An easy assumption to make is that Guy was an oppor-
tunist who snatched up the celebrated author of *Auntie Mame* like a
spider. That may or may not have been so, but, undeniably, Pat was
utterly smitten with Guy. Pat's good friend and *Little Me* editor, Peggy
Brooks, feels that Guy may actually have been a bit overwhelmed by
the force of Pat's attention. "My memory about Guy Kent," she says,
"was that this wasn't something that Guy had really looked for; he just
sort of went along with it. My feeling was that he was not equally
caught up in it. I don't know if other people saw it the same way,
because I never talked about it with them too much. Guy seemed sort
of smooth, sophisticated; the type you'd meet at a cocktail party. I
didn't have a feeling of liking or disliking him at all; I only had the feeling that Pat was so emotionally involved; and I felt that Guy was only
receiving it, and not knowing quite what to do about it, as if he were a
little floored by it. I don't think he was trying to promote anything for
himself from Pat particularly; I didn't see that."

But Pat's friend singer-songwriter Murray Grand views things a bit
differently: "Guy Kent? What an asshole! He was a gigolo, a user; he
latched onto Patrick because Patrick had fame and money. I don't at all
believe that Guy was ever madly in love with him." Grand, who accompanied Pat and Guy on a trip to Acapulco, continues, "I thought he was
boring and a little pompous, always trying to pass himself off as upper
class with an affected, pseudo-British accent. I never could understand
why Patrick had selected *him*. He must have had some hidden assets
that I hadn't noticed. And I certainly didn't see it in a bathing suit, so
it couldn't have been *that*."

As 1962 wore on, Guy Kent became more and more of a presence
in Pat's life. That summer, Pat and Louise took the children for a vacation in Venice. They were accompanied on the trip by their good
friends Dr. William G. Cahan and his wife, Sisi, and the two families
shared a cabana on the Lido. Undoubtedly by design rather than accident, Guy Kent turned up in Venice at the same time. He was around
for the rest of the vacation.

Pat's Council on Foreign Relations buddies Elaine Adam and Vivian
Weaver moved into the town house that summer and looked after it in

the family's absence. Pat left Elaine and Vivian a seven-page, single-spaced typewritten memo detailing everything they needed to know about the place. Here's a condensed version, featuring the choicest excerpts:

To: Mrs. Adam
     Miss Weaver

Subject: Our Gracious Home

Whilst enjoying the advantages of this smart tenement, there are some trivial details of housekeeping which may or may not attract your interest. They are listed below in alphabetical order:

CANDLES—Are in the nudge-door at the northeast corner of the dining room. (One nudges these doors to open them and to close them. Try it. It's *fun!*)

CLEANING EQUIPMENT—This is scattered generously around the house. . . . You won't use it anyhow, you sluts.

DISHWASHER—Is in the kitchen on the second floor. It is a model called the FU-70. I wouldn't touch it with a barge pole.

DOORBELL—If the doorbell ever gets stuck and won't stop ringing, drag ass downstairs and give it a poke. Remember that if the front door is bolted on the inside (as I know it will be with two gristly old hymens like yours to be protected) you *can't* open the front door by buzzing—only by hand.

FREEZER—If it should break down over the weekend, start eating and don't stop until the last rotting chop is consumed.

GARDEN—If we should have a prolonged dry spell, give it a little squirt with the hose. In fact, you might enjoy playing under the hose in your bathing suits.

IRON—There are two on the top floor in the counter in the large bathroom, I think. An ironing board is also up there. Although from the looks of the two of you, it's the last thing you'll be wanting.

LIQUOR—On the bar and in the cupboards above the bar sink. I know you won't let it evaporate.

LORCA, GARCIA—Loses so much in translation that it's really wisest not to read his stuff at all. Not even in Spanish.

MAGAZINES—Open them as they arrive, read them and put them in chronological order in the proper places. *P.W., Punch, Country Life, The Tatler, British House & Garden, Connaissance des Arts* and *Show* go in my office. *Time, The New Yorker, American House & Garden, Gourmet, Amepika* (a Russian-language rag) and the *Vassar Alumnae Magazine* go in Louise's office.

NEWSPAPERS—I cancelled those. You girls read entirely too much.

ORGASMS—Go right ahead.

QUEANS—Entertaining, yes, but will they lay you?

QUEENS—Stay out of it.

QUEERS—See QUEANS.

RECORD PLAYER—Turntable inside door just south of radio. There is also a way to shut off the speaker that blares in the master bedroom, but I thought it would be more of an adventure if you two could figure that out for yourselves.

REPAIRS—For mediocre work of all sorts, try the Allen Repair Service on Lexington Avenue about a block north.

TELEPHONES—Six in all and two numbers. You'll have oodles of fun pressing the buttons. They can all be turned off if you long for silence. The number is listed under Lancelot Leopard, Ltd.—*not* under Tanner.

TOOL CHEST—A battered bread box which once belonged to the *second* Countess Palffy—a fine old Hungarian name. It is behind the sliding doors at the north end of the kitchen—and God alone knows what else is there.

UTERUS—Don't strain it.

WINDOW WASHER—A Mr. Max Yuknitz comes every month while we are here. As you'll never be here in the daytime and as the curtains are drawn at night—unless you really *are* the exhibitionists that voyeur on Eighty-Third Street says you are—I see no point in having them done every month.

XYLOPHONE—Promise me you won't practice on it after ten-thirty.

YOUR RADIO SHOP—A most valuable address. His name is Henry and he is an oedipal Hungarian whose grim old mother is happily dead. I am in love with him and I *think* he likes me. Anyhow, he does all sorts of electrical repairs for almost nothing. He's most obliging, but you must telephone him before ten in the morning in order to be serviced, I believe that's the expression.

ZABAGLIONE—Place the yolks of 6 eggs in the Waring Blendor with one-half cup of sugar. Mix. With motor running gradually add two-thirds cup of Marsala. Place in a pan over boiling water and beat with a wire whisk until mixture foams and begins to thicken. Do not overcook. Serves 6 and is a highly overrated dessert.

Corry *says* that she'll be back sometime during the last week of August to fumigate the place. So get those Greek sailors out before she discovers what kind of girls you really are.

Check-out time is twelve noon on Labor Day.

Mi casa es su casa. (Sp.)

An idea of Pat's typing skills can be gleaned from the fact that the entire seven-page memo was fired out with barely a single error.

Autumn of 1962 saw the publication of one of Pat's most memorably wicked novels. For several years, Pat and Louise had been making winter trips to Mexico, which had become one of their favorite vacation spots. Pat grew fascinated by Mexico City's burgeoning Anglo-American expatriate community, so much so that he realized it would be the perfect setting for a none-too-subtle comedy of manners. The result was *Genius,* a lacerating satire of English and American arrivistes in early-sixties Mexico City, and the overbearing, bombastically gifted film director—a combination of Erich von Stroheim, Orson Welles, and Edgar G. Ulmer—who hoodwinks them all into financing his latest attempt at a low-grade comeback epic. In Leander Starr, the director, Pat created a character who was brilliant, selfish, unscrupulous, and utterly shameless—but utterly winning as well. By charming the pants off of Mexico's so-called International Set, Starr is able to produce and direct *Valley of the Vultures* in one week, and to maintain his princely style of living while always staying just one jump ahead of predatory widows, his ex-wives, and the IRS. The latter organization is represented by one of Pat's most comically endearing characters, Mr. Irving Guber, who has been sent to Mexico to dog Leander Starr's steps until he has secured the thousands of dollars Starr owes in back taxes. By utilizing one simple phonic trick—adding *ue* to every word of Guber's dialogue ending with *ng*—Pat suggested the thickest of New York accents emanating from Guber's lips: "Well, I'm not a drinkingue man myself. I mean I haven't got anythingue against it—in moderation. Rye and ginger ale at a social gatheringue—somethingue like that." Totally out of his element, Mr. Guber is dyingue to finish his business with Starr as quickly as possible and get home in time to spend the holidays with his wife, Shirl, back in Teaneck, New Jersey.

Pat narrates the story from the point of view of Patrick Dennis, as he did in the *Auntie Mame* books. Once again, he is the dismayed, dyspeptic observer unwillingly drawn into the mad antics of a larger-than-life title character. This time he includes Louise in the action, although he refers to her throughout as "my wife" and doesn't mention her by name. Just as in real life, she proves to be his ideal sardonic sidekick, a fellow writer who always has a daiquiri in hand and a wisecrack at the ready. Early on, when they first learn that the impoverished Starr is their neighbor at their hotel in Mexico, they decide to get back at him for having bilked them on a business deal ten years before:

> Immediately after my wife and I had downed our restorative drinks we set up office directly beneath Starr's heavily curtained windows. For the rest of the afternoon we played noisy duets on our typewriters. (My output was principally a letter to our son and "The quick brown fox jumps over the lazy sleeping dog," while my wife ran up a scorcher to the Vassar Alumnae Association and several versions of "Now is the time for all good men to come to the aid of the party.") Every now and then when, from sheer exhaustion, we stopped banging away at our typewriters, we launched into loquacious and totally fictitious dialogue about the brilliant things we were supposedly working on—oh, I tell you, the Lunts couldn't have put on a better show of the madly successful little couple. We had wild bits like:

> ME: Would you mind stopping whatever you're doing and casting an eye over this?
> SHE: Hahahaha! Funniest thing I've ever read. They'll love it at Warner Brothers.
> ME: Well, they're not going to get it unless I have approval of the director. That's absolutely definite in my contract.
> SHE: I don't blame you one bit. That's what I told them at MGM. I said, "I want a decent director—somebody young and reliable."

> My wife swears that she heard a low moan from inside Starr's apartment, and maybe she did, but her ears aren't half as keen as her imagination. We poured out more drinks and went back to

our clattering until we got bored with doing typing exercises. Then my wife led off with another body blow:

SHE: Funny as this piece is, do you think it's quite fair to stop working on that play you promised the Theatre Guild?
ME: Of course I've stopped. I've finished it over the weekend and sent it right off to Lawrence and Armina by airmail.
SHE: And you didn't let me read the last act?
ME: How could I? You were at that meeting with Dolores Del Rio about adapting that novel for her.
SHE: Oh, so I was. Well I do hope Lawrence liked it.
ME: *Like* it? They were *mad* for it. They've already signed Margaret Leighton and Rex Harrison for the leads.
SHE: Perfect!
ME: Now the only problem is finding a director.
SHE : Isn't it always. As I was saying to Josh Logan . . .
ME: Wouldn't you like another drink? *I* would.
SHE: Adore one.

This time, there was the distinct sound of a door being slammed furiously in Starr's apartment. . . . Between the hot sunlight beating down on us, the many, many, many drinks, the hectic typing, and our bravura performances, we could hardly stagger back into our own quarters at dusk.

Pat based many of the book's more bizarre and pretentious characters on the more bizarre and pretentious characters he had already met while making the rounds of Mexico City's incessant cocktail parties. Although *Genius* was farcical, it was as deeply rooted in truth as all of Pat's New York novels, and it performed a similar act of social surgery on the anglophone elite of Mexico City. It also skewered the rabid devotion accorded megalomaniacal artists by their sycophantic fans. And, like *Little Me,* it showed Pat's X-ray insight into moviemaking, which always runs the risk of being the most self-delusional of all enterprises.

Genius also gave Pat a chance to lampoon the women's magazine industry, to which he had been contributing the odd article and short

story over the years. In *Genius* he is working on a generic love story des-
tined for one of these publications:

> . . . It was a light, frothy piece for a famous women's service
> magazine that will buy any piece of fiction, no matter how bad,
> as long as it's wholesome and the author's name is sufficiently
> well-known to beef up the front cover. They have a something-
> for-everyone formula that is one hundred per cent foolproof.
> While the ladies in the fiction department put away about a quart
> of gin apiece at lunch every day before dashing off to their ana-
> lysts, the stories they insist on printing are simon pure. Nobody
> smokes, drinks, swears, or has any problem deeper than will-
> virtuous-Penny-get-dashing-Hillary-away-from-scheming-Marcia.
> The readers all know that she will, in three thousand carefully
> chosen words, but they've been happily reading the same story for
> more than half a century and still gurgle with pleasure and excite-
> ment when goodness and honesty triumph over wickedness. In
> the nonfiction department, however, anything goes, and the
> closer to pornography the better. Sandwiched in between fash-
> ions, recipes, beauty hints, model rooms, and stories of such a
> purity as to make *Our Sunday Visitor* look like *Playboy* are articles
> that would curl your hair—"Syphilis in Our Nursery Schools," "Is
> Your Daughter a Teen-Age Prostitute?" "The Orgasm and You."
> Still I don't have to read the magazine, just write for it, and one
> sweet, simple story (prefaced by a warning to the subscribers that
> I am very wicked) pays an awful lot of tuition.

Genius received largely positive reviews, and fans of Pat's work still
regard it as one of his best books. "Dennis has run amok again," read
the review in *Kirkus*, "and until someone throws a big net over him, he
will remain easily the funniest fellow writing today." In the *New York
Times Book Review,* motion-picture editor A. H. Weiler raved:

> With the appearance last year of *Little Me,* which hilariously kid-
> ded the myth of ghost-written autobiographies of stage, screen
> and TV stars, the emergence of *Genius* became inevitable. Ever
> since Cecil Blount DeMille et al. invaded Hollywood's citrus

groves with *The Squaw Man,* the theatricality of some movie-makers has been fair game for hypocrisy busters and lampoon lovers. Patrick Dennis, who is both sire and nephew of "Auntie Mame" (as well as the fictitious Virginia Rowans and the real Edward Everett Tanner III), is not the man to allow a literary lance to rust with such trophies to be bagged. *Genius,* his latest kill, may not set a precedent—but the towering director he has drawn and quartered emerges as a selfish, childish, arrogant but lovable deadbeat who, as one of the four ladies he married says, "was really a genius. But who can live with a genius?" Mr. Dennis (who has no illusions that he might be Dostoyevsky but is a professional adept at his form of fiction) has made it a pleasure . . . pretty socko, as the trade papers have it.

R. D. Spector, in the *New York Herald Tribune,* also praised the book, but the good review clothed a nastier slap at Pat's merits as a writer: "No critic can tell Patrick Dennis how to write a bestseller. His books are not 'good' literature, perhaps not even literature. . . . He has little concern for credibility and less for the niceties of character delineation. But with great gusto and a genuine gift for creating the wild and boisterous scene, farcical situations, and bizarre settings, he can't miss."

With a firmer plot thread than most of Pat's novels, not to mention its vivid comic characters and exotic locale, *Genius* would have been perfect as a play or film. Indeed, the motion picture rights were bought before publication by no less than Otto Preminger. Preminger, one of Hollywood's top-ranked directors at the time, had already made such landmark movies as *Laura, Carmen Jones, Bonjour Tristesse,* and *The Man with the Golden Arm.* Comedy had never been his strong suit, but there was more than a little Otto Preminger in the ostentatious character of Leander Starr. That, plus the prospect of making a movie that tweaked the movies, undoubtedly appealed to him. Under his production deal at Twentieth Century–Fox, he hired Ring Lardner Jr. (*Woman of the Year, Forever Amber*) to write the screenplay.

"I completed a first draft, a second, and probably a third," remembers Lardner today. "Otto gave me a lot of input while I was working on the script; he always had a lot to say about what he thought should be done. He would go through my first draft page by page, with little quibbles and suggestions; some of them quite good. He liked it, but he said he only wanted to do the film if he could get Rex Harrison, Laurence Olivier, or Alec Guinness to play Leander Starr. None of them were available, however, and he decided, on that basis, that there was nobody else he could think of for the part." Ultimately, due to the casting problems, the project lapsed.

The week of December 7, 1962, *Little Me* had just opened on Broadway to good notices and strong box office. *Genius* had been published three months before and was consolidating Pat's reputation as the leading comic novelist of his time. Pat was even the subject of a five-page article in that week's issue of *Life* magazine entitled "Auntie Mame's Nimble Nephew," in which he was photographed at home and was shown posing with *Little Me* cast member Virginia Martin backstage. Another shot showed him in the office of Otto Preminger, with the two men smiling warmly at each other from opposite sides of Otto's desk as they discussed casting possibilities for the film version of *Genius*.

At that moment, Pat was at the peak of his career.

By the time the article appeared, only a week later, he had attempted suicide and had been admitted as a mental patient at New York State Hospital.

FIFTEEN

"The Loony Bin"

Guy Kent had been the match that lit the fuse that led to the powder keg. Once Guy entered Pat's life, it was only a matter of time before Pat's carefully managed world would blow to pieces.

But if Guy Kent had not come along, it would eventually have been someone else. Pat's conflicted sexual nature, which he had been trying to repress for too many years, had finally gained the upper hand. With his love for Louise and his children remaining strong, Pat was caught in a miserable vortex of guilt, desire, and depression. He was drinking even more heavily than usual. To make matters worse, he began trying to curb his four-pack-a-day cigarette habit by taking Miltown, an anti-smoking drug that had just been introduced. For him, the drug brought on devastating side effects. "What it did," said Louise, "was to accentuate every suicidal tendency he ever had." Around Thanksgiving of 1962, Pat contacted Dr. Nordfeldt, the psychiatrist who had treated him some fifteen years before, about seeing her again.

On the evening of December 4, 1962, Pat returned home from a party where he had consumed a huge amount of liquor. He sat down and wrote three letters: one to Dr. Nordfeldt; one to Louise; and one to Guy Kent. Then he took nine Seconal and crawled into a hot bath, assuming that he would sink beneath the water and quietly drown as the drugs overcame him. But he hadn't taken into account his six-foot-two-inch frame. His long legs kept him propped up out of the water, his mouth and nose stayed safely up in the air, and he kept breathing during what turned out to be a long, deep snooze. This was how Louise found him several hours later.

Pat and Louise's friend Dr. William G. Cahan was the first person

Louise called when she discovered Pat in the bathtub. "I got a call late at night," he explains. "I was in bed. It was Louise saying, 'Bill, I think you'd better come up here. Pat is trying to do himself in.' I got dressed and rushed up there. Pat was coherent, so I hung around until he sobered up a little bit and got him dressed." Cahan talked Pat into letting him take him in a cab to Regent Hospital to dry out. For the occasion, Pat insisted on dressing in his usual Savile Row splendor and even sported a rakish straw hat.

He remained at Regent Hospital for three days, by which time Louise and Dr. Cahan had convinced him that he needed more intensive help with his problems. Rather grudgingly, Pat agreed to enter the psychiatric facility at the Westchester Division of New York Hospital, popularly known as Bloomingdale's due to its location on Bloomingdale Road. Despite his warm feelings for Dr. Nordfeldt, Pat was understandably skeptical about being shut up in—as he called it— "the loony bin." He knew that this, combined with the severity of his depression, could make successful treatment difficult. By now, however, he was so emotionally benumbed that he openly expressed a willingness to spend the rest of his life in the hospital—or else to try suicide once more.

At the hospital, Pat was administered a battery of psychological tests and was interviewed at length by the attendant psychiatrists. Manic-depressive psychosis was the official diagnosis. Pat's dissociative tendencies—his low "feeling function"—had resurfaced. The problem had temporarily disappeared when he married Louise, but now it loomed again after thirteen years of struggling with his homosexuality. To the doctors at Bloomingdale's he professed emptiness and boredom, a complete weariness with life. All he longed for, he insisted, was the oblivion offered by death.

As a celebrated author in the public spotlight, Pat felt particularly vulnerable. Not only did he have to keep his homosexuality under wraps, he also was living with the fear of imminent failure. Despite his enormous readership, despite the rave reviews, despite his huge income, Pat was still plagued by the feelings of shame and inadequacy he had carried with him since childhood. Most of the blame for that can probably be traced straight back to his bullying, despotic father, whose complete disapproval and rejection scarred Pat from an early age. Children tend to internalize their parents' perceptions of them, and Pat was no exception. In large part due to his father's constant disapproval, he felt basically unworthy of the success he had achieved and was fearful of being found out as undeserving. In fact, each time a new novel of his had been well received, it brought on depression rather than elation. When he entered Bloomingdale's, Pat was asked to fill out a psychological questionnaire. One of the components was a sentence-completion exercise in which he was to fill in the following blank: "The reason for my failure is_____." Pat wrote "success."

Ever the entertainer, Pat told the doctors that he felt Bloomingdale's would be "a fine retreat" where he would be content to remain. He was open about his problems and mentioned his fear of inadequacy, his gay activities, and his relationship with Guy Kent. It is heartbreaking to read that he described himself as "nothing" as a person, writer, lover, or husband and felt that one day he would succeed at suicide, because he saw no other solution.

But these feelings that Pat volunteered were meager and extracted with great difficulty. Pat cooperated little with the doctors in their probing and searching. Considering his sardonic, somewhat disdainful attitude toward his new surroundings (his new nickname for himself was Psychopatrick), it's not surprising that he was unable or unwilling to completely surrender to institutional psychoanalysis. His manner was simultaneously relaxed yet evasive, and he himself admitted that his indifference might well have been a mask to cover up strong feelings. In his psychiatric interviews, he insisted on categorizing himself as superficial. None of this indicated any hope for a speedy recovery. After their initial meetings with Pat, the doctors described his prognosis as uncertain.

With his sartorial flash and grand, eccentric manner, Pat made a striking impression on the other inmates. Most of them had already read that week's issue of *Life* magazine and were startled to have a celebrity in their midst. At first Pat kept to himself, reading, watching television, rarely conversing with anyone. Eventually he allowed himself more contact with the other patients. One of them, who was successfully treated and is now a bookstore owner on New York's Upper East Side, remembers Pat fondly. "Oh, yes, Pat Tanner," he recalls with a broad smile. "Very kind man, and very funny. He always kept us laughing. Do you know, he had such long legs, and he was so limber, he could sit and literally put his feet all the way up and cross them behind his head! Just like a yogi!"

The Christmas holidays came, but they only increased Pat's depression and accentuated his growing hostility toward the doctors at Bloomingdale's. By the end of the first month of his stay, he admitted to feeling seclusive and withdrawn and agreed he should make more of an effort to interact socially with the other inmates.

Another month passed, and Pat showed little improvement. Complaining of feeling even more discouraged, he began refusing to see visitors. He also said quite plainly that he was starting to feel certain that psychiatry was not going to offer him much help. The doctors agreed that Pat was too depressed at the time to benefit from psychotherapy alone and started dosing him with the antidepressant Tofranil. But the drug did not agree with him—all Pat got from it were unpleasant side effects and a worsening of his spirits. Eventually he only pretended to take the Tofranil. Instead, he would hide the pills in his beard.

Occupational therapy was not the answer either. Pat showed little interest in it and probably found it faintly ridiculous. Soon enough, he found it to be an effective vehicle for his hostility: he made a mug in the likeness of one of the staff physicians, then smashed it to pieces.

Meanwhile, Louise and the kids coped at home with the devastating situation. Louise never cared to discuss this difficult time. When asked years later how she got through it, she simply answered, "Just from day to day," and would say no more. Michael and Betsy were initially told that their father was working on a writing project in Florida, but that story was blown when Pat sent them a letter and eight-year-old Michael noticed that the postmark was from White Plains. Louise sat him down and gently explained that his father had had something called a nervous breakdown.

"Nowadays," says Michael (now Dr. Michael Tanner), "if you check the *DSM4* or even the *DSM3*, which is the psychiatric code book, you will not find the term *nervous breakdown*. What he had was a major depressive episode brought about by guilt over his affair and attempted suicide, and that's what landed him in Bloomingdale's."

Betsy, who was five, was told that her father was suffering from claustrophobia. "It made sense to me at the time," says Betsy. "I really didn't take it too personally. Now I think of what my poor mother must have been trying to do."

On January 28, 1963, Pat appeared before the entire staff of psychiatrists at Bloomingdale's to state firmly that he believed he was not the kind of patient who could benefit from institutionalization. What he wanted to do, he asserted, was resume a normal life outside and go back into analysis with a private psychiatrist, possibly Dr. Nordfeldt.

Facing a tribunal of eighteen doctors could not have been easy for Pat. He was questioned intensively by every one of them as they tried to ascertain whether he was indeed ready to face the world without doing further damage to himself. Unfortunately, Pat's bitterness and frustration were hard for him to hide, and he responded to many of the doctors' questions somewhat superciliously with short, affected replies. He also shook his foot nervously during the questioning.

Pat was grilled relentlessly on everything in his past that had led him to this point, from his father's hostility to his own sexual proclivities to his history of depressive episodes. He admitted to continuing feelings of depression and dissociation, but felt that he was no longer a danger to himself. At the same time, however, he said he had no fear whatsoever of death. He also made a sad, revealing comment: "No one would care about me if I died. They would be wasting their time."

After his hearing, the doctors concluded that Pat was still a danger to himself and should remain at Bloomingdale's for treatment of manic-depressive psychosis. His appeal for discharge was denied.

He only became more depressed. He began to smoke more than his usual four packs a day. His hands frequently trembled.

But at least he was able to resume work on his latest novel, which was already overdue at William Morrow. *First Lady: My Thirty Days Upstairs at the White House* would be a kind of follow-up to *Little Me:* another parody memoir liberally sprinkled with photos by Cris Alexander. This time, the mock autobiographer was one Martha Dinwiddie Butterfield, and the satire would be American politics rather than the movies. A native of rural Pellagra County, New York, where her family manufactured Lohocla Indian Spirit Water (190 proof and guaranteed to kill or cure), Martha would spend her brief term in the White House in 1909, her husband having been swept in by one vote. They would be swept right out again when the missing vote turned up in Lohocla's

Brooklyn warehouse. And she would eventually wind up—where else?—at the Bosky Dell Home for the Senile and Disturbed, along with her former Press Secretary, Patrick Dennis, and former Official White House Photographer Cris Alexander. For once, Pat did not lack inspiration for an ending.

Pat kept working on *First Lady*. By April 16, 1963, he had been in the hospital over four months and was more convinced than ever that the treatment was doing him no good. Once again he appeared before the board of doctors and requested release. But the doctors felt that release was still inadvisable, and Pat was officially certified to the hospital's care. Against his wishes, he was placed under continuous observation.

Next came shock treatment.

Before long, Pat spiked a fever to 104 degrees, and pneumonia was diagnosed. At first he refused to take medication, angrily asking whether he had to die to get out of the hospital. Eventually he recovered his health enough to resume his psychiatric sessions, but for weeks was filled with rage and barely spoke.

As the months dragged by, Louise came to share Pat's feelings that the doctors at Bloomingdale's couldn't do much for him. "The one thing that [Pat's hospitalization] did for me," she remembered, "was to make me realize that they did not have any idea how to deal with him. One of the doctors said to me, 'We're all baffled as to how to treat him, because his IQ is about twenty degrees above any of ours.' There was one idiot that came trying to take him out and teach him how to play golf! It was really the most ridiculous thing, as if that would do any good. Of course, anybody's attitude, under the circumstances, would have been hostile. I think the only thing that locking anybody up does is that they don't do any harm to themselves. As far as curing anything, I don't think it does one goddamn bit of good. I think he was able to function, but I think that whatever it was that was eating him continued to eat him."

Fortunately, Pat was able to plunge himself into the completion of *First Lady,* and his anger and hostility began to lessen. He also started to take a more active part in his therapy, going so far as to suggest more shock treatments, which he actually claimed to enjoy. Even the doctors were surprised to hear this. Pat's response was that he'd already begun the series, so he might as well complete it.

Soon Pat was receiving visits from his closest friends, which he had initially declined. "I was very taken by surprise, and shocked, and troubled, when he had his crisis," says Cris Alexander. "We couldn't believe it," adds Shaun O'Brien "We felt something must have snapped; we couldn't understand what had happened. We had never felt any sense of conflict within him. He never made us feel that he was anything except one of us. He was one of those people who wanted to have a wife and children and he did, and that was fine, too. We assumed it was all understood and that there was no problem. He never discussed any ambivalence; he always talked and joked about things very openly, but we never discussed personal sexuality or sex with him. I think he became more unbuttoned after the suicide attempt."

Indeed, Pat's crisis at least precipitated that one healthy step he had been unable to take: an acceptance, at last, of the homosexual side of his nature. Forty years ago, with Stonewall and the gay liberation movement still a long way off, this was a far harder thing to do than it is today. The circle of supportive gay friends that Pat had developed, in particular Cris and Shaun, undoubtedly served as a kind of role model for him as he finally grew reasonably comfortable with that part of himself. Although his fondness for Louise and the children remained strong, he felt that he could no longer return to his old way of life, or—for that matter—face the guilt and shame he was convinced he had inflicted on his family. He asked Louise to understand that he had to separate from her and, once released from the hospital, live on his own.

Summer came, and Pat was still desperate to leave, although the doctors remained firm in their conviction that he needed to stay. Finally, during a visit from his friend and accountant, Abe Badian, Pat said, "Abe, you've *got* to get me out of here. I don't belong here. I'm not crazy, and I'm no longer suicidal." Badian arranged for a specialist from the city to come up and interview Pat. After roughly three visits, the specialist concluded unequivocally that Pat was no longer a threat to himself. With this assurance, and with the knowledge of Pat's utter misery at being locked up in "the loony bin," Louise signed the authorization papers for Pat's release.

On August 1, 1963, Pat walked out of the hospital, discharged. He retained the diagnosis of manic-depressive psychosis, but now his condition was listed as "much improved." He had been an inmate for eight long months.

On August 11, Dorothy Kilgallen's syndicated column was headlined "Pat Dennises in Splitsville." The lead item read, "Patrick Dennis and his wife have parted. The author of *Auntie Mame* and other funnies has moved out of their luxurious town house and is living in a small apartment in Gramercy Park."

SIXTEEN

Splitsville

The "small apartment in Gramercy Park" was the home of Pat's close friend Hal Vursell, a vice president at Farrar Straus, to whom Pat had dedicated *Genius*. Pat stayed with Vursell a few days, then took a room at the Lowell Hotel on East Sixty-third Street. For the first time in eight months, Betsy and Michael Tanner were told they were going to see their father and found themselves with Louise in a taxi speeding down Park Avenue to the Lowell.

"At the hotel," says Michael, "they sat us down and said, 'The doctors have decided that it's best that we no longer live together. So from now on, you'll have two addresses.'" One would be the town house on East Ninety-first Street, the other would be Pat's new bachelor pad at 930 Fifth Avenue. Betsy, who was six at the time, remembers little of that day; Michael carries memories that are still painful. "We didn't want our parents to break up," he says. "I wasn't a fool; I realized this was it. It was a very, very upsetting afternoon. I remember saying a rosary every night after that that they would get back together. Because they always loved each other; that was very clear. There had never been a harsh word. My nightmare was that I'd be called into a courtroom and have to choose between them. And of *course* my mother was the more appropriate parent; no question about it. My father would have been the first to say that. But I didn't want to admit that I wanted to live with my mother instead of my father. I loved them both very much."

Pat and Louise also loved each other very much and were each other's best friend as well. In spite of the separation, no plans for divorce were considered. The situation could not have been more amicable, but Pat and Louise's close friends were stunned by the news. "I never knew why they had to separate," says Shaun O'Brien. "Why couldn't they just understand each other and not be apart? He came over one afternoon for a heart-to-heart while they were breaking up. I said, 'I don't know why you two can't just work this out—stay in the same house together and just do your own thing. You're such good friends.' And he said, 'Well, that's the trouble. Louise and I *are* such good friends. We could be locked in the same room together for a month and we would have such a wonderful time just talking and joking.' And it was true. We never had any sense of discord. We never saw any sign of it."

"When Pat told us he and Louise were going to separate," says Cris Alexander, "I said, 'Pat, that's the worst thing—selfishly speaking—for us. Because we've never had as much fun as when we're with you and Louise.' They were the most perfect team."

"The separation was very tough on their friends," says Joy Singer. "One thing they did not do, for which we were grateful, was divide the address book. It was made very clear to me that we could be friends with both of them; that it was a very amiable separation; that they were still very much in love with each other. As somebody said about it, 'It's the happiest separation I've ever seen. A more successful separation you could not imagine.' From the *outside,* the marriage was successful. Bizarre, but successful. The two of them really did adore each other and had the greatest respect for each other. Apparently they could not live together. He didn't often bare his soul to me, but clearly, he was in constant conflict with himself. He very much enjoyed his 'normal' life; he loved Louise and he adored the kids, and he didn't want to give that up. He certainly didn't want to give up his homosexual life either. But it really wasn't a time when you could have the two lives side by side. Pat was an extremely honest person. Deception was not something that came easily to him." That feeling is echoed by Pat's longtime close friend and CPA, Abe Badian: "I didn't appreciate or understand this characteristic of Pat's at the time, but he never, to my knowledge, said anything he didn't mean. He might make the most outrageous statements, and I'd say, 'Oh, Pat, cut the crap!' And he'd say to me, 'Abe, you know that I don't say anything I don't mean.' And that was absolutely true."

Louise would soon leave the town house, the care and maintenance of which had become a huge responsibility, and move with the children and Corry to a large apartment around the corner on Park Avenue, where she would continue to entertain old friends with parties and dinners while keeping up with her writing career and raising her kids. Pat's new Fifth Avenue place was on a high floor with a spectacular view across the park to the Art Deco towers of Central Park West. It came with a tremendously queeny old butler named Cecil, who liked nothing better than to don a frilly apron and bake cookies for Pat. He also favored Pat with a ruffled toilet seat.

One of the first dinner parties Pat threw at 930 Fifth Avenue was in honor of a new friend of his, someone who, up until the day before, had also been an inmate at Bloomingdale's and felt he was being held too long against his will. Shortly after Pat's own release, he and some pals devised a plan to spring him. They drove up to Bloomingdale's late one night and waited outside the main gate in their car until all was quiet. Then Pat signaled to his friend, who came down from his room, slipped through the gate, climbed into the getaway car, and was off to a new life of liberty. Pat gave him a black-tie dinner the next night in celebration.

Through all of this, Guy Kent was still very much in the picture. Although he and Pat did not live together, Guy spent many nights with Pat at 930 Fifth Avenue. Pat's close friends continued to have a hard time warming up to Guy, who often seemed determined to antagonize them. "I remember I was thirty-nine years old," says Shaun O'Brien, "and Pat had just moved into his pad on Fifth Avenue and he gave a little dinner party. Guy Kent said, 'Well? How old *are* you?' And I said thirty-nine, which I was. And he rolled his eyes and said, 'Oh, please! If you're thirty-nine, I'm twenty-six!' And he got very dopey and stupid about it, and I was, frankly, appalled, because I wasn't kidding. He also kept insisting that I had false teeth. He'd say, 'Of course they're false! Don't deny it! Nobody has perfect teeth!' I was a real object of scrutiny and disdain. But then I remember when Cris and I left, the door closed, and you could hear Pat just lacing into him: 'What do you mean by talking to my friends like that? How dare you?' So we quickly ran to the elevator." After that, Cris and Shaun did their best to arrange to get together with Pat alone, when Guy wouldn't be around.

With the manuscript for *First Lady* completed, Pat and Cris began the photo sessions for the book. Starring in the title role was *Auntie Mame* alumnus Peggy Cass. "Boy, there was nothing cheap about *him!*" she said of Pat. "I never even had to discuss the deal with him; he just told me what I was going to get, plus a percentage of the sales, and I said, *'Fine!'* There was not a tight bone in his body. He was a very generous man. There wasn't a check he didn't pick up. But I had a wonderful time doing it. We went to the Brooklyn Museum costume department, and I got to wear all kinds of wonderful Worth gowns. Some of them weighed so much you could barely walk around in them."

First Lady was an all-star effort, at least for theater buffs. In addition to Peggy Cass, the "cast" of friends Cris Alexander recruited for his photos included such names as Thelma Pelish *(The Pajama Game),* Allyn Ann McLerie (Irving Berlin and Moss Hart's *Miss Liberty),* Kaye Ballard *(The Golden Apple, Carnival),* Dody Goodman *(Wonderful Town; The Shoe String Revue),* Harold Lang *(Kiss Me, Kate; Pal Joey),* Sondra Lee *(Peter Pan; Hello, Dolly!),* and New York City Ballet stars Melissa Hayden and Jacques D'Amboise. Once again Louise, Corry, and the kids turned up in small roles, and the part of Generalissimo Junta y Flotilla was taken by Guy Kent. Pat played himself, literally kicking up his heels and raising gleeful hell in the elaborate insane-asylum collage on the book's final pages.

Character actress Alice Pearce, who had appeared in *Little Me* as Belle's reform-school friend Winnie, was cast as Martha's daughter Alice. During the photo sessions, Pat's father made a rare trip to New York and became utterly enamored of her. "Now, there was never anybody more truly enchanting than Alice Pearce," says Cris Alexander. "But she was certainly *not* Jayne Mansfield! Well, Daddy Tanner certainly had the hots for her. He would follow her around hoping to see her change her costumes!" Lumbering, elderly Edward Tanner Jr. pursued the mousy Alice Pearce around the studio until the straight vodkas he'd been tossing back finally caught up with him. Eventually he leaned against a wall, then slowly slid down it and passed out. At that instant, nine-year-old Michael came up and stood next to his collapsed, blotto granddaddy, and Cris managed to capture the charming moment with his camera.

By this time, Pat's relationship with his father was less threatening. Ed Tanner could hardly argue with the success and celebrity his son had achieved, nor could he be unhappy with Pat's having produced two lovely grandchildren for him. Pat and his father would never be close, but as Ed Tanner aged, he became less vicious and dismissive of his son.

First Lady was finally published, appropriately enough, in the election year of 1964. It was a big, lavishly produced extravaganza, but it could not begin to compare to the fresh outrageousness of its predecessor, *Little Me*. Pat spread his humor far too thinly through the book, which painfully reveals him laboring to stretch a one-joke premise over 283 pages. Even Cris Alexander's work falls short of the polished standard he had set in *Little Me*. Lewis Nichols in the *New York Times* gently suggested that Pat and Cris "try again," while *Time* magazine simply called the book "nothing but a drag." But considering Pat's state of mind when he wrote the manuscript—and *where* he wrote the manuscript—it's not surprising that his well-known wit was in short supply. That he was even able to finish it at all is some kind of miracle.

Michael and Betsy were now getting used to the new routine of visits with Daddy, which did not involve the usual trips to the zoo or the park or the ball game that are the province of most broken families. Instead Pat took the kids to his favorite restaurants—exclusive, elegant, formal Upper East Side French establishments such as Voisin and Passy. "You know, I would have much rather gone to the Soup/Burg," says Betsy. "But that was the way it was; I didn't ever really think anything about it. You realize you grew up in an unusual way decades later." During the elaborate dinners, Pat would insist that the waiters serve the kids wine, even though Betsy and Mike, at seven and ten, would probably rather have had Kool-Aid. Since Pat was a preferred customer and a well-known figure, the management would nervously oblige, using red tumblers for the kids' wineglasses and placing empty ginger-ale bottles on the table while remaining quietly terrified that they would get thrown into jail for serving alcohol to minors.

Sometimes Guy Kent would come along. Once, Pat took Betsy and Michael to see a taping of the *Bell Telephone Hour,* for which Guy was designing costumes. "It was tremendously boring," says Michael. "We spent all afternoon watching Jane Wyman. Afterwards we went to Serendipity for sundaes. We had no idea what was going on with my father and Guy. I thought Guy was fun; no one struck me as being obviously gay at that time."

Not at all surprisingly, divorce and its effect on children served as the basis of Pat's next novel, *The Joyous Season*. Although it fell squarely into the category of A Patrick Dennis Novel—social satire of America's upper classes, as narrated in the first person by an observer who becomes a reluctant participant—this one would be different. The narrator was a ten-year-old boy. Kerry and his six-year-old sister, Missy, are clearly stand-ins for Michael and Betsy as they watch their parents quarrel and separate during the holiday season on the Upper East Side. There's also a Corry figure in Lulu, their nurse, and the in-laws—especially both grandmothers—have elements of their real-life counterparts. Over the course of a year, Kerry and Missy's parents divorce and are both nearly ensnared into disastrous second marriages, but, this being a Patrick Dennis novel, all ends happily and the parents are reunited and remarried. (Once again, Pat had written himself into a corner and could not come up with an ending. And once again, his editor, Julian Muller, had to write the final two pages.)

For both Michael and Betsy, *The Joyous Season* was tremendously consoling. "It really was told from my point of view," says Michael. "That was very exciting for me. I loved that book; it sort of healed things when my parents were splitting up."

"I can assure you," adds Betsy, "that not one of those episodes in the book ever happened, but that it *was* us. There was no question! It was joyous for me to read, because things worked out in the book in such a charmed way. I've always thought that it was a very sweet gift that my father gave us."

The dedication page read, "For Betsy and Mike."

Among Pat's many targets in *The Joyous Season* was psychiatry, a subject he knew a thing or two about by now. To deal with his feelings about the divorce, Kerry is sent to a child psychiatrist three times a week:

> Everybody nowadays is so big on psychiatry that there must be something to it but, for the life of me, I can't figure out what. Or

maybe it's just Dr. Lorenz Epston. . . . The first day Dr. Epston made me lie down on the couch and darned if I didn't drop right off to sleep while he was droning away about trusting him and telling him everything that came into my mind, no matter what. After he woke me up he kept asking me what I was trying to escape from and he wouldn't believe me when I told him that I'd stayed up late the night before watching *The Nurses* (it was all about this dope fiend) and it would have been rude to say that also he was kind of a bore. But after that he let me sit up straight in a chair.

He kept telling me that everything I said or didn't say or did or didn't do or remembered or forgot was for a reason deep down inside of me. It seems to me that lots of times people just plain forget things and I said so. But he told me I was dead wrong. You're always wrong with Dr. Epston. Then one day, right in the middle of my appointment, his wife called up and gave him a terrible chewing-out for forgetting to meet the Miami plane with her mother on it. (What a set of pipes that Mrs. Epston has! I could hear every word clear across the room. And they were *some* words!) When I asked him what the real deep-down-inside reason was for not remembering to meet his mother-in-law, he said, "*Ver gehargct*, you smart little goy!" Golly, that psychiatric lingo!

The Joyous Season was the only time that Pat would tell a story from a child's point of view (in the *Auntie Mame* books, Patrick is an adult looking back), and Pat managed the feat with charm and sensitivity, although Martin Levin in the *New York Times* sniped that ten-year-old Kerry had "the savvy and some of the diction of Billy Rose" and felt that Pat's "nonstop japeries ring hollower than necessary." In his perceptive review in *The Saturday Review*, Nicholas Samstag wrote, "[Mr. Dennis] is wonderfully funny, although these are the central diseased nerves of our society that he twists into snares with which to catch the dancing feet of folly. . . . His sole purpose seems to be to amuse, and he accomplishes it exquisitely. But he has a sort of inaudible gravity drive that you feel in your bones like the whine of one of those high-frequency dog whistles. . . . It says on the dust jacket that Patrick Dennis's [books] have sold over ten million copies. Not enough."

Shortly after he got out of Bloomingdale's Pat also plunged into work on two theatrical projects. One was *Fancy Me,* a musical designed for Dody Goodman and Alice Pearce about a girl who enters a contest and wins a trip to Europe with her spinster chaperone. Pat wrote the book and lyrics; the music was composed by his friend Harry Percer. It was slated to open in October of 1964 in London, but it never got much further than backers' auditions and a demo record of the score.

The other project was *Good, Good Friends,* also a musical, based on a story idea by Charles Scheuer and Warren Enters. The score was by singer-songwriter Murray Grand. Nancy Walker was set to make her official directing debut, Onna White *(The Music Man)* was signed as choreographer, and the sets would be by Robert Randolph *(How to Succeed in Business Without Really Trying).* Scheduled to open on Broadway in March of 1964, it was to be produced by Fryer and Carr, the original producers of *Auntie Mame.*

The story was perfect Patrick Dennis material. Set in Hollywood in the 1930s, it focused on the rivalry between Glenda Manson and Irene Thornton, two stars vying to be Queen of the Lot at UMB Studios while always sincerely, passionately, publicly professing to be the closest of friends. Among the other characters were UMB's dance director, Aries Mars, its chief, B. K. Bumbleman, and Edna Fanshaw, described as "Hedda and Louella in one, dressed in high-fashion clothes that are all wrong for her and a huge cabbage-rose hat to match the Dorothy Draper wallpaper of her office." Ultimately Glenda and Irene both find their stardom snatched away from them by an eight-year-old, curly-haired kid who bears a distinct resemblance to Shirley Temple. Had *Good, Good Friends* made it to Broadway, it would have been Pat's answer to the musical of *Little Me*—his version of exactly what that show *should* have been. Unfortunately, the project started becoming too expensive, Fryer and Carr withdrew, and everything fell apart.

The show did finally get staged ten years later, for a run in San Diego, by Don Wortman, a producer who owned the Hotel San Diego's Off-Broadway Dinner Theatre. Wortman had been an agent at International Famous when *Good, Good Friends* was having its backers' auditions, and he had always loved the show. He decided it would be fun to mount it and hired John Bowab, who had been the associate producer of the musical *Mame*, as director. Jane A. Johnston, Eileen Barnett, and Isabel Farrell starred, and this scaled-down production with a cast of twenty and an orchestra of four was a big success locally. Since then, the show has once again disappeared, except for a brief flurry of interest in 1988 in a possible Broadway run.

But Pat and *Good, Good Friends* composer Murray Grand became friends and remained so for the rest of Pat's life. Grand enjoyed Pat's anything-goes sense of mischief. Once Grand was visiting Pat at his elegant Fifth Avenue apartment on a Sunday afternoon. A huge parade was passing far underneath the window, and a large cannon in the parade was going off at intervals. When the cannon fired a big blank below Pat's apartment, Pat threw down two stuffed birds, making it look as if they had been shot. "It was hysterical," says Grand. "These two birds came flopping down. People had their mouths hanging open; they didn't know *what* was happening. Leave it to Patrick."

By this time, Pat was turning into quite a handful, especially when he had had too much to drink, which was often. Before his crisis, Pat could usually be counted upon for fairly outrageous remarks, but not for inappropriate public behavior. That was now beginning to change. Perhaps it was a growing sense of desperation or the loss of Louise's stabilizing influence. Maybe it was his increased alcohol consumption, or just sheer go-for-broke hell-raising after eight months of being penned in at Bloomingdale's. But some of his antics may have served to sabotage the chances of *Good, Good Friends* getting to Broadway. Case in point: during a backers' audition, Pat disappeared into the men's room at a break and came out stark naked. "When he drank too much," says Grand, "he used to strip. Dody Goodman got hysterical. She was screaming with laughter. Everybody else was so offended, they just grabbed their tiaras and ran. That backers' audition was a fiasco. We didn't raise any money that night."

Another time, Pat and Grand went out to dinner with a wealthy woman from Texas who had agreed to put a lot of money into the show. "Ugly beyond belief," says Grand. "She looked like Wallace Beery in drag. She had on what we called 'important' jewelry. Pat said, 'Oh, may I see your necklace?' And she said of course, and he unhooked it off her neck and looked at it, and put it in his napkin. After a while, every piece of jewelry she had on was in the napkin. And then he called over the waiter and said, 'Would you please take this and throw it in the garbage?' Well, the look on her face was absolutely unbelievable."

It was 1965, and America was changing. The short-lived sophistication that had marked the Kennedy years was ebbing away and gradually being replaced, on the one hand, by the exponential explosion of suburbia and its poolside culture, and on the other, by the social upheavals brought about by the civil rights era, the burgeoning counterculture, and widespread recreational drug use. Although a Democrat, Pat found the country turning in a direction that left him bewildered and uncomfortable. His favorite satirical targets—social climbing, snobbism, the self-importance of both old and new money— were starting to seem quaintly dated. Just as he'd always predicted, Patrick Dennis was, quite suddenly, becoming old-fashioned.

He was ready for a major change in his life and felt that the United States was no longer the best place for him. It was also time to make an escape. New York was a continual reminder of his remorse, his waning celebrity, and his ostracism by a society that disapproved of the sexual identity he had finally come to accept.

During his travels, Pat had developed a fondness for Morocco, as had Guy Kent. He and Guy decided to leave New York for good and move to Tangier. Always known as a sunny place for shady people, Tangier offered tolerance, decadence, and a ready-made colony of American and European expatriates. It also presented another enticement: high living at low cost. In spite of being a committed Democrat, Pat had been making noises about wanting to live someplace where he could have "a footman behind every chair." Although his income was starting to shrink, his expenses were higher than ever, and the lengthy stay in Bloomingdale's had strained his financial resources. A move to Morocco meant living like a sultan for far less money.

In May of 1965, Guy went ahead to Tangier to move into the apartment Pat had already rented for them, while Pat spent the next few weeks packing up 930 Fifth Avenue and closing off his twenty years in New York. He also bought tickets for Michael and Betsy to meet him in Morocco after the end of the school year and to spend the summer with him. Then he went off to Tangier to join Guy.

He wasn't gone long.

It seemed that no sooner had Murray Grand seen Pat off for Tangier than Pat was back in New York at Murray's door. "I was supposed to go over and visit them," says Grand, "and suddenly there was this banging on the door, and there was Pat with his suitcase, asking me if he could come in. When Pat had arrived in Tangier, Guy announced to him that he was going to marry this blonde whose father owned a diamond mine. He *did* marry her. Pat had left Guy passed out on the floor. He literally thought he'd killed Guy when he'd left Tangier. I don't know whether it was a fistfight or what. It could have been one of Pat's hallucinations, because when he'd get drunk, sometimes he'd see things that weren't there. Here he had moved to Tangier because of Guy—he'd set this whole apartment up; Guy didn't have any money— and Guy announced that he was leaving him. Pat thought he was going off to find love and happiness, walking into the sunset. Well, it wasn't the sunset; it was disaster."

A bit more information can be gleaned from actress Paula Lawrence, whose long stage career extends back to the original production of *One Touch of Venus* and beyond. Guy had designed her costumes for the play *Season in the Sun,* and she had remained friendly with him. "The woman Guy married in Tangier was a friend of Orson Welles's first wife. She and Guy came to see me in New York several times from Tangier. She wasn't a terribly *interesting* woman, but sweet, and attractive, and of a certain social level. She seemed pleasant enough, but kind of—shall we say—short-sighted? She was not what one thinks of as a so-called fag's moll. She had inherited a bit of money, and she was a widow, and she had lived in Johannesburg, and Guy was just the most colorful person she'd ever met. There were great shopping tours and gloves being ordered, and I just had a feeling that no one had ever paid that much attention to her. And they were affectionate and pleasant enough with each other. I also got a feeling that there was a lot of alcohol going on."

Pat was devastated by Guy's action. Guy apparently wanted to continue his relationship with Pat on the side despite the marriage, but Pat would have none of it. Now, to compound all of his other psychic burdens—his guilt over hurting his family, his legacy of self-doubt from his father, his fear of becoming suddenly obsolete as a writer—he had to put the pieces of his life and his heart back together. While staying with Murray Grand and figuring out what to do next, Pat sought out his friend Carmen Capalbo. "Pat talked to me about Guy in great detail," says Capalbo. "It was an earthshaking event in his life. He also felt terrible guilt over what he had done to his family. Pat wasn't one of those mournful drunks, but if you were in the right conversation, his eyes would tear up—he had these big, bright blue eyes, and suddenly they would become rimmed with tears. You see, Pat was almost an innocent; in all the years I knew him, he was not the kind of guy who was always talking about sex and getting laid and chasing women or men. That was never an element. And all the people I knew who knew him—some of whom were homosexual—all said the same thing. Now, maybe at a certain point that changed, I don't know. But I never saw the slightest thing. He never once made any kind of a reference to or an overt move in the direction of anyone. Even when we were at Gurney's Inn in Montauk working on the script for *The Loving Couple*. His wife wasn't around; he could have done anything he wanted to. And he certainly never, *ever* came on to me in any way; that was not in the picture."

Although Pat's close friends rallied around him and were supportive as always, it's probably safe to say that few of them were going to miss Guy Kent. "I could never understand that," said Peggy Cass. "Imagine being heartbroken about *him!* Christ! He was a sight! A little gnome! Not a bit good-looking. And he could be obnoxious! He was like somethin' you'd filch out of a wastebasket! But he could be funny; and maybe it was his sense of humor that attracted Pat. To give the devil his due, I think Pat probably fell in love with that mind, which was very amusing and very incisive."

Guy Kent was virtually swallowed up in Morocco. Little is known about the rest of his life, except that he stayed in Tangier and apparently died there sometime in the early 1990s. It is assumed by those who knew him that he and his bride eventually drank themselves to death.

Since Tangier was now out of the question, Pat took eleven-year-old Michael and eight-year-old Betsy on a long trip to Paris, Rome, Tunis, Cairo, and Madrid. By the end of the summer, Pat had decided upon a new home for himself: Mexico City.

PART FOUR

Pat in Mexico,
early 1970s

SEVENTEEN

"The International Set"

Mexico City in the 1960s was a far more enticing place than it is today. Before it started choking on its own pollution, before its economy plummeted, before its population exploded and crime infested its streets, Mexico City was a magnet for people from all over the world who were finally discovering the country's vibrant culture. Muralists such as David Alfaro Siqueiros, Rufino Tamayo, and Juan O'Gorman had become cultural icons and were attracting and inspiring a new generation of artists, artisans, and historians. Magnificent museums were being built to house collections of modern and pre-Hispanic art. The Ballet Folklorico turned the country's native dances into dazzlingly memorable theater. Rudolf Nureyev and Dame Margot Fonteyn danced at the Palacio de Bellas Artes; great orchestras such as the Moscow Symphony and the New York Philharmonic made regular tours of the country, as did such classical superstars as Yehudi Menuhin, Beverly Sills, and Leonard Bernstein. Foreign dignitaries such as Queen Elizabeth, Charles de Gaulle, Haile Selassie, and even the pope were making official visits. As the world discovered Mexico, Mexico discovered itself, taking pride in its culture and cuisine, its history and traditions.

None of this held any particular interest for Pat.

But Mexico City *was* a great place for parties.

On his many trips to Mexico with Louise, and subsequently with Guy Kent, Pat had developed a fondness for the easy style of living that Mexico offered and had made many friends in its large community of American and European expatriates. In the second chapter of *Genius,*

Pat paints a detailed picture of the Mexico City social scale, revealing it to be perfect Patrick Dennis territory:

A lot of Americans, more or less fluent in Spanish, have tried to crash the Old Mexican Society. They can't but it would serve them good and right if they could. The O.M.S. is one of the most inbred, parochial, and dismal flocks ever to be seen. At their parties, the men gather at one end of the room and talk about business, while the women at the other end discuss such stimulating subjects as their children, how lazy their maids are, and the high cost of living. After two or three hours of that, the first glass of tequila is brought out, and a good time is had by all.

Even drearier is that one-hundred-and-ten-per-cent American colony made up of the representatives of such various United States products as refrigerators, calculating machines, farm equipment, soft drinks and canned goods. What with their D.A.R. and American Legion Post and Rotary Club and P.T.A. and general red, white and blowsiness, they have always been able to create a miniature Main Street in some of the most unlikely places in the world. Well, they're welcome to it.

Still lower are the Americans who are ashamed of being Americans. They are generally given to beards and sandals, arts and crafts, dirndls and dungarees. They are more native than the natives, denying their children (of which there are many, mostly born via variations of natural childbirth that would shock an Aztec) such bourgeois affectations as shoes and the English language. As the Mexicans will have nothing to do with them, they consort exclusively—and in Spanish—with other Americans who are ashamed of being Americans. They deserve each other.

On the other hand, there is a large and fluid group of perfectly pleasant people who are not much of anything at all. It is a constantly shifting society made up of Americans, English, a few French and Germans, a scattering of South Americans, and a lot of very cheery Mexicans who have lived elsewhere at some time or another and who have more interesting things to talk about than household and finance. They congregate in good, nontouristy restaurants like the Rivoli or the Derby or Ambassadeurs or Bill Shelburne's El Paseo. They give nice parties and better small ones. If times ever get dull, there are things like vacationing movie stars or minor nobility or con men or just visiting firemen to jazz things up. This clump of jolly, unclassifiable people is called, with heavy scorn, The International Set by all the locals who aren't part of it. The title makes it sound a great deal grander and racier and clique-ier than happens to be the case. What it actually is, is a bunch of fairly attractive people who like to see one another every now and then, and if you don't take it seriously you can have quite a good time.

Pat was more than ready for a good time. After the disasters and disappointments of the previous three years, Mexico City looked to be the ideal refuge. It was also a place where his money could go much further, and his tax burden could be somewhat lower. He soon found an absurdly enormous apartment—nine rooms plus servants' quarters—in a modern high-rise at 33 Calle de Varsovia, on the western edge of the chic Zona Rosa neighborhood. It was one of the first luxury apartment buildings to have been constructed in Mexico City.

Pat decorated his apartment lavishly in his trademark flamboyant style. Wastebaskets in tiger skin, bedspreads in leopard skin, his large antique-clock collection, his huge, ornate porcelain water heater from Hapsburg Vienna, and mirrored closet doors. A library with green carpeting, red velvet wallpaper, and white furniture—the whole evoking the colors of the Mexican flag. He even covered the inlaid wooden floor in the entry hall with black-and-white linoleum squares. The landlord almost had a heart attack.

Thirty-six paintings, all slightly askew, hung in the living room alone. One of them was a kitschy mechanical toy entitled "The Mirror of Venus." A naked Venus stood gazing into a round gilt frame held by Cupid, which was a hole across which passed little pictures of Sophia Loren, Elizabeth Taylor, Jacqueline Kennedy, Ringo Starr, and others.

Pat also got himself a highly decorative pair of weimaraners, whom he named Maximilian and Carlota. Refusing to be housebroken, they added their own unique accents to the color scheme.

Pat was ready to impose his Upper East Side lifestyle on the Zona Rosa, to bring Civilization to the Aztecs. The round of parties began.

One of the most memorable took place when Rosalind Russell visited Mexico City. Pat arranged a special dinner party for her at his home. After Russell walked in, Pat's overeager servant removed not only her wrap, but her coatdress as well, leaving her standing in her slip. Later, a slightly intoxicated guest confused her with the top-heavy actress Jane Russell. He made it a point to tell her how wonderful he thought she'd been in that Howard Hughes western with the scene in the haystack. Roz laughed, threw open her bolero jacket, and said, "Wrong Russell!"

When it came time to leave, two of the guests began snapping at each other over who was going to get to take Miss Russell home. As the dispute escalated, Russell sneaked off and disappeared down the elevator, leaving the two squabbling guests behind.

Not only was Pat throwing large affairs at Calle de Varsovia, he was also a highly desirable guest at parties and dinners throughout the expatriate community. In Mexico, everyone referred to him and addressed him as Patrick Dennis, and he seemed content to let them do so. Since much of his fame was allied to his pseudonym, he evidently shrugged and gave up on being known as Pat Tanner. The price he now had to pay was to assume another role, to play a character he had created that was already becoming old hat for him.

In Mexico, Pat was able to be considerably more relaxed about his sexual identity. If a member of the International Set was a little slow on the uptake and suggested setting Pat up on a blind date with an unattached female, Pat's usual response was, "Madam, I am a forty-five-year-old Protestant homosexual." Upon meeting the wife of a particularly attractive man, he had no compunction whatsoever about asking, "How much do you want for your gorgeous husband?" That kind of talk was awfully shocking in 1965, but it also made him an outrageous and entertaining party guest. "He was Patrick," says one friend, "and so he got away with murder. But he could be serious; he wasn't always frivolous. He had a deeper part of himself. He always contributed, and in a serious fashion, to serious discussions."

One of the friends Pat already had in Mexico City was Katherine Walch, a British expatriate who had originally fallen in with Hervey Jolin's camp circle in New York City during the Depression. She had been living in Mexico since the 1950s and had gotten to know both Pat and Louise well during their frequent visits. Walch had also been a guest at the Tanner town house on East Ninety-first Street. During one of Pat and Louise's first Mexico City trips, she had arranged a comically disastrous visit for them to the home of the famous Mexican film director Emilio "El Indio" Fernandez, which later served as the basis for a memorable episode in *Genius*. (She had also arranged for Pat to meet the great film star Dolores Del Rio for lunch, but Pat had to cancel—he was stricken with a powerful case of the trots.) Over the years, Katherine became close enough to the Tanner family that Pat made her one of the executors of his Mexican will (see appendix).

"Frankly," says Katherine, "I doubt that Patrick had much interest in what was going on around him in Mexico City. I have to admit not recalling any serious conversation with him about world affairs, and much less Mexico. He knew all the good *restaurants* in town; as for anything else, he couldn't have cared less. He seemed to live in an endless round of social activities, where he was always the central figure— witty, urbane, impeccably dressed, satirical in comment, very observant, and seemingly never out of humor—and yet somehow remote. It seemed that he was putting on a front to the world, and that the true Patrick was never revealed."

Michael and Betsy came down to be with their father for the first time during Christmas break. This began a long series of visits that they both view today with mixed memories. "We'd step off the plane," says Betsy, "and the first thing he'd do was—well, he wouldn't *burn* our clothes, but he'd take us right out to get new ones that were in line with his taste. He'd re-wardrobe you. It was a credit to him that he could get away with that. Of course, there's no question that he had better taste than just about anyone you're ever going to run into, so you couldn't really quarrel with that."

It was their school vacation, and Michael and Betsy had little to do but sit around Pat's expensive apartment during the day and go out with him to his favorite posh restaurants at night. "Going down to Mexico to visit him was difficult," says Michael. "It largely meant having a Coke fixed for us by the butler and sitting around chatting with Dad. It was never very comfortable. Betsy and I just wished we were back in New York, playing out on Ninety-first Street." Out of sheer boredom, Michael and Betsy were even inventing their own sports games—such as wrapping a bottle cap in Betsy's hairband and playing baseball in the living room. Pat was rarely pleased by this, especially when it resulted in broken windows and shattered vases.

"Imagine those two poor kids," says Katherine Walch, "cooped up in an elegant apartment, forced to learn bridge so as to be socially acceptable to their father's guests. Patrick ruled them with a rod of iron, shaming them into good behavior, never raising his voice or scolding. They never protested when I was around but were totally subservient to his wishes. He overawed them."

Katherine kept urging Pat to do *something* with the kids—take them out; expose them to Mexican history and culture—and Pat finally agreed on a visit with the kids to the Toltec ruins of Teotihuacán, just outside the city limits. He insisted that Katherine come along to act as tour guide and showed up with the kids at her apartment in his private chauffeured car, dressed not for viewing ruins but for taking tea with the Windsors. By the time they reached Teotihuacán, it was raining. "Out you go," he said to Katherine and the kids. "You can explore; I'll wait here." Katherine gave the kids a tour of the site; they climbed the pyramids in the rain, and everyone returned soaking to the car where Pat waited. Then they all went back to Calle de Varsovia. Katherine and the children each went off for baths in the apartment's three marble-and-onyx bathrooms, and that was that. Pat had done his bit toward exposing the kids to Mexican culture; except for the occasional bull-fight. "Which is probably why my sister has been a vegetarian since the age of fourteen," says Michael dryly. On the occasions when Louise would come along for their trips down to Mexico City, Michael and Betsy got out more.

During his first year in Mexico, Pat got to work on a new novel. Like *Auntie Mame,* it was a chronologically ordered set of episodes spanning four decades and centered on a single character and was once again narrated by Patrick Dennis as a first-person observer. But this book would be no breezy charmer. *Tony* marked a turning point for Pat: his novels, while still comic, would now be made of sterner stuff.

Tony is a smooth, sociopathic charmer who, like Woody Allen's Zelig seventeen years later, assumes different personae to help him infiltrate the various upper-class milieux that would normally shun him. The son of an impoverished dentist and a sluttish mother, he is totally self-invented, moving from accent to accent and alias to alias. Forever on the brink of crashing High Society, he always manages to take things just a step too far and, by the end of each chapter, has had all his plans blow up in his face. By sabotaging himself, he usually winds up pulling his innocent dupes down with him. As he swindles and social-climbs his way through life, Tony leaves a trail of broken hearts, emptied bank accounts, and even death behind him.

It all made for a Patrick Dennis novel that had darker undertones than anything he had ever written before. Like *The Joyous Season,* it was a personal work: Tony was based on Guy Kent. He was exaggerated, of course, for comic effect, but Pat insisted to Murray Grand that Guy was most definitely the inspiration for the character. Pat even set the final chapter in Tangier, where the washed-up, forty-six-year-old Tony has gotten himself engaged to a grotesque, wealthy, older British widow. Although Tony and the Patrick Dennis narrator never have an affair, they constantly find their paths crossing. Pat is in Tangier finishing a novel when Tony seeks him out:

"Crystal and I are engaged."

"That's just perfect. Good-by."

"She's a fabulous girl—and a great beauty, *I* think."

"So's Medusa, *I* think."

"All sorts of famous artists want to paint her—Henry Koerner, Sidney Nolan, Feliks Topolski . . ."

"I seem to see her blasted into the side of Mount Rushmore, where I heartily wish I could be at the moment—or someplace equally far from here."

"Don't you like Tangier?"

"I loathe it. It's Canarsie with minarets—a town that never made it filled with people who never made it. So it's ideal for someone like you. Now get the hell out of my house."

"Please," he almost sobbed. "I've had a rotten time of it these past few years."

"And you've deserved it. Why you're not in jail is a mystery.

And believe me, Tony, if I can ever do anything toward putting you there, I'll move heaven and earth to do it." I turned back to my typewriter. Mechanically Tony made one last stab at turning on the famous old charm, then thought better of it and left.

In spite of the scathing portrait Pat painted, or perhaps *because* it was scathing, he dedicated the book to "G.M.K."

Pat usually had a gay character or two in his books; they were there for comic effect and were all fairly stereotypical in their nelliness. In *Tony*, Pat finally created a gay character who engenders sympathy. Tatham Purdom is a well-off Southern boy newly arrived in New York who is smitten with Tony. Tony moves in with Tatham and becomes his kept man, bleeding him for all he is worth until Tatham's manipulative mother pays Tony off and Tony decamps to Palm Beach, leaving Tatham with nothing but a "Dear John" note. Tatham commits suicide—the usual end for a homosexual character in that era—but as Pat's crisis of only a few years before shows, such actions were never exclusively the province of fiction. Pat even pokes fun at his own troubled childhood when, as an editor at a publishing house, he reads the literary submissions of Tatham's numerous gay friends:

> . . . They were all thinly disguised autobiographies and after the first three I knew just where to turn to find what:
> Page one—"John [or Ralph or Christopher or Brooke] was not like other boys. . . ."
> Page three—"His gentle mother was a beautiful woman, warm, understanding, and gay. . . ."
> Page seven—"He hardly knew his father, a stern man who had little time for his family . . ."
> Page ten—"When the other boys chose up teams for baseball or football he was not invited to join in their fun. . . ."
> Page fourteen—"The scoutmaster [or Latin teacher or chauffeur or curate] laid his hand gently on John's [or Ralph's or Christopher's or Brooke's] arm. 'You're trembling,' said he. . . ."

Pat didn't have to look very far for his inspiration.

Not surprisingly, Tony is not the whole show. As Tony marches through time, from an Eastern prep school in 1936 to Morocco in 1966, each chapter finds him in a different setting in a different year with a different cast of characters. Pat pulls out his favorite tricks—bizarrely memorable supporting players, perfectly transliterated accents and dialects, descriptions of changing fashion and decor that give exquisite comic insight into the lives and eras at hand. New York, the suburbs, the publishing industry, the television industry, various walk-ups, penthouses, and country clubs all come in for Pat's wicked dissection job. Once more, his talents as a social reporter prove peerless in their pinpoint accuracy.

The critics were not terribly kind to *Tony;* they found the title character superficially drawn and were put off by the book's acidic tone. Although Erik Wensberg in the *New York Times* noted that the novel was driven by "a surprisingly fierce moral engine," he also damned it as "silly" and "woeful." In the *New York Herald Tribune,* Albert Goldman found the book funny but felt that it suffered from a "flashy leanness." *Tony* did not earn the sales figures it deserved.

Since then, America's fascination with wealth and celebrity has only intensified, making *Tony* more relevant than ever. Liars, cheaters, opportunists, and sociopaths will always abound, and it's probably safe to say that most people have been afflicted with a Tony or two in their lives. Pat's book was indeed driven by a "fierce moral engine," and he was one of the few American writers of his era who could successfully create an enjoyable, darkly comic novel from that point of view. His fierce moral engine was always running, firing its pistons all through his work.

Nineteen sixty-six saw the long-delayed Mexico City premiere of the stage version of *Auntie Mame.* Produced at the famous Teatro de los Insurgentes on a huge budget, it had two great Mexican stars—Amparo Rivelles and Andrea Palma—as Mame and Vera. Pat attended a few rehearsals, and when he saw the lavish set that designer David Anton had created for Mame's town house, he was overjoyed. He threw his arms around Anton, gave him a huge hug, and then ran up onstage and treated himself to several delighted trips up and down Mame's curving staircase. Although it ultimately suffered from what was said to be a poor translation, *Tía Mame* proved a success with Mexico City audiences.

In New York, Mame was taking on yet another life as the smash-hit Jerry Herman musical. Angela Lansbury, in the title role, reinvented herself as a musical-comedy star and left behind the evil manipulators and monstrous mother figures she had been playing in such films as *The Manchurian Candidate* and *The World of Henry Orient*. The show would run on Broadway for five solid years, and a parade of Mames including Celeste Holm, Janis Paige, Jane Morgan, and Ann Miller took turns starring. On the road and in subsequent revivals, Jo Anne Worley, Ginger Rogers, Patrice Munsel, and Juliet Prowse have made their way down Mame's great staircase.

Unfortunately, Pat's *Auntie Mame* contract did not include provisions for any musical comedy adaptations of the property. *Mame* was raking in huge amounts at the box office, little of which was going into Pat's pocket. Arbitration ensued, and matters would not be fully resolved until after Pat's death.

Pat refused to go to the opening of *Mame* and did not see it until the summer of 1967, when he was making a brief trip to New York. "I found it a crashing bore," he wrote his sister, Barbara. "Angela Lansbury was just too common for words, which is the one thing Mame cannot be. Celeste Holm should at least be a bit classier."

Pat's move to Mexico initiated lengthy streams of correspondence between him and the family that would continue for years. Michael Tanner has saved nearly forty of his father's letters. Not only do they make marvelously witty reading, they also show how Pat regarded his kids. Just as he never talked down to the children, he never wrote down to them either: his letters read as if they were intended for adults. Throughout the correspondence, he uses nicknames that refer to private Tanner family mythology: Pat was Lancelot Leopard, Michael was Manny, and Betsy was Minnie, sometimes Catso. All were leopards of royal lineage, except for Louise, who was a lynx that Lancelot had freed from a trap. In a letter to Michael and Betsy on June 4, 1966, following a short birthday trip to New York, Pat wrote:

Dear Minnie and Manny—

I'm home again and settling in gradually.

I have now blown my nose on Min's handkerchieves and read the book about Hemingway. Thank you both again.

Now that Hemingway is good and dead, I can add him to my list of overrated talents. They now run as follows:

1. Jesus Christ
2. William Shakespeare
3. F. Scott Fitzgerald
4. Ernest Hemingway

These gentlemen are listed in the order of their deaths, not in the order of their overratedness—except that Hhhhhe comes first on both counts.

At the time, Betsy was nine, and Michael was eleven and in Catholic school.

When the kids came down to spend the summer with their father that year, Pat at least had a few outside activities planned for them. They got to go ice-skating at local indoor rinks, and they spent two hours each morning at the nearby Crocker School learning Spanish. Meanwhile, the endless rounds of parties and dinners continued. To aid him in his entertaining, Pat hired a large staff of servants. In a letter to Lynxie, Minnie, and Manny, he wrote:

Yes, it's all too true about Florentino's third lapse. Minnie and Manny might also be interested to know that the interesting crash we heard in the kitchen was caused by Florentino's saying something very unflattering about Bonifacio's mother—palpably untrue, I gather, as Bonifacio brought one up from the floor and let him have it. Florentino is lucky that it was only an open hand and not a meat cleaver. Never fool around with no cook, cubs.

On the following day Florentino was replaced not once, but twice. To begin with, there is Pablo, aged 26, who is gigantic, so breathtakingly handsome that people stop on the street to gape, and so sweet, innocent, shy and *stupid* that he can't get to the corner without being helped. I plan to keep him that way. Then there is Jaime, 23, who is the cousin of Carlitos, the blackest of the three doormen, who is just Manny's size and much blonder. (An American tourist in the woodpile?) I'm not certain as to how long he's going to last, but at least he fits into Florentino's old uniforms and, at the rate things are going, I'm going to own more uniforms than the Mexican Army. . . .

I will say that the two young men work their asses off. The place was a bower of flowers, beautifully arranged and not, you can be sure, by the President of the Garden Club of Garrison, and all the rugs shampooed—and sopping wet—when I got home yesterday. I was not displeased . . .

Pat soon became so fond of Pablo—in a strictly platonic way—that he virtually adopted him. Pablo, who had been a butler at the Italian embassy when Pat hired him away, was indeed charming and hardworking. Pat even played matchmaker for him, encouraging him to marry Micaela, one of the maids on his household staff. Pablo did—even though he and Micaela were not particularly fond of each other—and the result was a baby daughter before Micaela locked her door to Pablo for good. Pablo became protective of Pat, particularly when Pat got drunk and needed some help. That was happening more and more often.

Meanwhile, Pat and his sister, Barbara, were coping with their parents, who were aging less than gracefully in Chicago. Barbara, who still lived there, was bearing the daily brunt of it, but Pat made heavy financial contributions. In 1965, Ed Tanner had taken a job with a prestigious Chicago real estate firm. What he didn't know was that Pat was, indirectly, paying his salary. Ed worked on commission, but was not terribly successful at closing deals. For each week that he didn't earn his draw, Pat supplied the missing portion of the base salary through the firm's payroll office, and that cost him approximately $600 a month in midsixties dollars. "No gripe," Pat wrote Barbara. "It's worth the money to keep him off the streets and out of the bars. No one knows who pays Edward's salary except [the real-estate firm] and Abe Badian, who signs the actual checks. I couldn't be quite mean enough to tell him, and he did keep me going for twenty-one years."

Both Ed and Florence Tanner were now more or less constantly inebriated. In a way, they were living up to a remark Pat once made about their never having gotten out of the Roaring Twenties. But by this point, it was no longer charming. Ed was drinking until he passed out. Florence spent her days drinking, chattering incessantly, and showing the signs of developing senility. ("If you talked to her just once," says Murray Grand, "you knew she was a fruitcake.") Her vaunted sense of chic seemed to have arrested itself years before; her favored household attire was the type of "baby doll" nightgown worn at the time by teenage girls.

Florence was wearing one of those nightgowns one day in 1966 when she accidentally set herself afire with a cigarette lighter. Fortunately Edward was home and happened to be soaking in the bathtub. He jumped out when he heard Florence's screams, took hold of her, and plunged her into the full bathtub. But by that time, she had already been seriously burned on her chest, arms, hands, and neck.

Pat immediately flew to Chicago, fearing the worst and packing two black suits in case of a funeral. He stayed by Florence's side at the hospital, and fortunately she recovered, although she was seriously scarred. When she was well enough to return home, Pat bought her several beautiful new robes to wear around the house—not of the "baby doll" variety.

During 1967, Pat turned out most of his fourteenth novel, *How Firm a Foundation*. A play on words, *Foundation* referred to the Fennessey Foundation, a fence set up to benefit upstate New York's wealthy Fennessey family under the guise of offering funding for the arts. The Patrick Dennis figure this time was an idealistic young fellow named John Wesley Smith, hired in the vague capacity of director of projects, who becomes unwillingly embroiled in the Fennessey family's unsavory machinations.

It was not top-drawer Dennis. Lacking the freshness of his best work, *How Firm a Foundation* at least made an enjoyable comic page-turner that offered some choice Pat Tanner insights into the world of the stingy rich. John Wesley Smith's first dinner at the Fennessey mansion, served to him and the rest of the Foundation staff, gives him an idea of just how parsimonious his new employers will be:

> The meal itself was good but not hearty. Like many of the very rich, the Fennesseys were not prodigal with food. There was one of everything: one cup of jellied consommé, one slice of chicken, one potato, one perfectly fluted mushroom, one leaf of lettuce, one dollop of lemon ice. Second helpings were not proffered. It required six people to prepare and five people to serve. The silver, the porcelain, the crystal, linen and flowers were exquisite, but hardly nourishing. A family of Sicilian immigrants, improbably invited to the Fennessey dinner table, would have considered the entire meal a sort of unusual antipasto, piled into their car and driven to the nearest pizzeria for the main course.

Pat had his usual troubles finishing the book. William Morrow was publishing it, and the firm sent senior editor William McPherson down to Mexico City to coax an ending out of Pat. (McPherson went on to become book editor at the *Washington Post*; he won a Pulitzer Prize for criticism and authored several novels, including *Testing the Current* and *To the Sargasso Sea*.) McPherson spent ten days in Mexico with Pat, first at the apartment on Calle de Varsovia and then in Cuernavaca at the Hosteria las Quintas resort. "I don't remember at what point I came into it," says McPherson, "but at that time the book was nowhere near finished. I would cajole him, and we would have these long liquid lunches, where we'd have lots of fun and laugh and he would say all kinds of funny things. Once he said something like, 'Well, you know, the Mexicans—they're all hung like minnows!' "

Pat entertained McPherson grandly in Mexico. "All those parties!" remembers McPherson. "He was such a wonderful host; so generous; and it was the most preposterous group of people. One of them was a widow from Minneapolis whose name was Doña Clarita del Lefkowitz—I'm not kidding! She had inherited some fortune from her husband. Pat kept referring to 'the del Lefkowitz pearls.' There was one woman I liked a lot who came from the town of Coffeeville, Mississippi. I also met Gore Vidal's mother in Cuernavaca, Nina Gore Auchincloss Olds. She had us to dinner one night, and across the ravine from her house was the home of Barbara Hutton, which was in a Chinese style. She had all these servants running around in coolie hats!"

It wasn't easy getting Pat to do much work. "We did make *some* progress," says McPherson. "We'd be at the Hosteria las Quintas in Cuernavaca and I'd say, 'Okay, Pat, you go to your room now and do some work, and I'll come check on you in a couple of hours and I'll read it.' But it was very hard to keep Pat on course, because he always wanted to drink or play or something."

Sometimes, Pat would let his guard down a bit with McPherson. "He loved his children," says McPherson. "I remember how he used to talk about how much he missed them. And he was very fond of Louise. Although he was very funny, and very intelligent, he was also very self-deprecating. He didn't give himself much credit; he just dismissed his books, I think. I have one particularly vivid memory of Pat from Mexico City. Pat always woke up very early. I got up one morning and he was on the terrace eating his breakfast, which was toasted Mexican bread with marmalade and coffee. And before he saw me approaching, he was kind of looking off into the middle distance. And he looked so very resigned, and fatalistic—it was not a happy expression."

During the ten days of McPherson's stay, Pat didn't accomplish much. Finally, he basically threw up his hands and told McPherson to go ahead and finish *How Firm a Foundation* on his own. "It's not that Pat couldn't do it," says McPherson, "he just didn't care. I went back to New York and worked very hard on it; I don't think I went out for about two weeks. I don't want to claim too much credit for it, but I remember being exhausted afterwards. And Pat didn't even want to see it; he didn't care what I did; he trusted me. He said, 'Do whatever you want.' "

Pat subsequently dedicated the book to McPherson. "He hadn't told me he was going to do that," says McPherson. "When I discovered it later, I was flabbergasted—and deeply touched."

By now Pat was such a fixture on the Mexico City expatriate social scene that he actually let himself get talked into appearing live onstage in the Mexico City 1967 Junior League Follies. "I convinced him," said an American friend, Pansy Kimbro, "because I told him he was such a jackass, he would fit right in! I said, 'You have to do this. You're an American living abroad; this is an American association for the poor children of Mexico.' And he said, 'I couldn't care less.' I said, 'Well, you're going to do it anyway.' " Not only did Kimbro get Pat to join her in singing a duet during the show's opening number, she also got him to appear in three other acts in the show, including an all-drag cancan chorus line. Just before that big number, Pat lost his bloomers backstage. "I was in charge of him; I was the troubleshooter," says Kimbro. "I said, 'My God, you can't go on without your bloomers and do the cancan! What have you got under there?' And ye gods, he showed me! He had *nothing* on! I screamed and said, 'Put yer god-darned dress down!' I asked him where he saw the bloomers last, and he said, 'In that room, where there are about thirty women dressing, all screaming at each other.' By the time we found his bloomers, the cancan music was starting. I screamed at him, 'Get these on and get to stage right!' Three of us helped him into the bloomers and he dashed out onto the stage. And he was one of the hits of the evening!"

On and on went the dinners at Rivoli and El Paseo, on and on went the parties at Calle de Varsovia and all over the city. Pat's old friend Katherine Walch watched him being sucked into the social whirlpool of Mexico's International Set and found herself starting to step back from him, despite her deep affection. At one of his parties, she remembers, Pat literally had to hire someone to stand at the elevator door and keep out the gate-crashers. "I don't even *know* some of these people," he said to her, surveying the room and shaking his head. At one point during the party, Walch looked over at Pat, who was surrounded by a crush of sycophants, and thought, "This man looks *despairing*. He's like a helpless swimmer." At that moment she began to withdraw. "I had to," she says today. "It got to me, finally. I really think Mexico was what finished him off. Instead of achieving anything, he was going from party to party. It seemed that he was putting on a front to the world. But his friendship was sincere, and I'll always be grateful for that."

One of Pat's few Mexico City friends whom Walch remembers with real fondness was Nina Quirós, an American citizen of Mexican and American parentage who was living in the city. "I liked *her*," says Walch. "She was a good influence, a steadying influence on him. She wasn't always trying to get him to have another drink and give another party." Nina had been one of the few positive things to come out of the relationship with Guy Kent. Guy had introduced Nina to Pat during a trip he and Pat had made to Mexico. Nina, a columnist for the *Mexico City News*, was a bit of an Auntie Mame type herself: middle-aged, social, fun-loving, broad-minded; always ready to try something new and to have a ball doing it. She and Pat became best buddies and, eventually, business partners. "We got a hell of a friendship going," Nina says today. "He knew how to have a good time and spend money. We had a very laissez-faire friendship. He never put great demands on his friends. He was very generous; if Pat had two dollars, you had one of them. He was *too* generous; he was always inviting everyone to his house, and everyone was eating and drinking him out of house and home. And Mexico wasn't *that* cheap at the time; let's be honest. Especially if you wanted to live on a grand scale. Of course it was cheaper than the United States, but still . . ."

Pat soon grew tired of the Calle de Varsovia apartment. He had completely finished decorating it and making it into a showplace and wanted to move on and do it all over again someplace new. He also felt the building was already starting to become run-down: elevator breakdowns and unreliable heat and hot water were taking a big toll on his patience. In the summer of 1968 he moved to a two-level penthouse in an even taller building at 160 Avenida Nuevo Leon, in the leafy, upscale Colonia Condesa neighborhood. Once again, Pat spent huge sums decorating the place. "I only spent five dollars a yard for these curtains," he'd tell friends. "Ah, but the lining! *That* cost *twenty-five* dollars a yard!"

The penthouse had an expansive terrace with a sweeping view of the city, and Nina Quirós and Pablo spent plenty of time planting and turning it into an aerial garden for Pat. "Then," says Nina, amused, "it would rain, and all the rain would come into the goddamn bedroom downstairs! That penthouse was a pain in the ass, I'll tell you!" Pat bought a huge ice-making machine for the kitchen, but the machine didn't work. After five calls to the dealer who had sold it to him, Pat was still waiting for a repairman to come. Finally he took the warranty he'd been given when he bought the machine, wrapped it around a brick with a rubber band, went to the dealership late one night, and tossed it through the plate-glass window. A repairman showed up at the apartment the very next morning.

That fall, Pat's parents decided to move into an apartment in Chicago's recently completed Hancock building. Although Pat found the building a modern abomination, he offered to decorate it for them long-distance. In a three-page letter to his sister, Barbara, on September 16, 1968, he gave a detailed breakdown of his decorating plans and added:

> Oi Gevalt, such an ugly building! . . . I am of more than two minds as to the wisdom of their moving into the Hand-Cock Building at all. . . . But, as Mrs. [Mary Baker] Eddy would have said, let's look on the Bright Side. The place, though overpriced and charmless, is possible and the two of them can drink themselves to death—quickly, one hopes—without going outside and slipping on the ice. No matter how much it costs, it's better than their living with you and *infinitely* better than their living with me. I have bronchial pneumonia at the moment and feel that my days are numbered to about two more. I am also nowhere as rich as I used to be. But I am probably mean enough and—let's hope—rich enough to outlast the two of them.

> . . . If only they were moving at any other time, I could bring Pablo up with me. He runs my household and *never* stops working. He also adores the two of them (you can see that he's not entirely bright) and they all get on like fleas in a crotch. Language has never been any barrier with our mother. *But* Pablo's wife, Micaela, is expecting a baby on April 28. It's very important to *me* that she have it and have it right. They've had three miscarriages in 11 months and, frankly, I'm far more concerned about spoiling a nice, new baby than I am about those two old maniacs.

> . . . Needless to say, I have barely scratched the surface of things to be done, recovered, cleaned, thrown out and so on. All of that

falls to you. And so do the daily—*hourly*—complaints. Had you noticed that *every* electric outlet in the new flat also contains a telephone jack—"even in the bathroom." Maybe if you could just cross the wires, they'd electrocute themselves.

Lak Ah sayd, Ah'm not mahse'f today.

Having fumed and farted for better than two pages, it all boils down to just one thing: It's all up to us, dentures clamped onto our tongues until the blood gushes, to pretend that everything is simply divine; that Ed is the smartest man, the best father,* the kindest grandfather, the ho-ho-ho-iest great-grandfather ever born; that Florence is the cutest trick since Salome—if not before—and that it's all going to be new shelf paper (you), new engraved letter paper (me), and that everybody loves them. We'll undoubtedly be just as impossible at their ages.

God is pain, there is no love—

P.

*Can you believe that he had the chutzpah to suggest to me last year that we had always been "good pals" and "liked each other"? Even I was at a loss for words.

Pat did succeed in getting the apartment decorated, and he went to Chicago to help Ed and Florence move in the following spring. By that time, however, Ed's health had taken a precipitous downturn, and he was diagnosed with cancer, cirrhosis, and circulatory problems. In addition, he had fallen several times and sustained a concussion, a cracked rib, and a broken hip. After he moved into the Hancock building, he began to need constant attendance.

In October of 1968, fourteen-year-old Michael suffered his first romantic heartbreak. In a long letter to his father, he plaintively unburdened himself and asked Pat why he and Louise had chosen to remain separated without divorcing. Pat wrote him the following reply:

Manny dear—

Thanks so much for your letter of the twelfth. Thanks, too, for your views on the divorce question. I agree. If the Lynx or I happened to fall madly in love with someone else and wish to be free to remarry, it would be a different matter. While it is, perhaps, silly to remain married in name only while living a couple of thousands of miles apart, I don't mind it in the least. We will have been married for twenty years in December while you will be down here (no anniversary presents, please) and I am in the *habit* of being married to your mother—even though it is only a legal position. I love your mother, anyhow.

Betsy is softer-boiled than you are, in addition to being three years younger. If a divorce, which neither one of us actually *needs,* is going to make her lot any harder, then I say screw the whole thing.

Here is an original thought: Isn't Life an effing mess?

Speaking of Life and messes, don't regret—ever—loving anyone. Love is something which we have always enough of to pass around—to squander, if we wish. You can castigate yourself for loving foolishly or for wasting your affection and time on someone unworthy of the gift, but to what advantage? What has been has been. (I'm just a little hotbed of original clichés tonight!) I'm sorry that you and Kersten have broken up, but if you did so, you must have had good reasons for separating.

You have ten years—more if you like—to make a final choice and settle down. Use the time. You will find lots of Alices and lots of other types as well. Only you can choose the right one for you.

And why the hell this "boyfriend-girlfriend" set-up anyhow? Is it a passing fashion like crew cuts or cascades of hair? Are you simply Out unless you conform and pretend—if you don't feel like it, you can do no more—to be in love? Well, *perhaps* you can explain it to me in December. If you want to be alone, then *be* alone. It isn't a sin.

Well, any old fart who has six months up on you can sit around and pontificate, offering free advice (which is worth exactly what it costs). I won't do it—or even attempt to do it—to you. Another original thought: All men grow older, few wiser. Oh, I'm just bristling with tiresomeness tonight.

Thanks, really more than I can say, for your letter. If there is anything about the marriage or the divorce or the separation or the status quo to discuss, we will all four talk about it—pure Parliamentary procedure—when you come down for Christmas.

I love you,

Lance

The separation did indeed continue to be utterly without rancor. Louise and Pat stayed in close touch, and Louise often came down for visits with the children. Sometimes during the summer, Louise would make the rounds in Mexico, visiting friends in Puerto Vallarta, Acapulco, and Cuernavaca, while also stopping in Mexico City and spending time with Pat and the kids. Communication—and fondness—remained constant in what was an unusual but workable relationship.

Christmas of 1968 saw Pat diving with almost childlike delight into a project that was perfectly suited to him. Mexico City's Anglo-Mexican Cultural Institute, a kind of locus for anglophone expatriates, staged an old-fashioned Christmas pantomime of the kind seen all over England during the holiday season. Like the traditional British pantomime—which had nothing to do with pantomime in the American sense, but was instead a stage fantasy for family audiences with songs, comic plot, and special guest stars—it was to be a gossamer-light entertainment.

Pat volunteered not only to write the script and lyrics, but to design all the sets and costumes as well. The whole show would be a team effort among pals; Pat's friends Murray Grand and Harry Percer contributed the music and Nina Quirós would be one of the stars.

Turkish Delight, set in England and Turkey in 1222, turned out to be a ribald comedy aimed primarily at the sophisticated adults in the audience and peopled with actors and extras in revealing costumes. Nina Quirós played the evil Queen Sadistica, holding British Crusaders as prisoners under a spell in her palace, and Pat—in conical hat, massive robe, and three-inch fingernails—played the small ensemble role of one of her slaves. The leading male role of Ted Haggis, who travels from England to Turkey in search of his captive father, was played by a handsome young opera singer named Carlos Montes, who was in his twenties at the time. "I was going to be wearing a see-through costume," says Montes, "and Pat put me on a week's diet, a protein diet of nothing but meat. I actually did lose weight, which was good, because I had to wear a Turkish costume that was nothing but bikini pants, with a transparent gauze covering!"

"*My* costumes would have been suitable for a burlesque queen," says Nina Quirós, laughing. "But I wore 'em! It was hysterical. I got carried in on a litter by my slaves. Carlos was a trained opera singer, and I had been trained in the bathtub, but I drowned him out with my singing!"

Pat was totally in his element during the conception, production, and staging of *Turkish Delight*. As he had intended, some of the audience members—particularly those who had brought their kids—were a bit horrified by all the risqué goings-on. The Mexico City branch of the Ladies' Guild of Christchurch was particularly displeased, because the odalisques onstage were their daughters and their costumes were flimsy to say the least. Of course the show was a smash, and plenty of local celebrities came to see it, including screen star Merle Oberon (*Wuthering Heights*), who was in Mexico at the time.

For Pat, the experience was a joy from start to finish. Such moments were becoming scarcer and scarcer in his life.

EIGHTEEN

Life in Death Valley

While working on *Turkish Delight,* Pat became quite close to a handsome young British expatriate by the name of Alan Stark. Stark was a dancer and dance historian who had come to Mexico City to study indigenous dance traditions, and he became *Turkish Delight*'s choreographer. Stark, like Pat, also played one of Queen Sadistica's slaves and helped Pat design the costumes.

"Patrick had a whale of a time during *Turkish Delight,*" says Stark. "He enjoyed himself enormously. He was so good working with the young people; he just loved it. Those were the times that I found him at his most natural, because he could be absolute hell when people were treating him like The Great Patrick Dennis. It was the *real* Patrick I liked, the one who was kind and quite dear, not the one that came out so often when he was drunk at parties. We had such fun together working on the costumes in his apartment. That was a different Patrick from the other one."

During their short relationship, Pat's behavior was never predictable. Stark once escorted him to an elegant cocktail party given by a highly regarded journalist who was soon to become Mexico's ambassador to Canada. "Patrick was impossibly drunk," says Stark. "Finally, I just said, 'This is enough; we're going home.' I took him home, got the staff to put him to bed, and went back to the party. Patrick was not in good shape."

Pat grew terribly fond of Stark and asked him to move in with him and become his permanent lover. "I remember that night in his apartment," says Stark, "when he said to me, 'Stay with me, Alan. Stay and be my lover. Stay and help me keep myself in line.' It was almost a *cri de coeur*. But that was an enormous responsibility that I wasn't prepared to assume at that time in my life. I *was* in his bed at times and *did* like to look after him, although I wished he'd behave himself a bit more. He got so fed up with being perceived as Patrick Dennis, the author of *Auntie Mame*, and I think his drinking in social situations was his way of dealing with that. Sometimes I think he might have gotten just as drunk on a couple of strong cups of English tea. When we were alone together, he was able to just be Pat Tanner, and *that* was the Pat that I was fond of."

During Pat's years in Mexico, such romantic involvements tended to be few and brief. Certainly most people who were close to him sensed his loneliness, his deep need to be loved, his longing to be appreciated as Pat Tanner rather than the nonexistent Patrick Dennis. But the drunk and difficult side of Pat was becoming more and more pronounced. It's hard to imagine anyone but a martyr, a masochist, or a saint putting up with it permanently.

Quite often, Nina Quirós had to cart Pat home from parties within minutes after they had arrived. "You know what liquor does to everybody," says Nina. "And in those days, it was much more prevalent. It was really incredible what he could drink. The wine during dinner, the drinks before, the drinks after—gee, that's enough to kill a horse!"

"I think Nina took very good care of him," says one friend. "I do think she was very good for him, because I don't think he could handle a lot of things himself." At one wedding reception, Pat arrived looking resplendent in a velvet dinner suit with ruffled blouse, and had to make a grand, Auntie Mame–like entrance down a long stairway from the front door into the sunken living room. Already tipsy, he had to be helped down the stairs by Nina. But as the party started and the drinks kept flowing, Nina sensed that one more nip might send Pat over the edge. "Patrick, I don't feel well," she murmured, and Pat gallantly, tipsily escorted her back up the stairway to their waiting car. Then, Nina opened the car door, gently pushed Pat in, told the chauffeur to take him home to Pablo and step on it, and returned to the party on her own. By now she knew just when and how to avert disaster.

Michael and Betsy were still making their semiannual visits to spend time with Pat during school vacations. For both of them, particularly Michael, it was getting harder. As Michael matured, he was becoming quite different from his father, and their range of interests rarely overlapped. Michael was athletically inclined and tremendously musical; Pat was neither. Michael was following the hippie fashion of the day and letting his hair grow long; his father disdained that look. Michael wanted to listen to his Jimi Hendrix and Jim Morrison albums; Pat always had the stereo system set to Mantovani. Michael wanted to be out playing ball; Pat was a decidedly indoor animal. "Why do you always have to be so damn *physical?*" he would often bellow at both Michael and Betsy.

And as Michael entered puberty, he began developing a strong interest in girls. An observant kid, he was also taking notice of his father's social set and started putting two and two together. It was 1968, Michael was fourteen, and he was finding himself crammed uncomfortably by his father into a Nehru jacket and a peace medallion and trotted out to parties that looked like a local production of *The Boys in the Band*. "Are Peter and Bob married?" Michael asked his father one evening. "Yes, Michael," Pat snapped, "they *are* homosexuals."

Finally one night after a particularly stressful dinner, Pat accused Michael of being "patronizing," although Michael barely knew what the word meant. Pat, as usual, had been consuming a good deal of liquor. Tensions between Pat and Michael were rising to the breaking point, and at the end of the evening Pat called Michael upstairs for a private talk. "My father came out to me that night," recalls Michael, "and it was a *crushing* blow, because he seemed so all-powerful and totally masculine to me. It was shocking; tremendously shocking. I'll never forget that. He sort of put it in the form of a question, saying, 'Don't you know I'm homosexual?' Of course, I did a tremendous take. And his next line was, 'I'm not going to make a *pass* at you.' I realize in retrospect that he was saying, 'I'm not a monster; I'm just trying to tell you something.' In a way it was kind of a gentle thing to say, but it had such a weird edge on it that it didn't help me at the time. And then he told me the whole story about Guy Kent, and about attempting suicide, and the truth that had been covered up for the previous five years. In Dad's defense, I think he told me as soon as I could handle it."

After his confession, Pat denounced himself in front of Michael, insisting that he'd been a terrible failure to him as a father. "That weighed on him very heavily," says Michael. "Of course, my response was, 'Oh, no, you've been great; you've been a wonderful father; everything's fine.' Kids want everything to be fine so much that they'll deny a *lot*. But afterwards I developed a sort of phantom GI complaint—abdominal pain—and I was missing school. He immediately began calling in doctors. I remember being examined by one doctor, and it was very embarrassing, because there was really nothing wrong with me. I was just having a tough time emotionally."

The affection that Pat sometimes had trouble expressing to Michael began to come out in disquieting ways. "He would get very drunk," remembers Michael, "and I'd be involved in these sorts of boozy bear hugs. There wasn't anything sexual about it, but that's certainly something I don't want to do as a father—become shitfaced in front of my kids."

Pat was in pain, and Michael knew it. It was not easy for the fourteen-year-old to see his father in the grip of such torment. One of Michael's strongest memories is of a night in Mexico when Pat was in another room but Michael was within earshot. Michael heard Pat let out a sigh of absolute hopelessness and despair. That cry has echoed chillingly to him down through the decades.

The next couple of years proved difficult for father and son. Michael maintained an emotional distance from Pat and plunged into the drug culture, which held no interest for Pat. Perhaps Pat found it easier to respond to other people's adolescents, as was the case with Carlisle Brazy, the daughter of two of Pat's good friends. "I knew Pat when I was a teenager," she says, "and he always treated me like an adult, which, I think, was one of the reasons I adored him. He never talked down to me. He treated me like an equal. He talked to me about everything; there was no forbidden subject. And there were many things we discussed that I felt I couldn't talk to my parents about. That, I think, was part of Pat's magnetism with everybody. And I always loved the relationship that he kept with Louise, because she would come down to Mexico and be part of the whole thing, and I found that very liberal. She was doing her thing, he was doing his, and they had a great respect for each other."

Early 1969 found Pat in a new role: he began producing and directing an hour-long variety show at Mexico City's Channel 8. With his book sales going into decline, he saw this as a way to generate more income and threw himself into it quite wholeheartedly, striding about his set in great Cecil B. DeMille style in jodhpurs and boots and carrying a riding whip. He even took a total-immersion Spanish course at Berlitz, but had no aptitude for the language. Throughout his stay in Mexico, his Spanish remained rudimentary at best.

American journalist James Harvey was passing through Mexico City on his way back from a trip to Cuba and was invited by Pat to be a guest on the show and to share his impressions of that country. Harvey's segment began with a group of chorus girls doing a sexy dance; they eventually dispersed to reveal the rather professorial-looking Harvey sitting on a cube with his feet dangling. Harvey was then interviewed, with his answers translated by an interpreter. "It was an agreeable experience," remembers Harvey, "also a bit surreal! Pat got me tickets afterward for the Mexican stage premiere of *How to Succeed in Business Without Really Trying.*"

Harvey spent a week in Mexico City and attended several parties with Pat, who struck him as being very much the center of a large group of people who, while not particularly decadent, had a lot of money and a lot of time on their hands. "The *Pravda* correspondent was very tight with these people," he says, "and the guy was very much a Soviet party-liner. When I was alone, he would talk contemptuously about how these people were never doing anything useful. Which was kind of funny, because during the week or so I was there, he never missed a party."

Pat soon grew bored with the inefficiency and confusion at Channel 8; he also got fed up with having to beg for his salary. When he quit the show after a few months, he was already owed several thousand dollars.

Pat had been on one of his infrequent "moral kicks"—eating right, avoiding booze and cigarettes—but those never lasted long. Soon enough, he was up to his old tricks, getting drunk, making outrageous remarks, and doffing his clothes at every opportunity. One of his most brazen escapades took place when he and Murray Grand, who was visiting from New York, went to a lavish costume ball in Acapulco as escorts to Nina Quirós. Nina wore an outfit that was straight out of the Ziegfeld Follies; Pat and Murray were dressed in black leotards and tailcoats with a big red sash going around the leotard. "I think we borrowed the idea from a Minnelli movie with Marge and Gower Champion," says Grand. Before going to the party, Pat and Murray had been served a special luncheon at the home where they were staying, and Pat had stuffed most of the silverware and linen into his crotch. "It stood out so far," says Murray, "that when he turned sideways, it was just eye-boggling. He had forks and spoons, and linen napery; he might have even put a cup in there." When they arrived at the party, they walked out of the limo and straight into a gaggle of paparazzi. Pat turned sideways to offer them the best view, and storms of flashbulbs went off. No sooner had Pat walked through the front door (announced by a pair of powder-wigged, liveried servants) than a middle-aged lady latched onto him and began telling him how he absolutely *must* have written *Auntie Mame* all about her. Paying her no attention, he walked right into the swimming pool and stripped. He took off everything. First the linen came floating to the surface of the pool, then the forks and spoons clattered to the bottom.

Pat emerged dripping triumphantly in his birthday suit. Then, for the finishing touch, he took his teeth out.

"People were aghast," says Murray. "Their jaws dropped open. Someone rushed up and draped a tablecloth around him. And the woman who had adored him snapped, 'Well! I'll never read another book of *yours!*' I think we left rather soon afterward."

Another time, Pat went to dinner with Nina Quirós and several friends at his favorite restaurant, the Rivoli. Plastered once again, he spat out a mouthful of wine after a sommelier poured him a taste from the bottle Pat had just ordered. After demanding a new bottle, he literally drank himself under the table. When he resurfaced and took his place in his seat again, he was naked. The staff wrapped him up in a tablecloth and rushed him out. Nina, of course, was humiliated.

"Really, Patrick with that naked department . . . ," she says today. "I don't know why he thought he was so gorgeous with his clothes off. None of us are! Or even were! He did it in Cuernavaca, he did it in Acapulco, he did it in Mexico City—I guess he figured he'd run out of places to do it in! Taking his clothes off was such an everyday occurrence; everyone eventually got used to it." Pat even had a portrait photographer do a full-length photo of him wearing nothing but a Spanish hat, with a rose clenched between his teeth.

The ceaseless parade of *Auntie Mame* admirers often evoked less than gracious responses in Pat. Once, while he was having dinner at the Rivoli, a female fan introduced herself and launched into a lengthy, fawning monologue. While nodding silently, Pat raised his long legs straight up and crossed his ankles behind his neck. Celebrities rarely enjoy being interrupted at dinner; still, Pat could have found a less insulting way to handle the situation.

Throughout all the madness in Mexico, Abe Badian of Teaneck, New Jersey, remained not only Pat's accountant but one of his most trusted friends. To most eyes, the two would have made an unlikely duo, but the facts-and-figures, pencil-pushing family man and the flamboyant eccentric became the closest of buddies. Twice a year Abe and his wife, Nan, would fly down to Mexico. After a day or two of business, Pat, Abe, and Nan would always take off together for trips to places like Acapulco, Puerto Vallarta, Oaxaca, and Guadalajara. "We had *wonderful* times together," says Badian. "Pat exposed us to a way of life we would never have experienced." When Abe and Nan's daughter had her thirteenth birthday, Pat arranged a special party and boat trip for her in the floating gardens of Xochimilco. He had the entire boat lavishly decorated in flowers, according to local tradition, with her name spelled out on the prow. "But don't put your hand in the water," he cautioned her. "It'll come out a stump!"

"Pat had utter trust in honest Abraham," says Nan Badian. "Many nights in Mexico City I would go up to sleep while he and Abe stayed downstairs talking. And I think he confided to Abe, not only about his business life, but his life. I know that's why he was always so very anxious for us to come down. He was always asking us why we had to wait to come till after tax season. He kept saying, 'Can't you come down sooner?' "

Abe did what he could to keep Pat's spending on track, but his efforts were basically futile. "Mr. Badian is, as always, fit to be tied," wrote Pat in a letter to Michael. "But if we spend our money and ask his permission after the evil deed is done, he always manages to dig it up from somewhere, somehow, some time later." Pat's newest plan was to build a lavish home for himself in Cuernavaca, seventy-five minutes from Mexico City, and move there for good. After only a year in his penthouse on Avenida Nuevo Leon, Pat had had enough of Mexico

City landlords and flimsy modern apartments. In a letter to Michael, he wrote:

. . . The penthouse continues to disintegrate and I can't wait for my landlord, Sr. Coq—who is a priq—to get back from the Orient so that I can break this long lease and settle down in some nice hotel suite where they are accustomed to such foreign eccentricities as expecting ceilings to remain up, hot water to be hot, lights to light, windows to open *and* close and repairs to be made. Mr. Coq typifies Mexican landlords—and probably all others, as well—in feeling that his responsibilities begin and end with collecting the rent—and raising it.

. . . I simply cannot wait to shuck this place and all the servants. (I'm now down to three; doing it gradually to avoid withdrawal symptoms.) I plain haven't the stamina for Gracious Living.

Cheery news from Chicago: Your grandparents are down in the dumps on the forty-sixth floor. He is riddled with cancer—I'm not certain whether he knows it or not—and walks with a cane. He has a year or two at the most left to him. At least he is not drinking. *She is.* At 83 she confounds medical science by being as strong as a horse—and not nearly as intelligent. Having been pronounced in perfect condition, she has taken to her bed with "total exhaustion," Scotch and sherry. Poor Barbara tries to lock up the liquor, get the dizzy old woman up and dressed and acting like a human being instead of some sort of root vegetable. Senile dementia.

Well, it appears that I will be an orphan before I'm fifty. I hope so. And I hope that the Lynx and I can arrange matters for you and Min *much* sooner. Geriatrics are just Jim-dandy, I suppose, but I do not fancy myself in the Senior Citizens' Sunset Trailer Court playing shuffleboard with my teeth in the back pocket of my Bermuda shorts.

. . . Is there anything of mine—furniture, pictures, books, clocks, china, silver blah, blah, blah—which you would like to have before I break up housekeeping? (*Don't* tell me that you want the porcelain stove, as that is a little difficult to ship.) I plan to take only the best Regency furniture for my new living room and the Charles X stuff for my bedroom-library-workroom. The malachite and the Bristol glass can come along, too. If there is anything you fancy, yell now.

Here's the bottom of the page and I'm not going to squander another on you. Write me before we see each other in November.

Always love,

Lance.

Ten days later, fifteen-year-old Michael sent Pat an emotional letter from his boarding school in Putney, Vermont. He poured out his heart to his father about his unhappiness at Putney, and the religious crisis he felt he was undergoing. Pat responded.

Dear, dear, dear Mike—

It makes me so unhappy to know that you're unhappy. The horrors of adolescence are said to be rather common. Being then, as now, shallow and frivolous, I never suffered. We would probably both be better off if you could give me some of your depth and I could give you some of my shallowness. Alas, that cannot be.

Even my own religious crisis wasn't a crisis. I was simply walking along a street in Evanston (Sherman Avenue to be specific) and suddenly a little voice inside me said, "No." End of religious crisis and I haven't thought about the subject in 35 years.

You are wise to anticipate a year or two more of misery. But do you also realize that it will come to an end?

. . . Michael, I do feel so terribly sorry for you and there isn't one blessed thing that anyone can do to help you except shut up and leave you alone. About the only comfort I can offer is to tell you that it will pass. And that's precious little.

. . . Big stink in San Miguel de Allende. Their bully-boy mayor has sent the police force out to shave the heads of hippies. While hippies have less than no appeal for me, it's no one's business how they dress or wear their hair and it's a very unhealthy symptom when some Fascistic little politician presumes to move in on people's civil rights. Lots of mild outrage about it, indignant letters to the press, etc. etc. That's a good sign. The cops here in the Federal District were going around snipping hair a couple of years ago and, if I do say so, my own nasty little letter to the *News* put a stop to it. Although, to give the Mexican police their due, they have had a terrible lot of trouble with big gangs of North American hippies who have moved in on helpless little provincial towns and absolutely destroyed them.

You've never told me about the Woodstock Festival. Please do. Or must I wait until Thanksgiving to worm it out of you?

Well, do try to be as happy as you can, considering the circumstances. I wish that I could help you, but I can only sympathise.

Love,

P.

Shortly after this letter, Pat contracted a case of typhoid that was nearly strong enough to kill him. After being bedridden for a month, he slowly began to mend. "Although more times than one," he wrote Michael, "the old Leopard heard the distant strains of the Celestial Calliope and the voice of the Great Ringmaster announcing Lancie's final leap through the Eternal Flaming Hoop, I am still here in this Vale of Kitty Litter. . . . Pablo has force-fed me like a Strasbourg goose so that my waistline is now up to 32 from 29. He is doing all the cooking and the food has never been better." Pat signed the letter "Typhoid Mary."

Edward Tanner finally succumbed to cancer in November 1969. Pat, who was in the middle of building his new home in Cuernavaca, dropped everything and flew to Chicago. After the funeral, he and his sister, Barbara, urged their mother to enter a nursing home where she could be cared for properly. Florence agreed and voluntarily moved into the Mary Haven facility in Wilmette, Illinois. (She would remain there until her death in 1974.) While Pat was still in Chicago, he and Barbara contacted the woman who had been Edward's mistress for more than forty years, and they took her out to dinner together. After he returned to Mexico, Pat wrote Barbara his thoughts on the experience:

—She is an awfully nice and attractive woman. They've been together since the twenties and I'm glad that we had dinner together and that she was treated like a human being and not simply dumped like the Scarlet Woman she's supposed to be. Unless he made some sort of private provision for her (but with what?) she is left with nothing and doesn't seem to expect, want or need anything. She lives very comfortably. I do think that it would be nice of us, however, to slip her some simple, personal memento of the old bastard. . . . It can simply be sent to her with a little note and that should take care of 40 years of devotion. It's like a re-make of *Back Street*.

On January 31, 1970, Pat officially gave up the penthouse and moved to temporary quarters in Cuernavaca, a city he had already nick-named Death Valley due to its high percentage of elderly retired Americans. He began putting up his new house in the tony Rancho Tetela neighborhood. Built to his own design, it may well have reflected his depression and deteriorating self-esteem: it was perversely turned *away* from the magnificent mountain views that its site offered. Only the maid and butler's rooms were planned to take advantage of the mountain panorama. "Views," sniffed Pat, "are for servants."

While waiting for his house to be built, Pat completed a new novel entitled *Paradise*. Another multicharacter extravaganza, it takes place at an exotic coastal resort hotel in Acapulco. When an earthquake separates the resort from the mainland and turns it into an island, stranding its inhabitants, the true personalities of the guests and the staff nakedly emerge. Meanwhile, unscrupulous TV news teams are competing to milk the misery of the situation for all it's worth. A kind of cross between *Grand Hotel* and Billy Wilder's *Ace in the Hole*, the book shows Pat at his nastily observant best, so much so that it was simply too dark for many readers. Even many old friends of Pat's, to this day, feel that the tone of the book is too unpleasant. But the characters who are selfish, conniving, and cowardly are balanced by good guys whom the reader is rooting for—such as the book's heroine, Liz Martinez, who owns the resort, and her best and most trusted employee—whose name happens to be Pablo:

> *"Senora?"*
> Liz turned. It was Pablo, her favorite among the servants. He was tall, good-looking, meticulously clean. How old? Twenty-five, Liz supposed. . . . Liz had never in her life seen anyone work as hard as Pablo. From seven in the morning, when he tapped on her bedroom door with her breakfast tray, until after midnight, when he put out the lights in the *sala*, Pablo was working. And everything was done with an air. Even now the little stack of letters addressed to Liz was piled upon a silver waiter, a wedding present salvaged from Liz's first marriage.

Through his ingenuousness and simple decency, Pablo ends up winning the heart of a plucky young American girl fed up with the snobbish, social-climbing world of her parents.

Although many of the novel's characters are clichés—a sweet, dumb hooker-with-a-heart-of-gold, a lecherous Spanish lounge lizard, an aging American queen and his sleazy kept boy—Pat's witty touch and vivid ear for accents and dialogue keep the book a fresh and funny read, and the plot's suspense increases as the newborn island keeps precariously shrinking in a series of landslides. Like *Genius*, *Paradise* glories in the culture clash of American tourists overrunning Mexico, and also like *Genius,* it would have been perfect material for a feature film. *Paradise* was, in fact, optioned for the movies several times, although it never got any further than the development stage.

Pat's editor on the book was his old friend Julian Muller, now at Harcourt Brace Jovanovich. This time, Pat needed no help from Julian to give it a satisfying ending. Nonetheless, Pat dedicated it to him.

While completing *Paradise,* Pat was asked by his friend and *Little Me* editor, Peggy Brooks, if he'd like to write a nonfiction book to be entitled *The Mexicans.* Pat wrote her and declined, with good reason, and also offered up his wrenchingly frustrated feelings about the *Auntie Mame* albatross:

I just don't feel up to writing a piece called *The Mexicans.* First of all, I don't feel confident of knowing enough about the subject even after nearly five years of living here . . . then if the book were too critical, they would probably deport me; but mostly because every point would have to be argued ad nauseam with bores at parties for the rest of my life.

Don't fret about my developing another Auntie Mame. It simply won't be done. All of my subsequent books, while perhaps lacking the slapdash vitality of A. M., have been better, but she is the heroine the public adores and will always identify with me. There are dozens of similar cases—Anita Loos has been stuck with Lorelei Lee for 45 years; A. A. Milne with that boring bear; Margaret Mitchell and Tom Heggen, had they lived, would have found a readership furious that their new characters were not Scarlett O'Hara and Mr. Roberts. A book *can* be too successful for an author's future and sequels are just too deadly to bother with. No, I must stoically content myself with modest successes of, say a million case-bound copies and a petulant public comparing every word with those in *Auntie Mame,* which they haven't read for ten years and only think they remember.

Pat went on in the letter to update Peggy on the latest news from Death Valley in his typically droll manner:

I'm getting a sty on my left eye. Pablo treats it with boiled cabbage leaves. These quaint Hispano-Indio cures actually work, although I smell like a side order of sauerkraut.

Three dashing New Orleans gentlemen are coming down to stay with me for Holy Week. Just a word at a dinner party on Monday and my telephone has not been still. I could really rent them out by the hour. With eight unclaimed balls under the same roof, every lovely blue-haired hostess in Death Valley has been clamoring, poor naïve things!

While squatting in Cuernavaca and waiting for his house to be finished, Pat often spent several days at a stretch in the home of his friends Thew and Katherine Wright, an American couple who lived much of the year in Mexico. Thew would go off on fishing trips, and Katherine would ask Pat to stay and help her take care of their eight-year-old son, Clinton. Pat was not exactly the baby-sitting type, but Clinton was a winsome, sophisticated little kid, a kind of real-life Young Patrick from *Auntie Mame,* and he and Pat enjoyed spending time together. "He was very sardonic," says Clinton today, "and I remember him always having a half smile on his face, sitting back ready to make a quip. He was very warm to me, though, and I remember that. Now, as an adult, I know what it is to be warm to children and to acknowledge their presence. It's easy not to do that. I liked him and looked forward to his visits. It was always a kind of adventure of its own."

Indeed it was. Pat would often help little Clinton with his third-grade English homework. One assignment was to make sentences out of a series of assigned words. *Fix* was one of them. The next day in school, Clinton proudly read aloud the sentence that Pat had given him: "My Granny needs a fix." Clinton's proper British schoolmarm glared at him like a Gorgon.

By May of 1970, the Cuernavaca house was nowhere near completion. Pat was blaming the architect, whom he considered young and incompetent. Pat was also beginning to have trouble with Pablo, who, according to him, was becoming "the rakehell of Cuernavaca." Pablo was already the owner of a Volkswagen for which he had never repaid Pat, and he was tearing all over town in it on alcoholic binges. "I have now beached his Volkswagen," Pat wrote Barbara, "save for essential trips to the market and such and am trying the silent treatment of icily polite monosyllables and refusal of all assistance. It has brought him to his knees so effectively that I may permit him to resume serving me around Saturday or Sunday."

But the problems did not end there. Pablo, to whom Pat had been like a father, started a scam against Pat that destroyed the relationship. While Pat was wondering why it was taking so long to get his Cuernavaca house completed, Pablo was stealing the bricks and concrete every night and selling them off to other contractors. Many of Pat's friends were not surprised; they had assumed from the beginning that Pablo was larcenous. "He even stole from *me*," says Katherine Walch, who had returned home from one of Pat's Calle de Varsovia parties to find her purse rifled.

Pat was so devastated by Pablo's actions, and by the feckless inefficiency of the architect and contractors, that he decided to wash his hands of the new house altogether. "The service quarters will be habitable on September 10," he wrote Michael, "and the moment the rest of the place is finished and furnished it's going onto the market. After all of the needless complications and delays in building it, I hate every one of its 12,000 bricks and will never be happy living there."

Pat abandoned the house in September 1970 at 80 percent completion. He simply walked away from it. Someone else bought it at a giveaway price, completed it, and turned around and sold it. Meanwhile, Pat was going to be stuck squatting in Cuernavaca. He had taken a year's lease on a house he didn't even particularly like and had poured huge amounts of money into rendering it habitable. By now he was just about broke.

Paradise was not going to be published for a good six months and Pat needed to make some money. He also needed something with which to occupy himself while waiting out his time in Cuernavaca. He began work on a new novel that—a first for him—would have bisexuality as its central theme. His old friend Peggy Brooks had recently become an editor at Coward-McCann, and Pat hoped desperately that she would be able to publish it. He had not been a hot commodity as an author for eight years, and there was no guarantee that Peggy would be able to convince Coward-McCann that Pat was an author worth publishing in a world that had changed so completely since the days of *Auntie Mame*. In a letter written to Peggy on November 11, 1970, Pat sets forth a plea so grave he is afraid to use the first person singular:

Yes, Peggy, darling, One *does* have a novel for you!

One has written half of the dearest, sweetest, shortest little book ever begun. (One hundred pages in two weeks!) It's about a happily married couple who both fall in love with the same guy—and One doesn't mean Kent. . . . One may be as out of fashion as an Empress Eugenie hat, but One still keeps on working (One must) and One is in dire financial straits. (What with taxes and One's idiocy, One can't even support One's children. Luckily, Louise still has her job at Schrafft's and the tips keep Mike in Putney and Betsy in Brearley. But her feet hurt.)

One needs m-n-y.

. . . It's a nice, clean book. No hay scenes. (Let the reader imagine whatever low, vile filth he wishes!) It has your name under its non-title. It's like that great non-seller, *Tony,* but much shorter and much, much better. And it has a happy ending!

. . . One decided that One's new house was a ghastly mistake and One simply stopped the whole construction at 80 per cent completion. One should have every one of its 12,000 bricks shoved up One's -rs (rectum) for being such a fool. But then, One has always been. But still, utterly adorable, Honest Abe is shitting bricks (all 12,000) about One's financial affairs. . . .

. . . It is now nearly seven o'clock in the morning and One is going back to bed before the standing army of carpenters, painters arrive to disturb One's cucumber eye masque. What is worse, they all have to be paid today. One could puke.

Come down. (It's called Editorial Work With a Difficult Author.) Bring John. One Loves You—

Fortunately, Peggy and her bosses at Coward-McCann—Executive Editor Ellis Amburn and President Jack Geoghegan—liked Pat's hundred-page sample. They offered an advance to Pat's agent, but it was less than he had previously received. The numbers on his last few books couldn't justify more. Nonetheless, Pat accepted the offer and was happy and relieved to find a sympathetic editor and publisher. On December 3, 1970, he wrote Peggy:

I'm so glad that you like the new book enough to publish it. The Coward-McCann offer is more than fair. Even generous, considering that this novel will probably never take off and soar. As it isn't bang-bang enough to be another *Auntie Mame* or dirty enough to shock its way to the top, it will be read and cherished only by people like the Beales and the Thorndikes [the novel's protagonists], who are, after all, the *best* audience. There just aren't enough of them.

. . . And while you're wallowing in that Lola Montez bathtub, please think of a title for this. Something short and sweet and to the point.

Well, thanks so much again for your belief in the book. Hope it will do better than we both think it will. But, at least, we're not expecting the moon.

Peggy Brooks had some good suggestions to make regarding Pat's new novel, and Pat was happy to incorporate them. Meanwhile, Harcourt Brace Jovanovich was set to publish *Paradise* in late March of 1971. From February 7 to March 3, Pat went to Central and South America and made a "shopping trip" to see whether there were any countries that he might consider moving to. The journey was not productive. "Costa Rica could be cheapa," he wrote Abe and Nan Badian on a postcard. "I would love to live in Rio de Janeiro," he wrote his sister, Barbara, "which is pretty and gay and where I know a lot of people. But I *don't* know Portuguese and really can't afford the move, as it's about three times as far away as Europe."

The publication party for *Paradise* was a huge extravaganza held in Acapulco, as much for the benefit of the new Hotel Paraiso-Marriott as for the book. It took place on the hotel's private beach, and Pat made a spectacular entrance. Like Botticelli's Venus, he arrived on the water, borne in on a surfboard by four hunky young Mexican beach boys and fully dressed in a shirt, jacket and slacks. *Paradise*'s editor, Julian Muller, was sent down to Acapulco for the party by Harcourt Brace Jovanovich. "It was a sodden affair," he remembers. "Some of the creatures who surrounded Pat at that time looked as though they'd come right out of the book. I don't know if that promotion did any good for anybody; it seemed pretty pointless to me. My acquaintanceship with Mexico remains happily thin. It seemed to me that this kind of life Pat was leading couldn't be anything but destructive." Then Muller adds with a chuckle, "That's my amazing observation after having spent twenty-four or forty-eight hours with him down there."

Paradise sold respectably, but was not a blockbuster. It only increased Pat's concern about the future of his writing career. With the series of professional disappointments piling up like a logjam, Pat could only keep up a merry front for so long. The shame of being rejected by his reading public was painful for him to bear, and additionally the threat of poverty now loomed.

On a brief visit to New York City, Pat ran into an old friend, Ross Claiborne, a former Franklin Spier employee who was now editor in chief at Dell. Claiborne suggested they have lunch together.

"It was a very, very sad lunch," says Claiborne. "Pat was really very lachrymose and said, 'You know, Ross, people really don't want me anymore. They don't want my frivolous brand of humor. I'm all washed up.' I said, 'Pat, that's not true! You're one of the most talented people I know; you've got this genius, this wit! Of *course* you're not washed up.' But I really couldn't pull him out of this mood of despair. I did everything in my power to buoy his spirits, but it didn't take. I ended that lunch feeling so sad. I said, 'Pat, send *me* something. I'm sure I can do something with it.' But he never did. He was at the lowest depths of his discouragement about his professional life. I think he left that lunch feeling just as discouraged as when he came in."

In spite of his depressed spirits, Pat had completed and christened his new novel. Now titled *3-D,* it was of average length—254 pages— not a quickie as Pat had envisioned. The book wasn't scheduled to be published until the following year, and Pat needed an income. In July of 1971, when the lease on his house in Cuernavaca was up, he returned to Mexico City and moved into an elegant old home from the Porfirian era on Calle de Tabasco, in the Colonia Roma neighborhood, not far from his former penthouse. Executives at Mexico's Channel 10 had offered him and Nina Quirós positions as writers; the two of them went to work there as a team. They developed a talk show called *Woman to Woman,* which Nina hosted in English and Pat produced and wrote. Unfortunately, the program was not successful, and Pat and Nina had trouble attracting advertisers. "I'm working like a dog and losing more money at it every day," Pat wrote his sister, Barbara. "If you thought Channel 8 was a little nest of inefficiency, you should see Channel 10!" Within a few months, the show was off the air.

Undaunted, Pat and Nina tried a new venture: public relations. The two formed Producciónes y Relaciónes, S.A., and operated it out of Pat's elaborately decorated Calle de Tabasco basement. With their International Set social contacts and their flair for throwing extravagant parties, the two were naturals for the PR trade. Nina already had publicity experience; she felt certain that Patrick's name on their letterhead would be a draw. And they didn't lack for business: Pat did turn out to be good at selling the firm and bringing in new clients. The problem was getting everyone to pay up. "Business improves daily," Pat wrote Michael in January of 1972, "but trying to collect from our clients is much harder than working for them. One bounced a rather large check on us last week when Nina and I were slaving our asses off in lovely Acapulco, which means that our rent check bounced and that the bookkeeping is total pandemonium."

Michael had graduated from Putney by that time and was attending Antioch College in Ohio after having spent the previous summer supervising a gaggle of kindergarteners at New York's Village Community School. His sister, Betsy, was now fifteen; she was beginning to ask questions, and Michael wanted Pat's permission to tell her about their father's sexual orientation. "Of course I don't mind your telling Minnie the truth about me," Pat wrote back. "Had she been your age at the time I told you, I would have included her in the conversation instead of sending her downstairs to feel excluded and unwanted. If a child is old enough and bright enough to understand the truth, it is ridiculous—and dangerous—to lie to him. He will eventually find out the truth and never trust you again."

Pat also filled Michael in on the details of some of the latest parties he and Nina had staged:

Acapulco is trashier than ever. But we have four clients there and must visit this suburb of Miami a lot oftener than we really care to. Last week we staged La Noche de los Tres Reyes (Epiphany) for the Paraiso-Marriott; the gala opening of Julio Chávez's Acapulco branch (overelaborate and overpriced gladrags); and a dazzling fashion parade at Coyuca 22 (an overelaborate and overpriced restaurant). Clients all and more trouble than your 20 five-year-olds.

The Night of the Three Kings was a beautiful and deeply religious occasion. Instead of bearing such attractive and useful gifts as frankincense and myrrh, *my* Magi descended in the Otis dressed in gorgeous caftans and headdresses by Julio Chávez (Melchor, the assistant manager; Gaspar, the accountant; Baltasar, the schwartzeh who sings in the nightclub), to pass out 800 *adorable* little figures (fortunately with very rough edges) among the gringo yokels waiting in the lobby, while the mariachis bleated out such lovely Yuletide airs as "Mama Loves Mambo" from the mezzanine balcony. *Rompope* (a horrid Mexican version of eggnog with *lots* of sugar) and *rasco* (a Twelfth Night cake that tastes like Mother Feinstein's matzohs) were served. Yummy! *Rompope* is a lot more potent than people think it is and so by seven-thirty there were kiddies throwing up, mothers passing out, hideous family quarrels and the whole thing filmed for coast-to-coast television. Another triumph for Nina and me. . . .

Now we are busily planning a *fun* leap year party which, malheureusement, the Lynx will miss. That poor cat was just born unlucky.

Then to think of a cute crucifixion on the Marriott beach for Easter . . .

Nina, who is now shrieking Spanish over the telephone, sends love. Now to confer about doing something clever for Brangus, Mexico's largest purveyors of quality beef. I suggested resoling our shoes with their porterhouse steaks. Nina doesn't like it. She has no feeling for true public relations.

After one of those big Acapulco events, a plastered Pat was waiting in the airport with Nina for the flight back to Mexico City. Suddenly there was a power failure and all the lights went out. In the momentary pitch-darkness, just before the lights went back on, Pat yelled out at the top of his lungs, "Nina! Get your hand *off my cock!*"

"I wanted to kill him!" says Nina. "We were surrounded by businesspeople who knew me. He passed right out on the flight, and when he woke up back in Mexico City, he'd already forgotten the whole thing."

If Pat and Nina could only have collected the money they were owed by their impressive client list (which also included Admiral Television and several large Pepsi-Cola bottling plants), they would have made Producciónes y Relaciónes a success. Unfortunately, that was not to be, and the firm folded after about a year.

Pat had spent most of that year depressed. He drastically curtailed his social life, stopped going to the International Set parties, and usually took his dinner on a tray in bed. Pat now felt that he had exhausted all possibilities in Mexico while enduring more than his share of adversity in doing so. He had little money left and no regular, dependable source of income. It was time to make another big change.

NINETEEN

North of the Border

While living in Mexico, Pat had become friendly with the American expatriate E. G. McGrath and his lover, the metal sculptor Victor Salmones. Based in Acapulco, McGrath and Salmones were co-owners of the Gallery Victor, which featured the work of Salmones and other prominent Mexican artists and sculptors. Salmones had become highly successful, and the Gallery was thriving. Pat suggested that it was time for a Gallery Victor in the United States, and McGrath and Salmones invited Pat to help them start one and become co-owner.

Pat went off to the United States with McGrath on a scouting tour of cities that might be good possibilities for the first American Gallery Victor. While there, the two stopped by McGrath's hometown of Sedalia, Missouri. Pat was introduced by McGrath to two elderly women, the Hicks twins, and he was fascinated by them. Before long, he had transmuted them into new characters and had renamed them Ethylle and Marjie—with a circle instead of a dot over the j. As far as Pat was concerned, Ethylle and Marjie Hicks had serviced the entire Sedalia High football team every year. His next step was to turn himself and McGrath into Marjie and Ethylle. McGrath even got letters from Marjie. "Pat eventually had Marjie taking up with a spic named Victor," says McGrath, amused today, "and opening a hot-tamale joint in Kansas City. He described their costumes and everything—off-the-shoulder Mexican blouses and roses in their hair. Pat loved inventing personas, you know."

Eventually Pat and McGrath settled on Houston as an ideal place to open Gallery Victor. So many wealthy Texans had been visiting Acapulco and bringing back Victor's sculpture that Houston already had a certain awareness of Victor Salmones and his work. Pat and McGrath chose the upscale new Galleria shopping mall as their location, where their neighbors would include Tiffany, Mark Cross, Neiman Marcus, Sloane's, Lugène, Dempsey & Carroll, Bally, and Sotheby-Parke-Bernet. The store would overlook the Galleria's huge indoor ice-skating rink, which formed the center of the mall's atrium structure.

Pat Tanner moving to a place like Houston almost sounds like a bad joke. But Pat knew he needed money, and, certain that this was the perfect way to get it, he approached the entire enterprise with an optimistic, open mind. When he announced his plans to Michael in a letter on June 14, 1972, he explained, "Houston is very nice; unbelievably cosmopolitan for Texas; rich, rich, rich; and starved for the kind of painting, sculpture and just plain junk which we can supply in vast quantities."

Pat left Mexico with little fanfare and moved to Houston with McGrath and Salmones in late August 1972. His seven-year stint in Mexico had been marked by frustration, depression, and dissipation, yet he had been able to enjoy plenty of good times and had made close friends. Behind him he may have left some ruined parties and some International Set hostesses who were just as happy to see him go. But he also left a good share of pals who would miss him and would always carry fond memories of one of the most colorful expats on the Mexico City social scene. As his Junior League Follies singing partner Pansy Kimbro says, "He was absolutely adorable. I love great characters, and he certainly was one of them. He was such a marvelous snob. Snobs can be so much fun!"

The Houston branch of Gallery Victor was due to open in September, but annoying delays of every sort popped up and kept it from opening until mid-November. Pat did a lot of waiting and thumb-twiddling in unpleasant circumstances. Most of his furniture had arrived from Mexico in shards, and one of the few pieces that was intact—his enormous antique sleigh bed—could not be fit through either the door or the window of his rented apartment at 1909 Brun Street. He spent his nights sleeping on a mattress on the floor in the sparsely furnished flat. Still, Pat made the best of it and in a letter to Michael described Houston as "a very pleasant town to live in."

While they were waiting to open the Gallery, Pat was taken by McGrath and Salmones to a famous drag bar in Houston called The High Camp. The queens all did special numbers in Pat's honor, and Pat, who always loved a good drag show, was delighted. His particular favorite among the performers was a three-hundred-pounder who had been a former halfback on a Miami football team. "Every Fourth of July," says E. G. McGrath, "he would pose as the Statue of Liberty."

Gallery Victor finally opened on November 19, 1972. In addition to Pat, Victor and McGrath, there were five other employees, all of whom were somewhat in awe of the great Patrick Dennis. "They couldn't help being impressed by him," says McGrath, "and he couldn't help letting them *be* impressed. Of course, he *did* try to turn Houston into Mayfair and Piccadilly, which you can't really do." Pat put in slavish twelve-hour days at the Gallery, and it seemed to be paying off: the gallery received plenty of attention and plenty of patrons. Pat, however, couldn't always disguise his somewhat supercilious view of the Houstonians. Many of his customers sensed his somewhat disdainful attitude and tried to put him back in his place. One man came in with his wife, pointed out one of Victor's sculptures, and asked his wife how she thought it would look in the rec room. Then he asked Pat how much it was, and Pat answered, "Oh, it's ten thousand dollars. I can just *imagine* your surprise, considering what you must have spent on your last purchase at Sotheby's." The man responded to this snotty remark by pulling ten thousand-dollar bills out of his wallet and handing them over to Pat.

"For once," says McGrath, laughing, "Pat was speechless. I told him, 'That'll teach you never to try to put a Texan down.' "

Within weeks after the gallery opened, 3-D was published. Set in Cuernavaca, it focused on two American married couples in their early thirties: Connie and Peter, who have turned an abandoned monastery into a luxurious home for themselves, and their close friends Hal and Jane, who are paying them an extended visit as houseguests. When a stunningly handsome but bone-stupid young man enters their lives, Connie and Peter both find themselves becoming obsessed with him. They start to play out their fantasies under Hal and Jane's disapproving eyes. Hal, who is a fairly progressive young minister, finds his self-proclaimed liberal tolerance stretched to the limit.

Married "swingers" were all the rage during the early seventies, as was the Unisex movement, which blurred the barriers of gender. Pat had set up a good premise that could have resulted in a trenchant, bitter satire of that era's newfound sexual liberation, and along the way he did score some effective points. Although the main body of the novel was enjoyable, the resolution was strained and disappointing. As Pat had decided from the start, nobody actually went to bed with anybody. Like the stripper who does little more than take off a glove, Pat just didn't deliver the goods. Instead he ended the book with the rather shopworn device of a situation almost identical to the one that began it, with the protagonists, having learned nothing, about to fall into the same trap. The cumulative effect was that of a shaggy-dog story—all that tease and titillation led to little of real substance.

"This is fiction for genteel sophisticates who seek glamour and risqué coffee-table reading," read the *New York Times* review, "something that isn't so outrageous as Terry Southern or so offensive as William Burroughs . . . as naughty comedy it belongs to an honorable tradition that includes *Getting Gertie's Garter, Up in Mabel's Room,* the blackout skits of the old *Vanities* and Dwight Fiske's ditties about Mrs. Pettibone and Ida the Wayward Sturgeon."

Faint praise indeed, and certainly a confirmation of Pat's fears of becoming old-fashioned. Even Peggy Brooks and the Coward-McCann editorial staff were disappointed by 3-*D*. "When we were reading it," says Brooks, "my boss as well as myself, everybody felt that it just wasn't as lively as Pat's previous work; that it was more trouble for him to write it; that he just didn't want to write any more books. There wasn't much meat in 3-*D*, really."

The weak reception for 3-*D* made Pat decide to put down his pen. With abundantly clear and unsentimental thinking, he wrote Michael: "I have written my last, as far as I know. Out of fashion and I've said everything I have to say. Twice. You can pick up the torch." (Michael was indeed showing signs of having inherited some of his father's writing talent and had already received encouragement from him along those lines, although Michael would not ultimately choose the profession.)

The gallery was Pat's last resort. It had to succeed.

And at first, it did. It sold not only Victor's sculpture, but the work of other artists as well, including a wide selection of paintings, tapestries, and antiques, and it did not lack for patrons. In a letter to Michael on January 12, 1973, Pat described the Galleria mall in detail, enumerating the world-famous upscale names of its shops, and then went on to say:

> And through its elegant portals pass the seediest slobs in the world. I don't mind wasting time and breath talking to people who can't afford to buy our junk as long as they are pleasant and interested. But I can walk away pretty fast from those chip-on-the-shoulder, my-boy-in-the-third-grade-could-paint-a-picture-better-than-that types. Lots of hippies blowing grass with dirty hair, Theodore Roosevelt moustaches, ill-kempt beards, and carefully torn and faded jeans—far more standardized than the gray flannel suits they were all rebelling against some years ago. However, they are capable of devastatingly brilliant passages of conversation: "It's like wow! But, man, I mean it's wow."

> . . . I believe that Lucille Ball is going to film the musical of *Mame*. . . . Miss Ball is a good comedienne, but a little too c-mm-n for the role. However, it has by now been played by so many women that it really doesn't make much difference who does it.

Mame was indeed filmed with a miscast Lucille Ball cavorting through overblown sets while croaking Jerry Herman's score. The entire package was fairly repellent and was denounced by the critics.

Pat was still putting in long twelve-hour days at the gallery and also trying to do the Houston "social bit" as much as was necessary to keep the gallery going. That meant, as he wrote his sister, Barbara, "that you can do two parties a day here—three on Saturdays, Sundays, and holidays." It was too much, and Pat had little desire to accept all the invitations that were coming his way.

Pat's *Little Me/First Lady* pal Dody Goodman was passing though Houston on a tour and stopped by the gallery to say hello. She hadn't seen Pat in many years and says, "I sensed that he wasn't really himself, and that he didn't really like what he was doing; that he didn't like having the gallery in a shopping mall where people were ice-skating. I think he thought, 'Is this what life has come to?'"

Gallery Victor had seemed to be a good idea, but after the first flurry of local interest, things slowed down considerably. Within six months after the opening, Pat, McGrath, and Salmones knew they would have a tough time making a profit. The gallery was struggling, and they were putting in sixty-hour workweeks.

In the early summer of 1973, Pat received a call from his old friend the producer-director Carmen Capalbo, who had just acquired the rights to the 1933 Cole Porter musical *Nymph Errant*. Originally staged in London with Gertrude Lawrence, *Nymph Errant* boasted a fine score that included such numbers as "Experiment," "The Physician," and "It's Bad for Me." But its book, credited to director Romney Brent, was in need of a complete overhaul. Capalbo knew that Pat was the man for the job. *Nymph Errant* had been based on a light comic novel by the British author James Laver, and Capalbo felt Pat was the only American writer who understood Laver's style. He called Pat in Houston and asked him to come on board as the new librettist. Although Pat had quit writing novels, he agreed immediately. Pat remembered the fun he'd always had working with Capalbo on their previous projects and was looking forward to that more than anything.

Taking a two-week leave of absence from the gallery, Pat made a secret trip to New York to do nothing but work on the *Nymph Errant* libretto with Capalbo in Capalbo's town house apartment at 21 East Eleventh Street. During that time, in what would be his final burst of creativity, Pat completely rewrote the original script. While retaining the basic thread of plot—a virginal young girl travels halfway around the world, from Switzerland to the Orient, getting quite a social and sexual education—Pat gave the show a sophisticated bite and flair, all the time remaining faithful to the book's spirit and keeping firmly in period. Capalbo had received permission from the Cole Porter estate to replace some of the score's weaker numbers with several cut and unpublished rarities from Porter shows of roughly the same era; these were skillfully integrated by Pat into the script.

Pat and Capalbo did have a great time working together, although

Pat's unabated drinking caused several precarious moments. The night Pat arrived, he sat down and drank an entire quart of Scotch with dinner. Before evening's end, he had passed out and had to be carried to his room by Capalbo and Capalbo's girlfriend. But when Capalbo rose the next morning at seven-thirty, he heard the sound of a typewriter. Pat had already awakened, showered, and turned out four pages of notes based on everything he and Capalbo had discussed at dinner the night before. If he had even the slightest hangover, there was no visible trace. "He was the most amazing writer in that sense," says Capalbo. "We'd sit and talk a scene out and then—boom!—he'd knock off three or four pages in an hour. That's two days' work for the average writer. And I'd say ninety percent of it was usable, which is also amazing."

While staying in New York with Capalbo, Pat experienced an unnerving episode of sleepwalking that may have been triggered by alcohol. Capalbo's seventeen-year-old son was visiting him; he had enjoyed getting to know Pat, who was kind and gentlemanly. Late one night, Capalbo was lying in bed reading after Pat had gone to sleep in the guest room at the front of the long apartment. At around 1 A.M., he suddenly noticed Pat walking down the hallway stark naked. As Pat passed Capalbo's door, he looked directly into Capalbo's eyes and, still walking, made a gesture as if to say, "It's okay; don't let me disturb you." Capalbo assumed Pat was heading for the bathroom, but instead Pat headed in the other direction—toward the door of Capalbo's son's bedroom.

Capalbo jumped out of bed and came up behind Pat just before Pat got to the bedroom door. He put his arms gently around Pat from behind and turned him around, quietly saying, "Come on, Pat, you should be back in bed." Pat, coming partially back to his senses, answered, "Thank you, Carmen. Thank you very much," and allowed Capalbo to lead him back to bed.

The next morning, as Capalbo awoke, Pat was pounding away at the typewriter as usual. When Capalbo entered the room, Pat said, "I'm awfully sorry I walked in my sleep last night." With great relief, Capalbo quietly accepted Pat's apology and left it at that, sensing his humiliation and knowing he had not been responsible for his actions.

The world is still waiting to see the *Nymph Errant* revival. Like Pat's other playscripts, it was never produced. Capalbo had wanted to premiere it in London, but with a glut of successful shows in the West End, no musical-comedy-sized house was available. After a full eighteen months of casting, designing, and money-raising, Capalbo and his coproducer, Jim Walsh, had to abandon the project.

Pat would ultimately be more disappointed for Capalbo than for himself. He had taken on the *Nymph Errant* rewrite only because Capalbo needed his input, and he had been happy just to spend time working with his old friend again.

However, while in New York, Pat did make a major decision about his career, and now had to break this news to Victor Salmones and E. G. McGrath.

Pat's life was about to take its most bizarre turn.

TWENTY

Serving Time

Inevitably, Pat concluded that the Houston branch of Gallery Victor, however promising, had been a bust. Despite the best efforts of Pat, Salmones, and McGrath, the gallery was clearly not going to maintain any great success. And never had a fish flopped farther out of water than Pat Tanner when he'd landed in Houston.

Exactly when or how Pat got the idea of becoming a butler is difficult to pinpoint. But the choice of profession, while surprising for a former bestselling author, is hardly mystifying. Pat knew he needed money, and he knew that one of his real talents was the art of living elegantly. Indeed, after many of his experiences with his servants in Mexico, he probably felt that he would have been better off acting as his own butler. He was already intimate with every detail that went into running a fine home; he loved to arrange lavish dinners and parties; he certainly had the grace, elegance, and tact—when he wasn't sloshed—that were required for the job. Add to this his precise knowledge of cuisine, clothing, and decor, and you have a majordomo worthy of the White House. As a butler, Pat would be an absolute natural. "He was a producer, you know," says E. G. McGrath, "and he produced through all phases of his life."

Being a butler meant that Pat could at last be living a blessedly circumscribed existence, in which security was a given and all of his duties would be comfortably set and spelled out. And best of all, it would be fun. Pat would be living inside one of his own novels, simultaneously observing and interacting with the class of people he had satirized through twenty years and sixteen books. He had sworn off writing, but he was about to embark on the sort of escapade that could easily have provided material for five more novels. "I think there were several things that precipitated it," says his good friend and accountant, Abe Badian. "Number one, he had really run out of money. It was necessary for him to find some way to survive economically. Number two, anonymity. He really wanted to get lost."

Pat decided that Palm Beach was a great place to get lost. Armed with a portfolio of references as to his "twenty-eight years of experience"—the most flattering of which was signed by the well-known author Patrick Dennis—he took out an anonymous ad in the local paper offering his services. In no time, he had secured a position in the home of Stanton Griffis, a retired former U.S. ambassador.

One might assume that Pat was taking a gigantic step down by entering this new profession, but he approached his odd new life with real pride and optimism. Pat announced his plans to Louise and his closest friends while visiting New York to work on *Nymph Errant* with Carmen Capalbo. Pat convened Louise, their housekeeper Corry, and Cris Alexander and Shaun O'Brien for lunch and told them, "I'm embarking on what is probably the best career that I will ever have."

"After we'd picked ourselves up off the floor," says Alexander, "he said, 'It's not that I'm written out. I am really out of fashion. I am *over*. I don't care to write anymore. And I'm going to do the best thing because, you know'—and he looked sharply at Louise—'I have always run our house!' And he said, 'It's the best thing I do. I do it with such ease; it pays handsomely; I'll have no expenses and I'll live in the lap of luxury.' "

"It was an odd thing to do," remembered Louise Tanner, "but he did many odd things. I think he was very, very proud of the fact that he could do something like buttle." Pat's niece Susan, who at that time had begun a new life of her own by entering the convent, says, "I was surprised that I wasn't *more* surprised that he did it. But he had said to me several times, 'I would make an absolutely fabulous butler.' He was right; he was good at it, and he knew how things should be done."

"Pat would have thought it a stylish thing for somebody who had been number one, three, and five on the bestseller list to go off and become a butler," says his longtime friend Joy Singer. "It would be a very wrong conclusion to assume that this was some kind of tragic fate for him. It was his idea of having a ball. He *loved* planning elaborate events, and seeing them through, and having a staff do all the work. He was also putting it over on everyone; he *became* a character from one of his books. Not telling them who he was, was all a part of the whole thing."

"When he told us about it," says his friend and *Little Me* editor, Peggy Brooks, "it seemed very much in character. It was as if he were Auntie Mame; that's the best way I can describe it. It's that side of him that was summoned up under these circumstances. You could see that his own intelligence had told him he could put this together in his own nutty way. You couldn't find another writer in the course of history, in two thousand years, that would have thought of this particular answer to his penury!"

Pat divested himself of most of his belongings before he left Houston. He even got rid of his extensive library, including his own writings, with three exceptions: his beloved copy of Thackeray's *Vanity Fair,* Emily Post's *Etiquette,* and a crossword-word puzzle dictionary. "I am delighted," he wrote his son, Michael, "to be shut of it all." In the same letter, he attempted to explain to Michael his new decision: "And why am I taking this insane step? I can't quite explain it to myself, so how can I explain it to you? Perhaps it's some sort of penance for my profligate life, like going into a Trappist monastery if I were a Believer, which, as you fucking-A-well know, I am not. If I ever understand it myself, I will try to explain.

"And I would be grateful if you told no one where I am working or what I am doing. It is not that I am ashamed of being a menial—after all, I chose it as being less boring than the Gallery Victor in Houston, which I still own 42½ percent of. It is simply that the news is too funny to keep. It would end up in someone's column and I'd be out on my ass, as they would be certain that I was working there only to spy on them and make sport of them in a new book."

Determined to drive himself down to Palm Beach, Pat bought a car in Houston. He went to a dealer, asked the salesman the price of a particular car, and wrote out a check on the spot. E. G. McGrath, who had come with him, was aghast. "I said, 'Patrick, you have to dicker with him! Nobody just pays the asking price!' And he said, '*I* do!' The salesman was actually disconcerted, because he had truly expected to bargain. He said, 'But, Mr. Dennis, don't you even want to kick the tires?' Pat said, 'No, I don't do that; here's the check.' He left town the next day, and that was the last time I saw him." (Gallery Victor would limp along in Houston for another year before it closed for good and reopened in Beverly Hills, where it thrives to this day.)

"Patrick Dennis is dead," Pat wrote Michael on September 14, 1973. "I killed him with a razor when I hit the Palm Beach airport. The beard is gone and so is the little that was left on top. You would never recognize me—I scarcely do myself. I was prettier the old way. Now I look like a cross between John Gielgud and a *very* old deep sea turtle. That beard covered a lot of sags and wattles." To complete the change of character, Pat gave himself a new name, Edwards Tanner, which he felt sounded more "butlerian."

Eighty-six-year-old Stanton Griffis had no idea that he had hired a bestselling author as his butler. Although during the 1930s he had been a top executive at Brentano's (not to mention Paramount Pictures and Madison Square Garden) and was fairly conversant in the arts, he had spent the latter half of his life in the fields of finance and world politics. Under Presidents Roosevelt and Truman, he had served as an ambassador to four countries and had particularly distinguished himself with his pioneering efforts toward collaboration between Washington and Madrid during the oppressive regime of Generalissimo Francisco Franco. As Red Cross commissioner for the Pacific Ocean area during World War II, he had received the Medal for Merit and the Medal of Freedom.

"It's a pretty house," Pat wrote Michael of the Griffis home, "and rather a small one; icily air conditioned, which is nice in the Palm Beach humidity. I will be paid a princely salary with very little opportunity to spend much of it (Wednesdays off). I have a lovely room (two exposures) and gray tile bath. And if I don't do something frightful like scald massa with a tureen of soup, I may even last. I've certainly trained enough servants of my own to know about serving from the left and removing from the right."

To no one's surprise, "Edwards" turned out to be a dream butler. Moreover, he thoroughly enjoyed his new profession. Seven weeks after his arrival in Palm Beach, he wrote Michael a lengthy letter in which he detailed the rush of new feelings and experiences:

. . . The great thing about it all is that I am an absolute sensation at my job and have never been happier. I rush about the Griffis house all day long at such a rate that my waistline is down to 30 inches . . . and I'm solid muscle. Decapitated, I would be stunning. Not even Cris Alexander could be as outrageous as a 1920's musical-comedy butler, and the more I lay it on, the better les Griffis and their *cursi* (a Spanish word with at least a dozen meanings, the best of which is "vulgar") chums like it. If they were nouveaux riches, it would be understandable. They are not; only Palm Beach, which rhymes. And in Palm Beach, Nice People talk only of money or the size of divorce settlements, which is the same thing with a light seasoning of s-x.

No, I do not assay an English accent. No need. In Houston, where people say "I might could give ya innythang y'd lak fer dunnah," it was generally conceded that your poor father not only spoke English but British. Anyhow, the Hon. Stanton Griffis is 86 and almost stone deaf, so it doesn't matter what I say, unless it's a whispered aside to the Little Bride. Then he catches every syllable.

Well, he's about the dreariest old fart on earth, with the manners of a pig and the morals of a goat. But at 86 his morals are mostly a faint memory. He was ambassador to Poland, Egypt, Argentina and Spain and not the president of Brentano's but the *owner* of Brentano's. Considering that *Auntie Mame* kept that defunct art-supply establishment in the black during both 1955 and 56, I was a little miffed when he said *"Who* is Patrick Dennis?" No longer. If anyone gave Geoffrey Chaucer as a reference he would have asked the same question. The Little Bride describes him as an "a-vor-i-cious" reader and indeed he is. He likes show-biz biographies, Democrat-slanted non-fiction (he has three copies of Margaret Truman's bio of her father, none of which has been opened, except by me), sex manuals (you'd think that he'd know how after 86 years of trying), and the novels of Jacqueline Susann. Not even any good pornography.

The Little Bride (they married the day before Edwards arrived) is a chit of 54, but . . . looks 35. I like her a lot. Cook says that she married him for his money. What else? Well, if she did, she's earning every cent of it. We're having a little problem trying to get her into the Social Register. With three ex-husbands under her belt, it won't be easy. I can't wait to see and wonder why it is so important to both of them. . . . Anyhow, she is nice . . . and she does appreciate the Leopard. Every day she gazes at me with welling eyes and says, "Oh, Edwards, I just don't know what we'd do without a well-trained ser . . . I mean employee, like you."

And now to get back to Lancelot Leopard of New York City: Well, kid, I'm a perfect whiz at my job. Being deaf, the Hon. Stan wears a Zenith hearing aid—about half of the time—which either gets police calls or just whistles. And so it's essential to bellow at him. Now I can't help overhearing from three rooms away that 1.) Edwards knows his place; 2.) Edwards is extremely intelligent for one of his station (Change at Jamaica); and 3.) Edwards is a perfectly trained servant of the Old School—you can spot them a mile away. And I can hear it two miles away.

Even the other servants are hoodwinked. At table—where, naturally, the Leopard Emperor sits at the head and dispenses loaves and fishes—they speak reverently of Other Butlers in Other Great Houses and say, "He was a first-class man, like you, Edwards."

I know that you and your mother and Abe—oh, especially Abe—are just undone by my new career. But I simply love it. A ham at heart. And when I switch out to serve dinner every evening I feel half actor and half prop man. It's fun. And it's also terribly profitable. The Hon. Stan . . . pays me a perfect fortune, which I have no opportunity of spending. I am beautifully housed . . . and given anything I want to eat and drink. My laundry is done for me and even the dry cleaner gives a 50 per cent discount just because so much work is thrown their way.

Dry cleaner, oi veh! Valeting the Hon. Stan is not easy. He is no *pulakis* (Greek for spring chicken) and if you or Minnie had had the same table manners 15 years ago, you'd be dead today. Anyhow, the Hon. Stan rather messes himself from any orifice not yet atrophied—and that's quite a lot. Fortunately, he creates lots of burns from blowing, instead of drawing, into his pipe. And so, if something is simply *too* horrid, I simply burn another hole into it and send it off to be cleaned and pressed, as well as rewoven.

Oh, Manny, baby, I can't tell you how wonderful it is to be able to do something well and to hear—or overhear—about it. Beyond the whole thing's being an utter camp, I now believe that I begin to understand what you impossible young people have in mind. Making a lot of money isn't important. I don't even want to know how many millions of dollars have passed through my hands on their way to Washington. Only God, Abe and the income tax people know. Or care.

Speaking of income tax, I even get tips. Tipping doesn't embarrass me at all, unless it's lower than $50—and it never has been. I simply bow lower, say, "Modom is too generous," and tuck it into my jock strap—having burned all of my brassieres. And it need not be reported.

It's fun, Manny. It's fun. Perhaps not for someone who wanted to see his name in lights or write popular books or be President (wouldn't that be a barrel of laughs?) but when your appetite is as jaded as mine—and when you're as effing old—you may begin to understand. I don't understand me, and so why should you?

People change. Your metabolism changes every seven years and, as you grow older, you change with it. I am, of course, stark, staring mad, but it is still possible to look back upon the changes in my own personality. The last time you and Min visited me in Mexico I was at the end of my (Mexican) Social Career. Except for a dozen close acquaintances, I saw no one for the last two years I lived there. And for the final year, I had my dinner on a tray in bed. . . .

How can anyone explain it to you? It is like a gynecologist trying to tell an expectant mother how to have a baby. You must simply live through it yourself.

Two months later, he wrote his sister, Barbara, "My address is no secret—only my profession. I'm still at it and still enjoying it. And I shall probably stay here until I drop as I could never reaccustom myself to paying out money for such fripperies as food, rent, utilities and telephone bills."

Small pleasures like movies began to hold an attraction for Pat once again. After years of abstinence, he started checking out the newer

American product, such as a reissue of *Midnight Cowboy* ("I liked it—but not as well as the book. Anyhow, I left with a damp handkerchief, which makes a film worth the money") and *Papillon* ("which again, wasn't as good as the book, but I thought the leper was cute").

Pat served many distinguished guests that the Griffises invited to their home. One of them, Charles van Rensselaer, had actually been friendly with Pat years before. At first Pat was a bit worried that his cover might be blown. But with his new name and his new look, he was utterly unrecognizable. Van Rensselaer left without ever realizing that the butler was his old friend Pat Tanner, and Pat was delighted—and relieved—that he had accomplished his masquerade with such complete success.

His old friends Abe and Nan Badian went to visit him in Palm Beach and spent a day with him. "We didn't meet at the house," says Nan. "I remember we were at the beach and we sat on a rock wall, just to sit and talk. We had lunch together. He told us about the guests that came to dinner, and the people he was working for. He made light of everything and saw the humor in the situation. He was in beautiful, well-maintained homes, which he appreciated, although sometimes he would say about his employers, 'Their taste is in their feet!' He would have done things differently."

The Hon. Stan and his wife took a lengthy European vacation during the summer of 1974, leaving Pat free to putter around the place naked in the summer heat, stretch out, and catch up with his reading. Michael, who was on his summer break from studies, visited. "When I went down to see him," explains Michael, "he was making eleven thousand dollars a year and living in a very small room. It was very monastic. He had done his own artwork on the walls—a sort of Mondrian knockoff—and he was actually very happy in that controlled environment. And of course, he was goofing on the whole thing. The butler move was unique. He truly enjoyed it. I think that's one of the coolest things that he did." During Michael's stay, the two took a trip to Disney World, which Michael remembers today with great fondness. Pat had looked forward to seeing Disney World with the anticipation of a child and wanted very much to see it with his own child, although that child was now a grown man of twenty. "Dad wrote a letter to his sister about the trip in which he told her that I was 'a very nice young man,' " says Michael. "That got back to me, and I was pleased that he thought I had turned out okay."

Pat would have been happy to remain in the Griffises' employ for many more years, but that was not to be. On August 12, 1974, Stanton Griffis finally blew rather than drew on his pipe once too often. He was in the Pierre Hotel in New York and accidentally set himself and much of the hotel on fire. Two weeks later, at Lenox Hill Hospital, he was dead from severe burns and smoke inhalation. His wife had survived the fire unharmed; she returned to Palm Beach and eventually sold the house. By early April 1975, Pat was out of a job, along with the rest of the household staff ("She's finally setting us house niggers free"). But he found a new position immediately in the home of a wealthy widow, Mrs. Clive Runnells, in Lake Forest, Illinois. He would be working in the very town where *Love and Mrs. Sargent* took place, only a few miles from his childhood home in Evanston, and would be neighbors once more with his sister, Barbara Hastings, and her husband, Jack. In a pleasant coincidence for Pat, his daughter, Betsy, would also now be living and working in the Chicago area. She had been hired as a stagehand at the Goodman Theatre as part of her first year of college at the Goodman School of Drama.

Pat referred to Mrs. Runnells as "a grand dame who still Does Things Right." And unlike Stanton Griffis, she "believes in treating her darkies right. Clothes, hospitalization, fringe benefits, travel expenses and all the rest of it."

Pat now headed a staff of ten. He also had an apartment on the property, separate from the main house, consisting of sitting room, bedroom, kitchen, and bath, with his own private telephone line. Pat was happy with his new employer, at least at the beginning. One month after starting work he wrote Michael:

This job is an absolute dream. Mrs. Runnells is a dear old thing of 82 who drinks a bit. About a fifth of Scotch a day. But a Lady to her fingertips. We have a French cook, a Polish chauffeur (who is an ex-barber and gives the men on the staff free haircuts), a Czech gardener with a Mexican assistant, a Dutch night watchman, two Italian chambermaids, an Irish lady's maid, two German housemen and a Cretinous (having nothing to do with the isle of Crete—indeed, never having heard of it) parlor maid who is leaving Friday after three weeks of my most intensive training. Oddly enough, they all get on beautifully, and the house is one of the best-run establishments I have ever seen. And all under the aegis of Lancelot Leopard and, of course, Mrs. Runnells' decayed gentlewoman secretary, who drinks twice as much as Mrs. R. and gets literally falling-down drunk. Luckily there is a corps of able-bodied men to lift Mrs. Long from the floor, load her into the back of the car (oddly enough, the cars are not a bit grand—two Fords and a Mercury) and send her home. We all speak piously about how slippery the floors are (Clifford and his waxing machine) and how treacherous Mrs. Long's blood pressure is.

Today is Wednesday, Edwards's day off, and I'm going to drive into that Toddlin' Town to visit the porno bookstores, the blue movies, three massage parlors and the Christian Science Reading Room. Thence to dinner at the Hastings's. I am fearless on the freeways and even into the Loop, although I tend to crash into the side of Marshall Field's.

Have a lovely time working the bookstore this summer. I finally got around to rereading *all* of *Remembrance of Things Past* and now wonder how I did it 30 years ago. Marcel could certainly do with a bit of editing. Perhaps if he ever makes the *Reader's Digest* condensed books I'll enjoy it more—and so will all those people who swear that his every word is golden.

By the end of the year, Pat's opinion of Mrs. Runnells had soured. "He didn't like Mrs. Runnells," explains his niece Sister Joanna. "He had found a parlor maid that he worked very well with, and that everybody else on the staff liked. But Mrs. Runnells didn't like her because she would never look her in the eye. Pat couldn't talk her out of firing her. He also talked about how he had to preside at some party she was giving for children on the Fourth of July. He was planning to come to my profession—I made profession [as a nun] on that day—and he was unhappy that he was forced to miss it."

Pat and the staff moved with Mrs Runnells down to her home in Hobe Sound, Florida, for the winter. On January 1, 1976, he wrote Michael: "Just how much longer I can endure this household is a difficult question. Not much more than a month I think. Mrs. Runnells suffers not only from Republicanism and megalomania, but also from galloping senility. My ulcers are back in full force after lying dormant for 15 years. As I have no personal problems, it has to be this job. I plan to be out of here and back in the frozen North by February. . . . Please God, we shall soon be reunited and I will be out of here."

On January 7, Pat tendered his resignation to Mrs. Runnells. "Next time," he wrote Michael, "I want to be in a one-servant house (apartment) right in the heart of town working for a single man who has a job that takes him out from underfoot every day. From now on it's city lights for me."

The following day, the *Chicago Tribune* ran a front-page article entitled "The Butler: Endangered—Not Extinct." "Edwards" was one of the Chicago-area butlers interviewed for the article. Pat obviously agreed to speak because his identity was safe: no photos accompanied the story; he concocted flagrantly incorrect autobiographical information; and his new single name was an effective mask. Pat figured prominently in the first third of the article:

Blaming it on the butler won't work anymore.

Yes, that dignified but devious favorite foil of fiction writers has become an endangered species, scarcely capable of shouldering another leering charge: "The butler did it!"

But if endangered, the butler is not yet extinct. The British television series *Upstairs, Downstairs* gave countless Americans their first glimpse of what an English butler is—or was. And research has turned up some interesting facts about Bicentennial buttling, Chicago style. For instance:

—Butlers say they're better dressed than the guests they serve

—They are almost always called by their last names

—They are mostly English

—They have no trouble getting jobs

—A well-trained butler gets $1,000 to $1,500 a month, except in Los Angeles, where they are overpaid, don't stay on the job, and usually are out-of-work actors

—They can save plenty of money because "room, board, and uniforms are provided, and there's nothing to spend money on except cigarets, underwear, and shoes," according to Edwards, a butler in Lake Forest.

Edwards is one of a vanishing breed. "We're practically extinct," he says in a world-weary drawl that makes him sound older than the years he claims. "I'm 54, and I'm the youngest butler in the business, aside from a few Latin men. I doubt there are 1,000 butlers left," he adds.

Chicago butlers can probably be counted on the fingers of one hand if "couples" are excluded. The majority work in New York, Newport, R.I., and Palm Beach. Edwards worked in all three places and Mexico before coming to his present post, which includes shuttling to Palm Beach for winters.

Edwards—resplendent in his black trousers, beige, double-breasted jacket and black tie—has worked for five families since getting out of the Army and has never had to look for a position. "I've been passed from hand to hand," he intones. "I've buried a lot of employers."

Occasionally he wears striped trousers and a morning coat, for formal luncheons, and in past positions he has worn white tie and tails. But never a tuxedo: "That's for waiters and bartenders," Edwards says.

No two households are alike, Edwards has discovered. In general, the butler runs the house, "unless there is a housekeeper, a real one." Where he is in charge, he hires and fires the help, takes care of the bills, and handles the administrative work. Sometimes the employer has a secretary who takes care of those details. Edwards is a good cook, but he would never want to own a restaurant. "That's a 24-hour-a-day job," he says. "A butler only works 15."

Meanwhile that money is piling up.

Several more butlers are interviewed in the article, but an unattributed quote that concludes the story is pure Patrick:

"After 30 years of listening to fatuous conversations," says a butler of his employers and their guests, "I'd rather wait on them than talk to them."

Within no time, Pat found himself a new employer. This situation would be the best of them all. Ray Kroc, the seventy-three-year-old founder of McDonald's, was in the market for a majordomo. Kroc had started from humble beginnings and didn't enter the burger business until he was in his midfifties. Beginning in 1954, he bought into Richard and Maurice McDonald's hamburger stand in San Bernardino, California, and rapidly turned it into a multimillion-dollar national franchise. An imposing, vigorous older man with slicked-back hair, impeccably tailored blazers, and a taste for large rings, he cut a commanding figure. He had married in 1956, and his wife, Joan, went on to found Operation Cork, a national program to help the families of alcoholics. Operation Cork was financed by McDonald's revenues through the Kroc Foundation. (Ironically, Ray Kroc himself struggled with alcoholism and entered a rehab center toward the end of his life.)

Pat got his wish to live in an apartment in the city: the Krocs' home was on the twenty-fifth floor of 1242 Lake Shore Drive, Chicago's most prized residential street, not far from the apartment where Pat and his parents had lived thirty-five years before. On March 18, 1976, Pat wrote Michael that his new job was "absolute heaven":

Mr. and Mrs. Ray Kroc . . . are the dearest people on earth—*nouveau riche* (20 years of super affluence) and frank to admit it. If anyone has to be burdened with several hundred million dollars, it ought to be the Krocs. Far from being ashamed of their money, they revel in it. They have a place in Florida, a ranch in California, and this posh apartment in Chicago where they occupy the whole twenty-fifth floor and I simply pig it on half of the twenty-sixth, all exquisitely overdecorated and quite good in a terrible way. They revel in their yacht, their jet, their helicopter, their private railway car, their baseball team (the San Diego Padres, who have never been known to win a game), their Cork Foundation (guess what that is spelled backward) to combat alcoholism, their 15 cars (only three of which are Rolls-Royces) and their Arabian horses (neither rides).

And they're not piggy about it like the Hon. Stan. To celebrate his seventieth birthday Daddy K. gave seven million to various worthy causes. They pay me $12,000 a year and full found and

want to give me more because I'm "indispensable." (How would
they know? They're never here. I've never laid eyes on Mrs. Kroc,
although we talk at length every day on the Watts line. She calls
me "Sweetie!") He likes to take his meals in our vast, chi-chi,
interior decorated kitchen and always makes me sit down and
have a drink with him. (True, it's not done, but what am I supposed to do? Spit in his eye?)

Until he was my age, Daddy K. knocked about doing any number of things, but mostly playing piano in famous old dance bands
of the twenties and early thirties, such as Isham Jones, Coon-
Sanders and Harry Sosnik. Then he opened the first McDonald's.
The rest is history. As a lonely millionaire, he wandered into a
restaurant and saw lovely Joan Beverly at the Hammond organ,
said, "That's the girl I'm going to marry," and for the past eight
years they have lived happily ever after. Ray is 73, looks 50, acts
30. Joan is nudging 50—a large, attractive blonde, to judge from
her many portraits and photographs—and by no means any common little tramp who hooked the U.S. Mint with her sluttish
wiles. Her speech, vocabulary and usage are excellent. She reads
good books and lots of them. She has a married daughter and is
now a grandmother. I mean these are terrific people.

I sense that Joan would like to soar a little higher in Society
than mass parties for the 3500 McDonald's franchise-holders.
Well, with Edwards to guide her, she certainly can. Her only
drawbacks are that she isn't a lush and isn't dull enough. But the
money won't hurt.

To prove my indispensability, I kidnapped Mannes from Mrs.
Runnells' to serve as Mrs. Kroc's Florida butler. He starts next
week. Mannes replaced me chez Runnells and is the world's only
Jewish butler. He is delighted to leave and says that Mrs. R. has
deteriorated so fast in less than two months that she's ready for
the lock-up. Ann, the Hobe Sound housekeeper of 14 years, and
Thelma, the parlor maid, are also defecting. I got out in the nick
of time.

In Mrs. Kroc's current scheme of things, I am to be more than
a mere butler. I am to be the major-domo, yet, and travel about
the various Kroc properties to chic things up. I am slated for Fort

Lauderdale on April 21 and for her seminar on alcoholism (in a supervisory capacity, you understand, *not* as a horrid example) in Santa Barbara in May.

Meanwhile I sit here as the only employee in this vast duplex, bringing it back from three months of total neglect and taking care of Daddy Kroc about one night a week when the jet soars in from whatever staid institution where he's been lecturing on hamburger. Last week was Dartmouth. . . .

Well, I just couldn't have fallen into a better place or with nicer people.

But that was not all the news Pat had for Michael in the letter. Throughout their fourteen-year separation, Pat and Louise had continued to remain in close touch, and now, with the children grown and out of the house, they found themselves once again turning toward each other:

. . . After 14 years together and 14 years apart, the Lynx and I are very seriously considering rejoining forces to go paw-in-paw down the Sunset Trail in Life's Autumn. Wouldn't that jar you. Minnie [Betsy] seems to be in favor of it in the patient way she has in dealing with idiots and the elderly, but I'm not sure. She's a deep one.

We talk on the Watts line (I have several Watts lines, dear boy, and make free long distance calls all over the country) and yesterday I spent 12 hours setting the whole thing—pros and cons—down in black and white. My only stipulations are that I won't be a kept gentleman but go on working in my menial capacity and that I do it outside New York, where there is anonymity. And that is about as adamant as I intend to be.

On the other paw, the Lynx has no objections to living part time, at least, in Chicago. She realizes that her fledglings have flown the nest, which is only right and proper, and, of course, she is lonely drifting around that vast, echoing apartment.

We are spending the month of March saying Yes, No and Maybe; oh-it-would-never-work and well-we-might-just-try.

It would be the Open Marriage of all time, but we may be old enough—if not mature enough—to handle it. We both agree that the happiest years of our lives were those spent together and, if time and separation have not altered us too much, we might have a few more in a rather eccentric sort of Togetherness which is too complicated to outline here and now. There's no one else I'd dream of being married to, and my feeling is that the least we can do is give it a try. And so, if the Lynx is still willing, perhaps we shall. Whether or not it will work, after all these years, is anyone's guess.

If you have any feelings on the matter, please air them quickly and frankly to both of us. Not that they will carry any weight with me. This would be our marriage; not yours and not Catso's [Betsy]. But it would be interesting to know your opinion. Meanwhile, I will keep you posted on any startling developments.

Betsy saw her father frequently while she was working and studying in Chicago and remembers a visit from Louise during which Louise and Pat discussed a reconciliation. "Which was sort of an interesting conversation!" Betsy says, laughing. "How much of this is true and how much of it is my own perception, I'm not sure. But they always did get along well together, and I thought it was very touching on both their parts." Shortly before Louise's visit, Pat had filled Betsy in on his affair with Guy Kent. "It was really a sweet conversation, and it took place when he was deciding to get back with my mother. He said, 'I never fell out of love with your mother. I just fell madly in love with Guy Kent.'"

Pat and Louise took their time considering a reconciliation, giving the idea a chance to gestate a bit rather than rushing back into each other's life. And before any final decision could be made, a matter of growing concern needed attention. For months, Pat had been losing weight at a rather alarming rate, and it clearly wasn't just due to rushing up and down the back stairs. Between November 1975 and April 1976, he had lost forty pounds, only twenty-five of them intentionally. "While I enjoy having an adolescent figure," he wrote Michael, "emaciation is more than I bargained for. Nor, for more than a month, have I been able to keep down so much as a glass of wine. I'm vomiting like a pregnant woman and no one seems to know why. I had a complete physical and that horrid barium X-ray thing last week. Not a trace of ulcers. I truly wish that ulcers were the problem as I have coped with the duodenal variety before and they are quite easy to control and even cure through boring diet. Tomorrow I go off for a gastroscope. I can hardly wait."

TWENTY-ONE

Paw in Paw down the Sunset Trail

The Leopard returned to the Lynx in May of 1976. He gave up the job
with the Krocs and came back to New York, there to start a new life
that would really be a continuation of the one he had abandoned fourteen difficult years before. It had taken him that long to come to grips
with his wracking sense of guilt and shame; to finally understand that
his wife and family had always adored him despite the problems and
were happy to welcome him back. Gay, straight, bisexual, asexual—
such categories could simply no longer be applied to Pat. He was
returning to Louise, who, through all of the torment and all of the
trauma, had been the one great and constant love of his life.

Betsy had just finished her first year at the Goodman School of
Drama in Chicago, and she and her father drove back to New York
together. By this time Pat had given up on the doctors in Chicago, who
had been unable to diagnose his debilitating illness. After settling back
in with Louise, he was going to have more tests taken in New York. "I
hope," he told his old friends Cris Alexander and Shaun O'Brien, "that
I'm not coming home to die."

Michael was finishing his senior year abroad in London. In a touching gesture of welcome and conciliation, he sent his father the key to
the door of the family's apartment in New York. Shortly before he
returned to the United States, Michael received the following letter
from Pat:

Thank you so much for the birthday-cum-welcome-home gift.
The key actually opens the front door. I have yet to investigate the
notched one. Perhaps it's the key to your heart?

Yes, smart-ass, we do have sex.*

Except that everyone is older, life continues as though I had
never been away and I am very happy. I only hope that everone
else concerned is, too. The poor Lynx. She asked for a play-mate
and it seems that she is getting only a burden.

My health is not good. I feel miserable about half the time and
wretched the rest of it. This makes any kind of social life next to
impossible and Lynxie gallantly, loyally (idiotically) refuses to go
places alone.

To make matters grimmer, the hot-shot specialist whom my
Chicago specialist wants me to see is away all week at a stomach
convention in Miami and so next Tuesday morning is the first
possible moment for our wild, sweet coupling. Then it will
undoubtedly be more tests in more hospitals and more time and
money wasted without any definite answer about anything.

When do you land? As many as are ambulatory plan to meet the
ship. Just tell us when. Or do we have to open the *New York
Times* and look up the hour of docking?

Thanks again, lub, see you next week.

Lub,

L.

*Now that you and Catso [Betsy] are adult and so helpful around
the house, we thought it would be nice to start another family—
at least one baby and possibly many more. The experience would
be good—nay beautiful for both of you, and it would save you the
embarrassment of inheriting too much money . . .

When Pat did finally get to see the New York specialist, the sentence
was soon pronounced: pancreatic cancer. It had taken both Pat's father

and grandfather, and the disease was often associated with the abuse of tobacco and alcohol.

Pat entered the hospital for a time, but little could be done to help him. He soon returned home to Louise, who took the most tender and attentive care of him. He spent all of the summer and most of the autumn slowly dying.

Stalwart, noble Corry Salley, who had been retired for several years, returned to the Tanner home to help Louise take care of Pat. Soon Corry was learning how to give him morphine injections to control the vicious pain that was overtaking him.

For most of the summer, Pat remained sequestered, seeing few visitors. Then, with the arrival of autumn, he began letting his close friends come to see him. Under the proper medication, he had a clear mind and little pain for about two hours every afternoon. And every afternoon, Cris Alexander and Shaun O'Brien would visit. Pat had an amazing collection of silk kimonos in shades of scarlet and fuchsia; he would pull himself together and don one each time he received guests. Even in his emaciated state, he retained his command and force of personality. "He looked fantastic, like some kind of wild saint," says Cris Alexander.

He remained the same Pat that everyone had adored. He refused to allow his spirits, his playful personality, to be devoured by the illness. "He didn't seem to be a beaten person," says Peggy Brooks. "Not a bit. His own little self was very much there. Witty is such an easy way to describe him. It was that *zany,* witty imagination that was still very much part of him. It couldn't be peeled away; it was so much his essence. He still had that eccentric, marvelous view of things that you find in his books and letters."

Ever the liberal Democrat, Pat made sure that one of the last things he did was to vote for Jimmy Carter in the presidential election by absentee ballot.

To feel the love of his family and his old friends; to see the familiar faces from his past; to know what a difference he had made in the lives of those who loved him—all had an enormous impact on Pat during the final weeks of his life. When his friend Ross Claiborne came to see him toward the end, Pat took his hands and looked into his eyes tearfully, saying, "Oh, I can't tell you how grateful I am." Carmen Capalbo paid

Pat a final visit, and Pat broke down sobbing in his arms, unable to speak. As Capalbo hugged and kissed him, all Pat could do was to keep patting him tenderly on the back.

During his illness, Pat had asked his friend Dr. William G. Cahan for enough sleeping pills to end his misery. "Ethical considerations prevented me from doing that," says Cahan, "much as I pitied his plight. He used to say, 'I can't use a gun on myself because I can't shoot straight, and I can't jump out a window because I'm afraid of heights.' But I did give him pills, and maybe he secreted them away. I prescribed medicine which, I think, was in the morphine group. And from what I suspect, he saved them for one massive effort. I'm not sure, but I suspect that. He was in a great deal of pain."

Whether or not Pat finally did, for once, make a successful attempt at suicide is a secret he took with him to the grave. But the end came on November 6, 1976. Corry had given him his morphine injection and asked if she could do anything else for him. "Yes," Pat murmured. "For God's sake, will you put in your dentures?"

Pat remained strictly in character a few moments later when he spoke his final words: "Louise, there's a spot on your dress . . ."

He was only fifty-five years old when he died. In his will, he had specified that he wanted no funeral or memorial services of any kind. "My body is to be cremated and disposed of in the quickest, cheapest manner possible," he wrote, "(flushed down the toilet, scattered to the winds, sunk into an unmarked hole in the ground, etc.) at the expense of my estate."

It is often difficult for survivors to feel a sense of finality or closure when honoring such wishes. Funerals are for the grieving, not the grieved; they are a way for loved ones to begin their attempts to carry on. But the Tanners respected Pat's orders, which they communicated to their friends by way of a death announcement containing a moving tribute. It was written by Michael and signed by Michael, Betsy, and Louise:

Friends of the Tanner Family:
Patrick Tanner, the head of our family, died on the morning of

Saturday, November 6. We have decided to honor the instructions set forth in his will that no services be held on his behalf, and ask you to understand that we place his wishes foremost.

To all of us who knew him, Pat's life served as a reminder that life is a joyful and delightful thing. Blessed with an uncanny ability to generate laughter, he was fortunate enough to see the fruits of his wit reach millions of people. As a writer and as a man, he managed to strike a balance between a reckless imagination and an impeccable sense of correctness. His life, though cut short, was fully realized; he lived intensely and fulfilled his many dreams. Pat was a true gentleman, a man whose first concern during his last months of illness was that he might be inconveniencing us.

We would like to thank all the people who with their charity and concern helped our family through this difficult time. We have been heartened beyond words by your support. Pat lived and died among extraordinary friends.

Epilogue

An early-spring storm swept through Manhattan the night of March 31, 1997. In secluded Gramercy Park, the trees rattled and shook, and driving winds whipped the rain through the streets.

Within the Gilded Age rooms of the National Arts Club, in the former Samuel J. Tilden mansion overlooking the park, the lights glowed and a party was in full swing. Cris Alexander and his partner, Shaun O'Brien, were making a rare visit to New York City from their home upstate in Saratoga Springs, and their buddy Louise Tanner was throwing them a party.

The average age of the guests was around seventy, and the affair was virtually a *Little Me* reunion. Thirty-six years after its publication, the survivors among *Little Me's* photographic cast of characters were together once more. The book's editor, Peggy Brooks, chatted with Louise, whom Pat had drafted to play Belle's pal Pixie Portnoy. Dody Goodman, who was Helen Highwater, and Elaine Adam, who had vamped and camped as Belle's archrival Magdalena Montezuma, caught each other up on their lives. Meanwhile, Cris Alexander was still wielding a camera, though this time it was pocket-sized. He lined up a picture of two of the men in Belle's life—Shaun O'Brien (Mr. Musgrove) and Kurt Bieber (the Hollywood stud Letch Feeley). Now white-haired and a bit stooped from sciatica, Bieber muttered playfully, "I don't know about this . . . I don't look much like Letch Feeley anymore."

A sumptuous buffet was brought out, and the party went on into the night. It was just the type of affair Pat Tanner would have loved, had he been alive to enjoy it. Now, twenty-one years after his death, Pat's presence in the room seemed palpable, evoked by the collective memory of some of his closest friends.

In spite of all his shortcomings, all his troubles, Pat left the fondest of feelings in his wake. Mention his name to anyone who knew him, and it triggers a huge smile as memories of grand times come flooding back. Those to whom he was closest, those whom he inadvertently hurt—Louise, Michael, and Betsy—treasured him in their thoughts. Louise, who never remarried, always wiped away tears when discussing Pat's final days. Michael insists, "I loved him *very* much," despite the stresses their relationship was prone to, but admits, "In retrospect, it's much better that I was brought up by my mother. I was going through the whole hippie thing, and it's just as well that we weren't under the same roof for that." Betsy simply states, "As far as I was concerned, there were no problems between us. I really loved him, and I think he loved me."

The Tanner family has continued to thrive. Betsy remained at Manhattan Theatre Club for twenty-three years, eventually reaching the post of technical director. She left the company in May 2000 to pursue a freelance career. Michael supported himself as a piano tuner and professional musician until he decided in his late twenties to attend medical school. He now is medical director of the primary care clinic at Bellevue Hospital. In 1997 he and his wife, Mary Anne, produced Henry Patrick Tanner, who would have been Pat's first grandchild.

In addition to her five books, Louise contributed extensively to *Films in Review* magazine and worked actively as a director of the National Board of Review, one of the leading organizations devoted to recognizing the best efforts of contemporary filmmakers. She also remained deeply involved as a supporter of progressive political and social welfare programs.

Louise's life ended the morning of May 15, 2000, following an illness of several months' duration. Shortly before she died, she told Michael and Betsy that she could hear their father's voice.

On May 19, Louise was laid to rest in St. James's Cemetery in Stony Brook, Long Island. When her coffin was lowered into the ground, Pat was with her once again, this time for always: The urn containing his ashes was cradled in her arms.

And what of Pat's legacy? What remains of his influence in contemporary American literature? "Light Summer Fiction" as Pat practiced it has been extinct for a long time. The average beach read is now a bodice-ripper, a Stephen King novel, or a Harlequin romance. Robert Plunket *(Love Junkie)* still writes comic novels and considers Pat one of his prime influences. A cluster of New York–based gay writers produced some memorable comic novels ten years ago: Paul Rudnick *(Social Disease, I'll Take It)*, Joe Keenan *(Blue Heaven, Puttin' on the Ritz)*, and Charles Busch *(Whores of Lost Atlantis)*. All have since gone on to write for stage, screen, or sitcom; they seem to have turned their backs on the novel form for now.

Even as he wrote his books, Pat knew that he was one of the last authors of the comic novel. He foresaw his eventual fall from fashion as early as the *Auntie Mame* success. That he was able to keep writing and selling his books all the way into the early 1970s, seventeen years after *Auntie Mame*'s publication, was astonishing. That he is remembered now primarily as the author of *Auntie Mame* is tragic. His sixteen novels may have been intended as entertainment, but they were shot through with the insight of a social chronicler who had an unerring eye for all-American snobbery and pretense. Today, his best books—*Auntie Mame, Little Me, The Loving Couple, Genius, Tony, The Joyous Season*—reveal a corrosive, critical mind, unwilling to condone the sheer fatuousness that has always been the province of the would-be American elite.

Pat was usually the first to deprecate his gifts as a writer, and to use the vaguely pejorative term *light* in reference to his creative output. Today, *light* has virtually become a critical condemnation. Toward the end of his career, Noël Coward suffered similar disapprobation. In a television interview of the late 1960s, Coward offered thoughts that could easily have applied to Pat:

> Despair is the new religion, the new mode. It is in the books we read, the music we hear, and far too often in the plays we see. Nowadays, a light comedy whose sole purpose is to amuse is dismissed as trivial and insignificant. Since when has laughter been so insignificant? No merriment, apparently, must scratch the grim, set pattern of these dire years.

Pat's primary purpose, in his life and his work, was to entertain. He could always offer this gift despite the dark, depressive clouds that would overwhelm him. Readers who appreciated the elegance of his prose and the Swiftian underpinnings of his writing knew that Pat's best books amounted to considerably more than mere "Light Summer Fiction." They were a rich, funny social critique of mid-twentieth-century America and those who aspired to its upper reaches. Fundamentally, Pat displayed a strong sense of justice, although he knew full well that ours is not a world in which justice can easily flourish.

Many of Pat's closest friends cherish a similar souvenir of him. It is the memory of an expression that often found its way to Pat's face—a quiet, secretive smile, coupled with a faraway look that made it appear that he had just awakened to something—as if, quite suddenly, he had discovered some delightful fount of knowledge that would keep him endlessly amused.

Pat rarely divulged what he was thinking in such moments. But the result remains for us to read in sixteen novels that are now mostly to be found, musty and forgotten, on the tables at church bazaars and in the darkened corners of used-book shops. Within their covers they contain the most engaging twentieth-century American social history ever compiled. Like keys to a lost civilization, they await rediscovery.

APPENDICES

I. Pat's article in *The National Herald,* August 15, 1943:

Greek Soldiers Are Deanna Durbin Fans
by Edward E. Tanner 3rd

They know the Durbin repertoire by heart and Deanna is still the queen of Greece.

The Greek soldiers' spirit is indomitable. They laugh at everything. Death, starvation or deprivation can never defeat them.

Because many Americans think mainly in superlatives, they can visualize only two kinds of Greeks: the meek Greek and the chic Greek. In other words, the American picture of a Greek is either the lovely Duchess of Kent and what she's wearing this year . . . or the quiet little black-eyed man who runs that dingy restaurant on Sixth Avenue. These are the Greeks, just two kinds—high and low; nothing in between. I thought so too, until being attached to the Royal Greek Army, where one acquires not only an understanding of these people, but an undying devotion for them as well.

They are the most complete individuals in the world but they do combine certain marked characteristics which make them unique as a people as well as separate beings. Greeks are extremists in everything. In extravagance and frugality, love and hatred, joy and sorrow.

They are instinctively gentlemen: hospitable, friendly and generous to the breaking point. The first night we American Field Service men descended upon the ADS (Advanced Dressing Station), the reception tent was emptied and turned into AFS headquarters. Every Greek in the unit voluntarily pitched in to make us comfortable. Each man paid a brief polylingual social call armed to the teeth with cigarettes, fruit, precious sweets from Egypt, helpful suggestions and beautiful smiles.

All Greeks are vastly cordial . . . even with prisoners. At El Alamein the Greek soldiers gave their bread—and they love bread—gladly to the same captured Italians who had sold their rationed roughage to the women of starving Athens at twenty dollars a loaf. Not that any one Greek lives who wouldn't take personal pleasure in knifing an Italian, German or Bulgarian (especially the Bulgarians) in active combat, but a guest is a guest.

The Greek Army is democratic to almost frightening degrees. During the day, men and officers stick strictly to business with a good deal of saluting and "Yes, Sir" and "on the double," but after duty they mix freely to sing or box or sip gin and lime, which they pretend to like (Greeks are chain smokers but only half-hearted drinkers), with no feeling of inequality. English liaison officers are usually appalled to see a Greek captain wrangling with his orderly about politics or the cinema or the relative merits of Alexandria or Athens over the backgammon board; or to hear a corporal calling down his major across the bridge table—"What do you mean bidding on a hand like that? Don't you know how to count your honors yet?" No army in the world can operate this way except the Greek.

The Royal Greek Army also travels from front to front with the gay abandon of a country day school moving to the sea shore for the holidays. They adore animals and always make sure their dogs, cats, lambs, birds and monkeys are given first consideration, then the luggage and finally the soldiers themselves gingerly carrying their lutes and guitars. Perched precariously atop a teetering lorry, the Army sings—and beautifully—every inch of the way; songs in French, Spanish and Italian and one particular Greek favorite, "Begin the Beguine." They love American music and worship Deanna Durbin. The dentist with our brigade croons "My Own" to his unconscious patients during extractions. The mechanics bellow "I Love to Whistle" while rebuilding demolished trucks; and the Greek soldiers, who are members of the Boy Scouts until late dotage, whistle "Be a Good Scout" all day long.

In cleanliness, a Greek is completely cat-like. On the desert a soldier will go without drinking water in order to wash himself every day. At Baalbeck (Syria) I have seen the men in the Second brigade dash naked through the snow to bathe in the icy stream which flows through the town. Being primarily a handsome race with beautiful hands and infinitesimal feet (average Army size 6 to 6½) this may be attributed to mere vanity but I hardly think so. Greeks deplore filth; flies are actually repulsive to them. A soldier will cross the street before going through a throng of milling squalid Arabs. He will shave his hair if he cannot wash it often enough and will wash his uniforms before entrusting them to a so-so native laundry.

The Greeks are sociability itself. They are curious by nature and love gossip. Any choice bit of news from headquarters, any new rumor, will cover the camp in six languages in less than an hour. The Egyptian Greeks (of which there are approximately 60,000 in Alexandria alone) all speak English of a sort, in addition to French, Arabic, Italian and their native tongue. They are prolific letter-writers and anxiously await the twenty-five word messages which travel for four months from Athens via the International Red Cross.

Occasionally a Greek will break down and confide that his mother froze to death in Athens . . . that his younger brothers have been shot by the Germans, Italians or Bulgarians . . . that his babies were starving to death when he escaped to join the Army assembling in Egypt. They tell of the hospital which was bombed on Easter Sunday at Jannina where 80 broken bodies—doctors, patients, nurses and stretcher bearers—were shoveled into nine coffins and buried. But the Greeks are vengeful. These crimes will not go unpunished. Today the Army in the Middle East controls the bands of rebels in the mountains of Greece. Every move, every scuffle, every bit of sabotage, is carefully planned in Egypt, Syria, Tunis or Turkey. No lone Italian or German dares to walk the streets of Salonica unarmed or unaccompanied. The Axis will pay ten-fold for every hostage it has taken and killed. The invasion of Greece will be done mainly from within. It will be cleaned out by the sad-eyed men who have the will and spirit to bury a daughter at twilight and attack an Italian sentry after dark. Athens will be avenged and it will be avenged by Greeks; by the stocky Cretans, the moody men from Samos and the limber soldiers of Chios.

The article as published ends rather abruptly here—it was probably cut down for space reasons.

II. In 1957, three years after its first publication, *House Party* was reissued by Crowell. For this edition, Pat—under his Patrick Dennis pseudonym—wrote a special introduction, an eloquent defense of comic novels, a genre already on the wane.

Of all the novels by Virginia Rowans, *House Party* remains my favorite.

It was first published in 1954 during that peculiar season of the year when a deluge of Light Summer Fiction is unloosed upon a public presumably all but done in from an onerous winter of Toynbee, Tolstoy and the tougher English novelists.

Except for a cosy reception from the critics, very little happened to poor old *House Party* at the time of its birth. Some five thousand kindly souls— give or take a couple of hundred—sauntered out and bought copies to send to friends who were sick or traveling. (Since my own books, as well, seem to be the constant companions of the bedpan and the bon voyage basket, I accept—but do not condone—this inevitable destiny of the "funny" novel.) I can only assume that several all-expense tours and compound fractures were made brighter by the presence of *House Party* during the dog days of 1954.

By the following fall, however, such serious works of art as *The Power of Positive Thinking, Royal Box* and *Love Is Eternal* were again commanding the reading public's gravest attention; and poor, frivolous *House Party* was cast aside with tennis racquets, musty bathing suits, travel-folders and temperature charts by its fair-weather friends—half-remembered, half-forgotten, like that summer romance or the winsome night nurse.

Nor did the book enjoy any of the subsidiary delights that often accompany original publication. No reprint firm came gallantly forth to provide *House Party* with a high-bosomed paper cover and a mass market of millions at twenty-five cents a throw. It was bypassed as "too sophisticated and not sexy enough for the drugstore trade." The book floundered, lost, in that never-never land of table settings, fashions and household hints—the Women's Magazines. For that is a world where no nice girl smokes, drinks or swears, and some of the ladies in *House Party* do all three—expertly. ("Of course *we* love it, here in the New York Office, but it's a little too *fast* for our readers.") None of the firms that specialize in cutting the works of Proust down to a novella which can be read in twenty minutes flat considered *House Party* suitable fare to be predigested for its customers. The London and Continental publishers damned the book as "too American to sell here." Several motion picture studios maundered over *House Party* without ever buying it to film, and there was even a dim attempt to adapt it into a play for the New York stage. That, too, died aborning.

Critically, *House Party* was a huge success (even if only in the category of hot-weather therapy). Commercially, it was a flop.

But *House Party,* an unpretentious wisp of a novel to say the least, had its own unintellectual coterie of admirers who read the book, reread it, told other people about it and even wrote the author asking for more. (About a dozen letters in all. Writers do not, by and large, receive the volume of crank and fan mail that people think they do.) Except for talk—and rather small talk, at that—nothing became of *House Party.* One by one, the existing copies were bought up, and eventually the novel become O.S./O.P. (Out of Stock and Out of Print), lamented by only a very few.

Publication of *The Loving Couple,* however, increased the Virginia Rowans audience to ten or twelve times what it had ever been before, and a gratifying trickle of requests for copies of *House Party* came in once again. Since there were no copies of the original edition on hand, the book is now being reissued—"by popular demand."

The term "by popular demand" always gives me the chills. It makes me think of a broken-down old actress who, bored with idleness in her hotel suite, decides to set out on her ninth—*and positively the last*—farewell appearance in *Sabrina Fair,* "by popular demand." It reminds me of that reticent, giggling hostess who allows her eager guests to bully her into singing "The Bell Song" from *Lakmé.* Or it calls to mind the superannuated politician, "drafted" by his adoring circle of ward heelers to run for just one more term, "as a service to the nation."

In other words, I don't believe it. I don't believe that "by popular demand" signifies very much either of popularity or of demand. And I can't bring myself to feel that a novel as unpopular and as little in demand as *House Party* can be causing *quite* such a stir.

Still, as long as *House Party* is being published once again, let me say that I am delighted. Since its original publication I have read the book six times—three times for business, three times for pleasure—and I know it well.

It has many faults. It is too long. It is densely overpopulated. (There are fourteen major characters, as many minor ones and God only knows how many bit-players. Such a cast would be permissible, perhaps, in *The Forsyte Saga,* but it's difficult to keep track of quite so many people in a novel that covers one weekend.) As in every other Virginia Rowans novel, the author makes the mistake of being either too feverishly gay or too waspishly cross while attempting to satirize the contemporary social scene. As in a Grade B Western the Good Guys are all too good, the Bad Guys are all too bad. And the plot is straight out of an old Shubert musical. It depends childishly on the long arm of coincidence; on implicit and explicit misunderstanding; on overheard conversations; on acts of God; and even, so help me, on mistaken identity. I can't *recall* a secret passage, but I don't know how the author ever managed to overlook one.

On the other hand, *House Party* has quite a lot of virtues, too. It's witty and cheery and might very probably please someone who finds himself unexpectedly in a hospital bed or in a dismal resort hotel on an inclement day. You could conceivably be concerned about the eventual fate of some of the characters, but I think that even the most obtuse will be able to foresee a happy ending. At any rate, the happy ending is there for all to enjoy. The dialogue is rather peppy and there are lots of places where you can laugh or chuckle or smile, depending on your mood.

Although it's not salacious enough for the twenty-five cent market, it undoubtedly contains enough racy material to satisfy the armchair devotee of cut-rate pornography, who must, by now, be inured to a disappointing disparity between the carnal delights advertised on the covers and the rather straitlaced material contained therein. Too naughty for the household magazine crowd, I don't believe that there is anything in the book that would seriously impair the morals of a ten-year-old child if a copy should be placed in his or her little hands. (This presupposes, of course, that you are accustomed to placing books in the hands of ten-year-olds and that the ten-year-old of your choice is dogged enough to read more than a couple of pages.)

All in all, *House Party* is a very pleasant little book. It can do you no harm and might even provide you with a certain amount of entertainment for your money. Try it. If you don't like it, you can always pass it on in good-as-new condition to a sick friend or someone who is contemplating a trip. It is, after all, Light Summer Fiction.

But I do hope that on this, its second time around, you and many others will buy it, read it and enjoy it. As I said before, *House Party*—for all its flaws—is still gay and merry and full of fun. And it still remains my favorite of all Virginia Rowans' novels. In fact, I wish I'd written it myself.

III. Pat contributed the following foreword to Vanguard's original edition of the *Auntie Mame* playscript:

Having had nothing to do with writing the play *Auntie Mame*, it is easy for me to be quite detached and objective about it. And I can say, right along with the critics and the thousands of people who have seen it, that it makes a wonderfully entertaining evening in the theatre.

If you are looking for a conventional little play suitable for the Freshman Frolic or the church basement—the sort of thing summarized in the catalogues of dramatic publishers as "Comedy; one interior; modern dress; three acts; four men; five women"—keep right on looking because *Auntie Mame* isn't it.

Like Mame herself, *Auntie Mame* is in no way conventional as a play. Nor could it be, because my novel, *Auntie Mame*, from which the play is derived, isn't even a novel, really. It is, instead, a couple of dozen episodes that take place in a couple of dozen localities over a couple of dozen years. I can't quite label it myself, but the matchless Rosalind Russell, who originated the role of Mame, who *is* Mame, calls this offering "a revue without music," and her definition is better than any I can supply. Both novel and play are freaks, then—but such *popular* freaks that their lavish eccentricities cannot be entirely despised.

Not every episode in my book is in the play. To get them all in—not that every one is worth dramatizing—would require passing out box luncheons, blankets, and toothbrushes to a rough-and-ready audience of slavish theatregoers weaned on Eugene O'Neill and the *Ring* series. But an astonishing number of the episodes in the book *are* in the play; enough so that the casual reader is convinced that every word of the novel has been translated to the stage. If that isn't catching the "spirit" of a book, I don't know what is.

And Jerome Lawrence and Robert E. Lee have gone yet a step further in their dramatization, for they have caught—far better than I—the moments of heartbreak that are also in *Auntie Mame* and placed them on the stage so deftly that, between the guffaws and giggles, snickers and snorts, there are audible sobs and visible tears at each and every performance. That is what I meant to do in the novel and, I am afraid, failed. To me, comedy is measured not only by its laughs, but by its tears. With every pratfall the heart should also ache. In this play it does, and I still cry just as hard when I drop into the Broadhurst Theatre now as I did on the night the play was out in Wilmington. Two handkerchiefs are par for the course.

But enough of the clown longing to play Hamlet. To quote from *Hamlet* itself, "The play's the thing something, something, something the king." And here it is, a warm, rich, sprawling, unorthodox comedy that I am proud and happy to have inspired.

IV. The following review by Pat of Tennessee Williams's *Garden District* appeared in *The New Republic* on January 13, 1958:

Ever since his superb *A Streetcar Named Desire* I have grown less and less fond of the plays of Tennessee Williams in a sort of geometric progression that resulted in leaving *A Cat on a Hot Tin Roof* [sic] and not even attending *Orpheus Descending*. However, with *Garden District,* a double bill appearing at the tiny York Playhouse, it's nice to see that Mr. Williams has something powerful to offer once again.

The curtain-raiser, *Something Unspoken,* is a short, telling dialogue between a rich, power-driven, ignorant snob of a New Orleans widow, nicely played by Eleanor Phelps, and her genteel, browbeaten secretary-companion, beautifully handled by Hortense Alden, who is probably the most exciting actress to appear on the stage this season. It's a dandy little one-act piece, demonstrating nicely Mr. Williams's understanding of the Southern gentlewoman, but it's short and slight and very easily forgotten after the tremendous impact of the second play of the evening.

Suddenly Last Summer is the heavy artillery of *Garden District*. Since every other critic who has tried to describe the play in any detail has fallen flat, I shall try to tell you just enough—but not too much—about what goes on.

Violet Venable is a wealthy old widow whose whole life has been wrapped up in her son, Sebastian. Sebastian, as Mrs. Venable tells it, was a paragon of all virtues—chaste, a lover of beauty, a devoted son, and a great poet, whose literary output amounted to one beautiful, beautiful poem for each summer he spent in smart European watering places with his mother. But Sebastian is dead. It happened last summer when, with Mrs. Venable laid up with a slight stroke, Sebastian took his impoverished young cousin Catherine abroad as his travelling companion. Because Sebastian's death occurred under circumstances that were hardly poetic, filial, beautiful or chaste, it is important to Mrs. Venable to maintain the silence of the only witness to this melancholy event—Catherine.

So far Mrs. Venable has managed very nicely. Because of the horrendous fashion in which Sebastian died, Catherine has been sufficiently unnerved so that Mrs. Venable has been able to keep her in a series of private mental institutions. But now Mrs. Venable, attempting an oblique bribe to a gifted young doctor, would like Catherine stilled even more effectively by means of a frontal lobotomy.

Catherine is brought to Sebastian's garden in the company of her foolish mother, her venal younger brother and a mental attendant. The doctor injects her with a truth drug and there, before Mrs. Venable, she tells the whole gruesome story of Sebastian, his life and his death.

I can give you ten good reasons for passing up *Garden District*:
1. It is an evening of unrelenting horror.
2. Neither offering is a play in any sense of the word.
3. There are just six amusing lines all evening long.
4. Most of the people involved are woefully unpleasant and decidedly from the wrong side of Queer Street.
5. The dialogue often tends to be arty, abstruse and highfalutin'.
6. If you stop to think about *Suddenly Last Summer* it all becomes unbelievable.
7. There's just something *about* boys named Sebastian, anyhow.
8. The theatre's not easily accessible.
9. Seats (there are only 299 of them) are difficult and costly to obtain.
10. A distressingly large percentage of those seats are occupied by unescorted young men who protest sibilantly that Tennessee Williams is really writing about the norm.

But both pieces, while far from perfect as plays, are vintage Williams, exquisitely directed and performed.

Hortense Alden, who, in a coquettish red wig, plays the vicious Violet Venable, brings to the role a terrifying mixture of Medea and Mrs. Phelps. She has a voice that is equal parts velvet and sandpaper and she is able to remind me of Elisabeth Bergner, Eugenie Leontovich, Luise Rainer, Judith Evelyn, Beatrice Straight and Miriam Hopkins while being absolutely original. In both plays and in two vastly different roles she is electric.

Anne Meacham, as the bedeviled Catherine, overcomes the obstacles of seeming taller than any girl in New York and of having an accent that could spring from any place *except* New Orleans (I speculated on Scotland twice; Czechoslovakia once), by turning in a spellbinding performance of a role so taxing that one false move could have made it ludicrous. Robert Lansing is perfect as the doctor and everyone else is just as good. The same can be said for the settings, the costumes, the lighting and the music.

V. For the December 12, 1962, issue of the *Chicago Tribune Magazine of Books*, Pat wrote a short story featuring Leander Starr from the just-published *Genius*. Here is its complete text:

'Twas the Night before Christmas in the Railroad Station

Leander Starr is no stranger to Chicago. He has visited many times between alighting from the Super-Chief and boarding the Twentieth Century, and vice versa, on his pilgrimages from one coast to the other. While in town, he has run up considerable tabs in the Pump Room, as all good Hollywood citizens are expected to do.

It is perhaps because of those large luncheon checks, still unpaid, that he prefers now to fly over the city. But the Christmas I speak of happened a long time ago when hotels hadn't yet assumed aliases and were called simple things like the Stevens, the Medinah Club, the just plain Blackstone or Congress, and when Starr was the hottest director in the picture industry.

It was Christmas Eve. Chicago was caught in the grip of a blizzard. The Super-Chief had been 19 hours late and the Century wasn't even planning to budge. The "L" could barely make it out to Evanston. Starr arrived in a white polo coat and a white heat of fury. It was a white Christmas, all right, and every hotel Starr had ever heard of—as well as quite a lot he hadn't— had marooned guests sleeping on cots in the corridors.

"I'm ever so sorry, Mr. Starr," his valet said after three hours in a pay telephone booth at the station, "but there's no place. Not even the Y.M.C.A. can take you."

"To think that I, a man who has maneuvered Carole Lombard, Jean Harlow, Gertie Lawrence—every goddess of stage and screen—to greatness, can be so victimized by fate and the elements; a castaway in this squalid station. Very well, get my things and we shall make do with a humble railway bench. Please ask those people to move."

As Starr had planned to spend nearly two weeks in New York, his "things" consisted of two trunks, a shoe trunk, six alligator hat boxes, golf clubs, tennis and squash racquets, five suitcases in graduated sizes, a portable radio, book case, desk, bar, the traveling pharmacopoeia (he was something of a hypochondriac), and the picnic hamper. It made quite a display and he suddenly was out of small change for tipping the redcaps.

Starr's valet, risking heart and muscle, walloped the "things" into a semicircle around the bench, making a sort of private apartment. Martinis were mixed from the portable bar, champagne appeared—none too cool—and the hamper offered up an adequate repast of smoked trout, celery knobs, tinned squabs (boned), a Westphalian ham, hearts of palm, and some *babas au rhum*.

"When I think," Starr fumed, "that I could be having a decent meal at 21!" But, fortified with three martinis, he was able to dig in with something of his old gusto when he became conscious of a face on either side of his own.

"Hello, Mr. Man," a small voice said.

"Go away," Starr growled.

"We're hungry," the other face said. They were two small children, obviously brother and sister, somewhere between 6 and 10. Starr was as bad about other people's ages as he was about his own.

"There's an appalling restaurant just over there. Ask your mother to buy you something."

"Our mommy isn't here. Sister Mary Alexander from the school left us here to wait for her but the train's real late and . . ."

"Here, take this ham and some rum cake and go."

"And we're thirsty, too."

"You can have some of this champagne, if you'll just leave me alone. Not properly chilled, but a good year. Now shut up."

"I guess we're not gonna see Sanny Claus," one of the children whimpered.

"Of course you're not, child. Now do be quiet and stop panting down my neck."

Starr sent his valet to the newsstand for copies of *Vanity Fair, Judge, Ballyhoo,* and *Theatre Arts* and began to read ostentatiously. Drugged by the champagne and the stale heat of the waiting room, the children stretched out on their bench and dozed off. But the station, once stifling, became cool, then chilly, then downright icy. The children shivered and stirred restlessly.

"I can't endure this for another minute," Starr snapped at his valet. "Put a coat over them."

"Your white polo coat, sir?"

"Certainly not. Look at those galoshes! Use the cashmere with the sable lining. Here, I'll do it."

As Starr covered the children, the girl opened her eyes. "Sanny Claus? Oh." She began to sob quietly.

"Go back to sleep, child. He'll be along in due course. Miserable little beggars," Starr said to his valet. "Not much of a Christmas for them—not to mention poor me. Tell me, did you pack that red silk smoking jacket?"

"Oh yes indeed, Mr. Starr."

"And my black riding boots? And is there cotton among my med'cines? Now get out a pair of socks—good long ones."

"Your silk stockings, Mr. Starr?"

"Do you think I'd wear rayon? Certainly the silk ones. And now just fetch me my *boîte de bijoux.* There must be some old watches and tie pins and other baubles in it. And then buy a couple of oranges and chocolate bars or whatever poison brats stuff themselves with."

"Really, Mr. Starr?"

"Do as I tell you. Now, give me those clothes. I'll be changing in the gents' room. When I come out, start jingling the luggage keys like a thing bewitched."

Five minutes later he reappeared, as skittish a Father Christmas as ever was turned out by Pearl's or Sulka's.

"Ho ho ho!" he boomed. The drowsing waiting room came to life with a jolt. "O, ho, ho, ho. Merry Christmas to all and whatever it is!"

The children, thoroughly awake now, sat up wide-eyed as Starr capered across the waiting room toward their bench.

"Sanny Claus!" they said in unison. "Right here in this ole train station!"

The next morning things began moving in a confused, sluggish way. A special train to New York had been assembled from old bits and pieces of rolling stock in the car yard. Starr, having insisted on a drawing room or at least a compartment, settled for an upper berth. He sat furiously dipping the last of the rum cakes into a cardboard container of coffee while he dispatched his valet and the children to the station restaurant.

"Anything to get them out of my sight," he said.

The children, each swinging a Patek Philippe watch by its thin platinum chain, went off happily enough to bacon, eggs, pancakes, waffles, and crullers. One by one, Starr's "things" were carted off to the cold, waiting train.

A harried woman in a worn cloth coat hurried in. "Pardon me, sir, but have you seen two kids—a boy and a girl—wearing . . ."

"I have seen nothing else, madam, more's the pity. They are at breakfast."

"Who with?"

"Why, with my valet, who else?"

"Some people's idea of what's funny!" the woman snapped and hurried off.

"We're all ready to go now, Mr. Starr," his valet said. "I'm to ride with the baggage."

The great white polo coat flung about him like an ermine mantle, Starr made his stately way across the station.

". . . and Mommy," the children were shouting, "Sanny Claus came. He reely did. Right here in a station."

"Will you shut up!" Starr snapped.

"G'by, Mr. Meeeeee-an!"

"Children," their mother said, "how many times have I told you not to talk to strangers! You never know what they might be up to."

VI. To supplement a previous American will specifying his legacies to Louise, Michael, Betsy, and Corry, Pat drew up a will in Mexico during the late 1960s. It was written in English for his law firm to translate into Spanish. Here are some excerpts:

I, Edward Everett Tanner, 3rd, also known as Patrick Tanner and Patrick Dennis, being of sound mind and body blah, blah, blah do hereby will and bequeath blah blah blah.

1. My body is to be cremated and disposed of in the quickest, cheapest manner possible (flushed down the toilet, scattered to the winds, sunk into an unmarked hole in the ground, etc.) at the expense of my estate.

2. No funeral or memorial services of any kind.

SPECIFIC BEQUESTS

1. All table silver (Mexican, Spanish and American) to Mr. and/or Mrs. Abraham Badian.

2. To Guy McMaster Kent: Ten pictures (hanging in the drawing room) painted by Guy McMaster Kent—six anatomicals and four Moroccan figures.

3. To Murray Grand: all personal jewelry (watches, cuff links, studs, cigarette cases, lighters, etc.).
4. To Salvador Campos Icardo: The sum of 10,000 pesos as a small token of my gratitude for his wit, charm and patience at trying to teach me the Spanish language.
5. To whatever household servants as may be in my employ at the time of my death: one year's salary apiece; their liveries and uniforms, and letters of reference to be written by the executors of my estate.
6. To Sras. Katherine Walch and Patricia Roane—unlimited selection of my household furnishings, china, crystal, rugs, hangings, pictures, bibelots, etc.
7. To Cris Alexander—the portrait of me painted and signed by Mr. Alexander in 1959.

GENERAL REQUESTS
1. Wardrobe: Suits, coats, hats, linen, shoes, etc. are to be divided among the gentlemen of my acquaintance resident in Mexico whom they best become and fit. In case of disputes, the executors of my will are to decide who looks best in what.
2. To my friends and acquaintances resident in Mexico (those whose names are checked in red in the green velvet address book to be found by the executors of my will near the telephone in the library of my residence), free selection of my unclaimed household possessions . . . without limitation. The executors of my will are to appoint a specific hour during one Sunday when my belongings are to be disposed of on a first-come-first-served basis in the futile hope that avarice may make my Mexican friends a little more punctual. Whatever wines and liquors remaining in my household are to be served.
    (It would please me if this *piñata de la muerta* could be conducted in a polite spirit of friendliness, generosity and understanding on the part of the ghouls. But as I shan't be present to be offended or angered by the behavior of my former companions over my possessions of either large or small value, it doesn't really matter. In any case, all disputes are to be settled by las Sras. Walch y Roane and Sr. Badian, the executors of my estate.)
3. All possessions not disposed of in this will are to be sold specifically or at auction. Proceeds from such sale are to be placed in the bank account of my estate. All monies remaining in my estate after payment of bills, debts and taxes incurred before and after my death are to be divided into thirds and given, anonymously, to three Mexican charities selected by the executors of my will as a token of my gratitude to the people who have harbored me so graciously and comfortably in their enchanting country.

    Blah blah blah blah blah and all the rest of that legal shit.

EDWARD EVERETT TANNER, 3RD

Salvador—
Please translate this into the sort of Spanish that will read as though it had been written by a human being and not some idiot at Goodrich, Dalton,

Baker, Bots, Porterhouse, Nightsoil and Desbagar. Say what I have said about the ghouls (*profanadores de cadávares*) so that they will all *try* to act like ladies and gentlemen and not go to war over my last necktie, and keep the language simple enough so that el Sr. Notario Cretino can understand it. And don't waste a lot of words. I'm paying you by the page.

S. S. S. y Capellán,

PATRICK

VII. When *Little Me* was reissued in trade paperback in 1982, Pat's son, Michael, contributed the following foreword:

Preface to the New Edition

What Is a "Classic"?

To think that twenty years have gone by since dear, dead Mr. Dennis guided my hand through *Little Me*! Who then supposed that my life story would become an immortal, ageless "classic"? Not those certain short-sighted "critics" (long since forgotten) who misunderstood my work. Not the stuffy, stubborn Swedes of the Nobel Committee who recently passed over me for the twenty-first consecutive year. No, this new edition owes its existence to those most important critics of all: my adoring "fans," who absolutely *refuse* to allow me to retire from public life despite all my many attempts.

Malheureusement, the publishers have ignored my *specific* instructions that the new edition be printed on scented cream-colored vellum watermarked with the Schlumpfert coat-of-arms and bound in limp calfskin, with a carved ivory silhouette of my face mounted on the cover above the title in gold leaf. *They* call it being cost effective—*I* call it chintzy, stingy, and *pas comme il faut.*

A legendary screen star, a best-selling author, twice the toast of Broadway . . . what mountain is there left for me to climb? Why, *The Belle Poitrine Story*, scripted by me for the screen, of course. Choosing a director remains the only "snag." One can't be too careful—Hollywood has gotten so *vulgar* in the years that I've been away. Yassir, my eleventh husband, says Federico Fellini (a well-known Italian director) is the only man alive who can do justice to my screenplay, whereas I lean toward Ken Russell. But I digress . . .

Here, then, my *chèvre d'oeuf*!

BELLE POITRINE
—As dictated to Patrick Dennis Jr.
(Michael Tanner)

VIII. Who's Who in *Little Me*

Many *Little Me* fans are curious about the "cast" of the book—who the people were that posed for Cris Alexander's wonderfully campy photos, and what happened to them. Here is a "Where Are They Now?" update:

JERI ARCHER (Lulubelle, Belle, Isabelle, Christabelle) continued her modeling career. She died of cancer circa 1970.

KURT BIEBER (Letch Feeley) appeared in such Broadway plays as *The Teahouse of the August Moon, Wish You Were Here, The World of Suzie Wong,* and *Wonderful Town.* He has been an extra in almost every movie ever filmed in New York City. Kurt says he is "still around and still cruising Christopher Street."

CRIS ALEXANDER (Fred Poitrine, the Dowager Countess of Baughdie, Elated Nurse) has retired from acting and photography and has spent the past thirty years in Saratoga, New York.

SHAUN O'BRIEN (Mr. Musgrove) continued to spend another twenty-five years as the leading character dancer of the New York City Ballet. His roles have included Dr. Coppelius, Herr Drosselmeyer, and the Father in *The Prodigal Son.* He has also spent the past thirty years in Saratoga with his companion, Cris Alexander.

DODY GOODMAN (Helen Highwater) continued her acting career, appearing in *Nunsense* and the film version of *Grease.* She resides on New York City's Upper West Side.

ALICE PEARCE (Winnie), a popular stage, screen, and television comedienne, had made a memorable film debut as the sneezy roommate Lucy Schmeeler in *On the Town.* Following *Little Me,* she appeared in such films as *My Six Loves, The Thrill of It All,* and *Kiss Me, Stupid.* A regular on the TV show *Bewitched* as the befuddled neighbor Gladys Kravitz, she was diagnosed with cancer but continued working. She filmed a *Bewitched* episode on the last day of her life.

HERVEY JOLIN (Morris Buchsbaum, Mrs. Palmer Potter) is now a nonagenarian living in Easton, Pennsylvania. Still known to his intimates as Mrs. Rhoda Fleming, he is involved in "horticultural pursuits, including propagating pansies developed from a Swiss strain. A large ruby red is to be named 'Little Me,' patent pending." He is also, at this time, "Director of the Rhoda Fleming Memorial Library." Each year he receives a Mother's Day card from his daughter, Florence Fleming (Cris Alexander).

ELAINE ADAM (Magdalena Montezuma) continued working for many years at the Council on Foreign Relations. She is now retired and divides her time between New York City and her upstate home in Columbia County.

JANE LAMBERT (Billie) grew up in Oklahoma with Cris Alexander and was, according to him, "a midwestern fag moll from the word go." His nickname for her was Dudley Bumpus. She went on to marry a millionaire and to do small parts, usually as mothers, in such films as *The Fury* and *Oh, God!* and on television in *Happy Days* and *Sanford and Son.* She died in 1979.

VINCENT WARREN (Lance Leopard) was a dancer who became a member of the Canadian National Ballet.

IX. Eulogy for Louise Tanner, delivered by Michael Tanner, May 19, 2000, St. George's Church, New York:

As I was going through my mother's things, this photograph fluttered down from the top shelf. It's from my parents' trip to Russia in 1959. It was a group tour. Dad was working on a fictional account of it called *Ill Wind Tour* that never came to anything. And as you can see, here is my mother, Louise, on a street either in Tashkent or Alma Ata bestowing coins and chewing gum on a group of five very insistent street urchins.

Several things strike me about the picture. My mother looks young and healthy and beautiful. The children are very poor—this one is barefoot. But what really strikes me is the smile on Mom's face—far from being intimidated by the situation, she looks genuinely amused and very happy. This put me in mind of chapter 9, verse 7, of St. Paul's letter to the Corinthians: "So let every man give as he feels in his heart; not grudgingly or of necessity: for God loveth a cheerful giver."

That was Louise—a cheerful giver.

The first thing you'd have to say about my mother is that she was fun. I will always be grateful to her for the general tone of discourse that she established in our family, which can be summarized: "Never a harsh word." I speak with her friends, who tell me: "You know I haven't spoken to my father for fifteen years. *He* can call *me* if he wants to." So sad. . . .

Our family, on the other hand, can best be described by a lyric written by Stephen Sondheim, one of Mom's favorites: "No fits, no fights, no feuds and no egos. . . ."

Mom was responsible for the very relaxed, tolerant, and loving atmosphere that has always prevailed in our family.

She was so easygoing. She was constitutionally unable to sustain anger for any length of time. Because, more than anything, she loved to laugh. Betsy and I were keenly aware of this. No matter how mad she was, if you could get her to laugh, Mom had this wonderful way of melting. She was a *melter*. The madder she got, the harder she'd laugh once the melting process was under way. And then we were off the hook—permanently. She was quick to set anger aside and forget about it—a wonderful character trait. It was just not in her to bear a grudge.

And then, of course, there was her wonderful sense of humor.

It was all going on in so many languages . . . Spanish, Latin, Yiddish, Chapin French, Vassar German, Berlitz Total Immersion Program Russian.

Not that she could actually *speak* any of these languages—she *couldn't*. My mother's approach to a foreign language was to learn about five-hundred words of it and sift through those five-hundred words for the ones that struck her as being amusing or cool-sounding, and then to pepper her English conversation liberally with these foreign words and phrases. And she didn't do it to be pretentious or lord it over people—that was just the way she spoke. But no one has ever spoken like my mother. No one! Never!

Let's take a typical Louise sentence. Mom would open her mouth, and you'd be off on a trip around the world. You'd start out in France, travel through time and space to ancient Rome, and wind up on the Lower East Side of Manhattan.

Example: "*Malheureusement*, Mike, it now dawns on me that my *lares and penates* may become a source of *tsuris* to you and Betsy."

And then often she would NOT FINISH THE SENTENCE. She'd pull up halfway and expect you, armed only with *lares, penates, tsuris*, and *malheureusement* to take it the rest of the way on your own.

Betsy and I always knew exactly what she was talking about.

Her other most characteristic verbal mannerism was the way she accented certain syllables and words *really* hard—especially when she was exasperated.

Example: "It seems like *EVERY* time you *TRY* to throw a *DINNER* party these days, there's *SOME*thing *SOME*body can't eat!"

So funny . . . Just naturally hilarious . . .

And, of course, she was generous. Louise was the most generous person I've ever known, and I mean generous in every way.

Mom was a soft touch. Charities loved her. The homeless were crazy about her. Waiters and cabdrivers did double takes upon seeing what she had left them. She always wrote a thank-you note. She volunteered at PS 96 for ten years, volunteered at Covenant House, volunteered at church soup kitchens. And she loaned money to anyone who needed it without expectation of repayment. Anyone, really, who happened to get within arm's length of my mother ran a significant risk of having a considerable sum of money bestowed upon them.

And most important, she felt a deep, lifelong obligation to aid the poor. For all of her profound ambivalence about the Catholic Church, in this regard she was truly Christian, a great Christian.

She was a huge influence on me. It's not a coincidence that I ended up working at Bellevue—a city hospital serving the poor and indigent ten blocks from her house.

My mother had a wonderful life. She made me a great counter of blessings, and it now gives me pleasure to count hers.

She had loving parents, her mother, Helen Frith, and her father, Henry Stickney.

In 1945, she took a job at Franklin Spier, the most eccentric book advertising agency in New York. There she formed a nexus of friends that would be there for the next fifty years: Peggy Brooks, Joy Singer, Isabelle Holland, the late Stuart Harris. Others joined her circle and stayed: Robin Little, Viv & Elaine, Cris Alexander & Shaun O'Brien

She fell in love with and married one of the most fascinating and unusual men who ever lived: my father, Patrick Tanner.

There were years of Glamour and Celebrity. I remember the two of them coming to say good night to Betsy and me, dressed for the theater. Dad handing a phone number to Corry and announcing: "Your mother and I are going to see this *dreary* Eugene O'Neill play and then we'll be at the Algonquin." Dad so formidable. Mom looking so beautiful, the whole room redolent of Chanel No. 5. They were so splendid together.

She traveled the world.

She published five books.

She gave birth to two children who adored her, and each other.

And, although my parents separated for many years, Pat came home to spend his final year with us. Dad died in Mom's bed. And my father's ashes are now in this casket, in an urn, cradled under her arm.

She was blessed by wonderful people who worked for her . . . William Palmer. Anne Palmer. The late Corry Salley.

And she lived to see me marry . . . *"finally."*

Then she gave me the greatest gift a mother can give her son once he's grown up: she loved my wife.

For her last three years on earth she was the proudest of grandmothers. Henry, I promised you last night that if you were a good boy and kept quiet during the funeral, I would speak to you, my baby boy, directly. Well, here it is: "Henry, you won't remember her when you grow up, but trust me. Grandmother loved you very much."

In April, when she could still appreciate it, I let Louise know that a second grandchild was on the way. To be named Louise if it's a girl. Or a boy.

She enjoyed superlative good health for the first seventy-five years of her life, followed by a catastrophic illness which was mercifully brief.

She presented with back pain on March 27th. I expected it to get better in a week, but it got worse.

On April 24th, a CAT scan showed carcinoma metastic to the lumbar spine, a hopeless diagnosis.

By May 4th, she was a hospice patient. I would like to thank the people who took care of my mother so lovingly during her last days: Rose, Estelle, Valerie, and Deanne of Partners in Care; the wonderful people from Visiting Nurse Service's hospice division; and Mom's physician, my dear friend Alan Dechiario.

Julie got us something off the Internet about caring for the hospice patient, and one sentence I found very inspiring: "Affirm the person's ongoing value to you and the good that you will carry forward into your life that you received from her." After she could no longer speak, I spent the last two weeks of Mom's life with my thumb on her radial pulse, just trying to soak it all up—the last of her tremendous goodness.

She died nineteen days after being diagnosed—in her own home in her own bed with me, Betsy, and her cat, Bruno, in attendance.

As she said: "One of my mottos has always been: 'Get it over with.' "

She was very stoic. One thing she never said was: "My back hurts."

She lay in her own bed under a whole wall of family pictures, with absolutely no medical instrumentation, not even an IV.

Her last words were: "Oh boy."

One of the only sad things about my mother's wonderful life is that, far from being complacent or self-satisfied, she was perennially insecure. Louise felt that she owed the world a debt that she could never repay. No matter how much of herself she gave, she never thought it was enough. Mother, look at all the people here whose lives you gladdened. You gave plenty, Mother. It was plenty.

THE NOVELS OF
EDWARD EVERETT TANNER III

Oh, What a Wonderful Wedding! by Virginia Rowans. New York: Thomas Y. Crowell, 1953.

House Party by Virginia Rowans. New York: Thomas Y. Crowell, 1954.

Auntie Mame by Patrick Dennis. New York: Vanguard Press, 1955.

Guestward Ho! by Barbara C. Hooton as indiscreetly confided to Patrick Dennis. New York: Vanguard Press, 1955.

The Loving Couple by Virginia Rowans. New York: Thomas Y. Crowell, 1956.

The Pink Hotel by Dorothy Erskine and Patrick Dennis. New York: G. P. Putnam's Sons, 1957.

Around the World with Auntie Mame by Patrick Dennis. New York: Harcourt, Brace, 1958.

Love and Mrs. Sargent by Virginia Rowans. New York: Farrar, Straus and Cudahy, 1961.

Little Me, The Intimate Memoirs of That Great Star of Stage, Screen and Television Belle Poitrine, as told to Patrick Dennis. New York: E. P. Dutton, 1961.

Genius by Patrick Dennis. New York: Harcourt, Brace and World, 1962.

First Lady by Martha Dinwiddie Butterfield, as told to Patrick Dennis. New York: William Morrow, 1964.

The Joyous Season by Patrick Dennis. New York: Harcourt, Brace and World, 1964.

Tony by Patrick Dennis. New York: E. P. Dutton, 1966.

How Firm a Foundation by Patrick Dennis. New York: William Morrow, 1968.

Paradise by Patrick Dennis. New York: Harcourt, Brace, Jovanovich, 1971.

3-D by Patrick Dennis. New York: Coward, McCann and Geoghegan, 1972.

NOTES

Prologue

page xiii–xiv   Quotes from Paul Rudnick: Paul Rudnick to EM (1-18-97).

1. Kid Stuff

page 4   Details about 1574 Asbury Avenue: David Peterson to EM (2-1-98); also David Peterson to EM (2-1-98).

page 4   Grandma Thacker at the burlesque show: Gordon Muchow to EM (1-8-98); also David Peterson to EM (2-1-98).

page 4   Background on Mary Williams Tanner: Michael Tanner to EM; Louise Tanner to EM (3-22-98).

page 5   Background on Edward Tanner Jr.: Sister Joanna to EM (7-4-97); Michael Tanner to EM.

page 5   "Pat's childhood friends": Katie Kelley to EM(1-5-98); Forrest Williams to EM (8-31-98).

page 6   Details of Pat's birth: Sister Joanna to EM (7-4-97).

page 6   " 'And did you know' ": Louise Tanner to EM (3-22-98).

page 6   "he had a favorite morning ritual": Katie Kelley to EM (1-5-98).

page 9   "Dispensing beauty advice": Keith Stevenson to EM (9-7-98).

page 10   "The older Pat got": Michael Tanner to EM (6-19-97).

page 10   "Pat's father blowing up at Pat" : Keith Stevenson to EM (9-7-98).

page 10   Ed Tanner's financial problems during the Depression: Sister Joanna to EM (7-4-97).

2. Growing Pains

page 12   "One night Ed came home": Anne Noggle to EM (1-4-97).

page 12   Ed Tanner's mistress: Michael Tanner to EM.

page 13   "he used his humor and sophistication": Anne Noggle to EM (1-4-97).

page 14   Boy Scout skit: Courtesy of Webster Jones.

page 18   Pat's high school record: Courtesy of Evanston Township High School.

page 18   "Katie's mother had been an actress": David Peterson to EM (2-1-98).

page 18   The drama program at Evanston Township High School: Katie Kelley, Millie B. Jones Mathers, David Peterson to EM.

page 20   "When not studying or rehearsing": Anne Noggle, Millie B. Jones Mathers, Katie Kelley, David Peterson to EM.

page 20   "Pat and his friends also": Webster Jones to EM (12-19-97).

page 25 Background on Finale Productions: Anne Noggle, Millie B. Jones Mathers, Katie Stockbridge Kelley, David Peterson to EM.

3. "A Great Big Town on a Great Big Lake"

page 27 Description of 3202 Lake Shore Drive: Sister Joanna to EM (7-4-97); David Peterson to EM (2-1-98).

page 29 "As usual, Pat was using levity": Michael Tanner to EM.

page 32 "In spite of the good times": Ibid.

page 32 Details of Agnes Noggle, the Rosenberg sisters, the nuns, and the insolent kid: Forrest Williams to EM (12-15-98).

4. Across to Africa

page 38 Background on the American Field Service: American Field Service archives, New York, N.Y.

page 40 "Pat did his best to contribute": Webster Jones to EM (12-19-97); Kirk Browning to EM (8-3-97).

page 40 "Pat had managed to get himself engaged": Letters from PD to Webster Jones, December 1942.

page 41 "Pat had already been to New York": Letter from PD to Webster Jones, April 9, 1943.

page 42–44 Details of the ocean voyage to Africa: Records at the American Field Service archives, New York, N.Y.; C. B. Squire to EM (10-18-97); William Weaver to EM (10-18-97).

page 44 "The volunteers on board the *Atlantis*": William Weaver to EM (10-18-97).

5. The Combat Zone

page 56 "At first, Pat was happy to be in Italy": Dean Fuller to EM (12-18-97).

page 56 "On January 19, 1944": Medical records of American Field Service archives, New York, N.Y.

page 57 "In February of 1944": Forrest Williams to EM (3-8-98).

page 58 "Midway through the Monte Cassino bombing": Ibid.

page 58 "On April 22, 1944": Medical records of the American Field Service archives, New York, N.Y.

page 59 "Pat's duties were every bit": Sister Joanna to EM (7-4-97).

page 61 "Pat's sense of humor": Robin Little to EM (7-21-97).

page 62 "By July of 1944": Dean Fuller to EM (12-18-97).

page 62 "Pat and the rest of Section One": Ibid.

page 63 "Pat continued doing his best": Michael Tanner to EM.

page 63 "More and more": Forrest Williams to EM (8-31-98); Kirk Browning to EM (8-3-97).

page 65 "Decades later": Records of American Field Service archives, New York, N.Y.

6. New Boy in Town

page 70   "One of the first things Pat did": Michael Tanner to EM.

page 72–74   Description of Franklin Spier based on recollections of Louise Tanner (3-22-98), Joy Singer (8-7-97), and Peggy Brooks (11-18-97) in interviews with EM.

page 74   *New York Herald Tribune Weekly Book Review* quote on *There's a Fly in This Room!:* November 24, 1946.

page 76   "Pat was terribly concerned for Frances": Kirk Browning to EM (8-3-97); Peggy Brooks to EM (11-18-97).

page 77   "Before long, Kirk invited Barbara": Barbara Browning to EM (12-3-97).

7. Social Register Rescue

page 79–80   Description of Creative Age Press: Marilyn Amdur to EM (1-25-98); Isabelle Holland to EM (10-4-97).

page 80–82   Descriptions of Louise's childhood, Pat entering her life, wedding ceremony: Louise Tanner to EM (3-22-98); Michael Tanner to EM (12-22-97).

page 82   Pat's problem with his "feeling function": Michael Tanner to EM.

page 83   "Earlier that month, Louise gave a party": Lydia Anderson to EM (9-16-97).

page 83–84   Quote from Louise Tanner regarding Pat's sexuality: To EM (3-22-98).

page 85–86   Joy Singer's recollections: Joy Singer to EM (8-7-97).

page 86–87   Background on Council on Foreign Relations: Mission statement from Council on Foreign Relations Web site; also, *Continuing the Inquiry: The Council on Foreign Relations from 1921 to 1996* by Peter Grose, published by the Council on Foreign Relations, 1996.

page 87   Pat grows back his beard: Vivian Weaver to EM (1-26-97).

page 87   Descriptions of Council personnel: Elizabeth Valkenier to EM (2-9-98).

page 88–89   Comments from Vivian Weaver and Elaine Adam about Pat's interaction with employees: To EM (1-26-97).

page 89   The long lunch at Oscar's Salt of the Sea: Roger Ross to EM (3-15-98).

page 90   Pat standing up for the secretaries at the Council: Vivian Weaver to EM (1-26-97).

8. Noms de Plume

page 91   Pat's falling-out with Dr. Nicolas Nyaradi: Louise Tanner to EM (3-22-98).

page 91   *New York Herald Tribune* quote on *My Ringside Seat in Moscow:* February 3, 1952.

page 91   *The New Yorker* quote on above: February 23, 1952.

page 92   *New York Times* quote on *Oh, What a Wonderful Wedding!:* June 28, 1953.

page 92   *Chicago Sunday Tribune* quote on above: April 26, 1953.

page 92   *New York Herald Tribune Book Review* quote on above: April 19, 1953.
page 93   *San Francisco Chronicle* quote on above: April 10, 1953.
page 100   Quotes from Lucy and Abigail Rosenthal: To EM (9-24-97, 9-27-97).
page 101   "At Michael's christening": Nan Badian to EM (10-15-97).

9. "A Simple, Single Woman . . ."

page 102   "Pat spent nearly a year working": Julian Muller to EM (10-24-97).
page 102   Quote from Vivian Weaver: To EM (1-26-97).
page 103   "During the meeting": Julian Muller to EM (10-24-97).
page 104   "Convincing Vanguard": Ibid.
page 105   *Chicago Sunday Tribune* quote on *Auntie Mame:* March 6, 1955.
page 109   " 'I found Pat to be tremendously acute' ": Julian Muller to EM (10-24-97).
page 111   Quote from Robert Fryer: To EM (6-30-97).
page 111   Morton Da Costa quote: From Richard Tyler Jordan, *But Darling, I'm Your Auntie Mame* (Santa Barbara, Calif.: Capra Press, 1998).
page 112–13 Quotes from Peggy Cass: To EM (10-4-98).
page 113   Quote from Julian Muller on Pat not changing: To EM (10-24-97).
page 113   Abe Badian on Pat's generosity: To EM (10-15-97).
page 113   Louise Tanner on fame: To EM (10-22-98).

10. "Will the Real Auntie Mame Please Stand Up?"

page 115   " 'The contract with Warners' ": From Sidney Field's "Only Human" column in the *New York Daily Mirror,* November 2, 1956.
page 117   " 'She *was* very interesting' ": Louise Tanner to EM (3-22-98).
page 118–19 Quotes from Frank Andrews: To EM (6-29-97).
page 119   Quote from Dr. William G. Cahan: To EM (1-12-98).
page 120   Quote from Peter Swords: To EM (8-17-98).
page 120   " 'She was a first-class pain in the ass' ": Abe Badian to EM (10-15-97).
page 122   During the next month: Michael Tanner to EM (6-19-97).
page 124   Quote from Elizabeth Bishop: To EM (2-17-98).
page 124–25 Quotes from Nancy Hoffman: To EM (8-26-97).
page 126–27 Quotes from Libby Lyon: To EM (10-3-97).
page 127–28 Quotes from Marilyn Rogers: To EM (9-25-97).
page 128–29 Quotes from Ann Wyatt: To EM (9-16-97).

11. Bosom Buddies

page 133–34 Descriptions of Ninety-first Street town house: Louise Tanner to EM (3-22-98); Cris Alexander to EM (7-25-97).
page 134   Anthony Cahan trapped in the elevator: Dr. William G. Cahan to EM (10-97).
page 134–35 Descriptions of Corry Salley: Louise Tanner to EM (3-22-98), Cris Alexander and Shaun O'Brien to EM (7-25-97); Joy Singer to EM (8-7-97); Michael Tanner to EM (6-19-97); Peggy Cass to EM (10-4-98).

page 135–36   Cris Alexander's description of the first *Auntie Mame* read-through: To EM (7-25-97).
page 136–37   Hervey Jolin's description of the camp circle: To EM (9-13-98).
page 138–39   Loyola's big night: Cris Alexander to EM (7-25-97).
page 139–40   Pat and the diamond necklace: Shaun O'Brien to EM (7-25-97).
page 140   Miss Modessa Priddy: Cris Alexander to EM (7-25-97).
page 143   *The Loving Couple:* Review in *The New Yorker.*
page 143   *The Loving Couple:* Review in *Saturday Review.*
page 143   *New York Post* interview: August 24, 1958.
page 144   "After taxes": *Time,* July 15, 1957.
page 144   " 'He would be the last person to say so' ": Cris Alexander to EM (7-25-97).

12. The Children's Hour
page 145   Louise Tanner on Dorothy Erskine: To EM (3-22-98).
page 148–50   All quotes from Betsy Tanner: To EM (12-29-97).
page 148–50   All quotes from Michael Tanner: To EM (6-19-97).
page 150   "Once Michael was given an assignment": Ibid.
page 150–51   "He also took her on a trip to Europe": Sister Joanna to EM (7-4-97).
page 151–52   Anne Noggle's visit with Pat in Paris: To EM (1-4-98).
page 154   "I don't like to bite the hand": *Newsweek,* August 25, 1958.
page 155–56   Julian Muller finishing *The Loving Couple* and *Around the World with Auntie Mame:* Julian Muller to EM (10-24-97).
page 156–57   Pat's quarantine on Staten Island: *New York Herald Tribune,* August 5, 1959.

13. The Birth of Belle Poitrine
page 158–61   "Following the success of *Auntie Mame* onstage" to "Like so many projects, the musical of *The Loving Couple*": Carmen Capalbo to EM (10-9-97).
page 162   *New York Times* review of *Love and Mrs. Sargent:* January 3, 1961.
page 162   *New York Herald Tribune* review of *Love and Mrs. Sargent:* January 22, 1961.
page 164   *"Little Me* sprang from an idea Pat had": Cris Alexander to EM (7-25-97).
page 169   "Unfortunately, one nasty episode": Ibid.
page 171   *New York Herald Tribune* review of *Little Me:* November 5, 1961.
page 171–72   *The New Republic* review of *Little Me:* November 13, 1961.
page 172   *New York Times* review of *Little Me:* November 5, 1961.
page 172   Kurt Bieber comment: To EM (3/00).
page 172   Robert Plunket comment: To EM (7/97)
page 173   Quote from *The Bay Area Reporter:* July 4, 1996.
page 174   "Pat was too much of a gentleman": Carmen Capalbo to EM (10-19-97); Cris Alexander and Shaun O'Brien to EM (7-25-97).

14. The Fat, Hairy Old Thing
page 175   "Pat became a frequent visitor to the Luxor": Michael Tanner to EM (6-19-97); Cris Alexander and Shaun O'Brien to EM (7-25-97).

page 175   "ride couldn't possibly last forever": Cris Alexander to EM (7-25-97).
page 175   Sometimes he even stayed out all night: Michael Tanner to EM (6-19-97).
page 176–79 Descriptions of Guy Kent: John Boxer to EM (8-10-97); Cris Alexander and Shaun O'Brien to EM (7-25-97); Peggy Brooks to EM (11-18-97); Murray Grand to EM (7-2-97).
page 179   Guy Kent in Venice: Dr. William G. Cahan to EM (10/97).
page 186–87 *Kirkus* review of *Genius*: September 1, 1962.
page 186–87 *New York Times* review of *Genius*: October 21, 1962.
page 186–87 *New York Herald Tribune* review of *Genius*: October 21, 1962.
page 187–88 "I completed a first draft": Ring Lardner Jr. to EM (6-18-99).

15. "The Loony Bin"

page 189   Miltown and its side effects: Louise Tanner to EM (3-22-98).
page 189   Pat and Dr. Nordfeldt: Michael Tanner to EM.
page 189   "On the evening of December 4": Dr. William G. Cahan to EM (10/97); Michael Tanner to EM (6-19-97).
page 190   "Rather grudgingly, Pat agreed to enter": Dr. William G. Cahan to EM (10/97).
page 190   "he openly expressed a willingness": Michael Tanner to EM.
page 190–96 "At the hospital, Pat was" and all other hospital-related information: Ibid.
page 192   "Michael noticed the postmark": Michael Tanner to EM (6-19-97).
page 192   Quote from Betsy Tanner: To EM (12-29-97).
page 194   Quote from Louise Tanner: To EM (3-2-98).
page 195   Quotes from Cris Alexander and Shaun O'Brien: To EM (7-25-97).
page 195   "Finally, during a visit from his friend and accountant, Abe Badian": Abe Badian to EM (10-15-97).

16. Splitsville

page 197   Michael, Betsy, and Louise's visit to the Lowell Hotel: Michael Tanner to EM (6-19-97).
page 198   Comments from Shaun O'Brien and Cris Alexander regarding the separation: To EM (7-25-97).
page 198   Comment from Joy Singer: To EM (8-7-97).
page 198   Quote from Abe Badian: To EM (10-15-97).
page 199   Pat aiding the Bloomingdale's inmate's escape: Cris Alexander and Shaun O'Brien to EM (7-25-97).
page 199   Comments from Shaun O'Brien regarding Guy Kent: To EM (7-25-97).
page 200   Quote from Peggy Cass: To EM (10-4-98).
page 200   Edward Tanner and Alice Pearce: Cris Alexander to EM (7-25-97).
page 201   *New York Times* review of *First Lady*: August 2, 1964.
page 201   *Time* magazine review of *First Lady*: August 7, 1964.
page 201–02 Michael and Betsy's memories of their visits with their father and *The Joyous Season*: To EM (6-19-97 and 12-29-97).
page 203   *New York Times* review of *The Joyous Season*: January 17, 1965.
page 203   *The Saturday Review* review of *The Joyous Season*: January 16, 1965.

page 204   "Fryer and ,Carr withdrew [from *Good, Good Friends*]": Murray
            Grand to EM (7-2-97).
page 205   Information on San Diego production of *Good, Good Friends*: John
            Bowab to EM (11-19-97).
page 205–06 Murray Grand's anecdotes: To EM (7-2-97).
page 207   Pat's return to New York from Tangier: Ibid.
page 207   Quote from Paula Lawrence regarding Guy Kent: To EM (7-18-97).
page 208   Quote from Carmen Capalbo: To EM (10-9-97).
page 208   Quote from Peggy Cass regarding Guy Kent: To EM (10-4-98).
page 208   "It is assumed by those who knew him": John Boxer to EM (8-10-
            97).

17. "The International Set"

page 213   Description of Pat's apartment at 33 Calle de Varsovia: *Mexico City
            News*, November 13, 1966; plus Nina Quirós to EM (9-11-97).
page 214   Pat's party for Rosalind Russell: Alan Stark to EM (11-1-98); letter
            to EM from E. G. McGrath.
page 214   "In Mexico, everyone referred to him": J. B. Johnson to EM (1-23-
            98).
page 214   Pat's sexual identity in Mexico: Joy Singer to EM (8-7-97); Jean
            Garay to EM (8-12-98).
page 215–16 Quotes from Katherine Walch: Letters to EM, plus interview (6-5-
            99).
page 215   Quotes from Betsy Tanner: To EM (12-29-97).
page 215   Quotes from Michael Tanner: To EM (6-19-97).
page 216   The trip to Teotihuacán: Katherine Walch to EM (6-5-99) plus let-
            ters.
page 217   "Tony was based on Guy Kent": Murray Grand to EM (7-2-97);
            Nina Quirós to EM (9-11-97).
page 220   "greatly reduced the amount of money": Louise Tanner to EM (3-22-
            98); Peggy Brooks to EM (11-18-97); Ross Claiborne to EM (8-9-
            97).
page 222   "Pat even played matchmaker": Letter from E. G. McGrath to EM;
            letters from Pat to Barbara Hastings.
page 222   "Pat was . . . paying his salary": Patty Sommer to EM (9-8-97); let-
            ters from Pat to Barbara Hastings.
page 223   "Both Ed and Florence Tanner were now . . . inebriated": Letter
            from Pat to Barbara Hastings.
page 223   Quote from Murray Grand: To EM (7-2-97).
page 223   Florence's fire: Sister Joanna to EM (7-4-97).
page 224–25 William McPherson's stay in Mexico with Pat: To EM (8-17-97).
page 226   Pat's appearance in the Junior League Follies: Pansy Kimbro to EM
            (1-25-98).
page 227   Quotes from Nina Quirós: To EM (9-11-97).
page 227   "Once again, Pat spent huge sums decorating": Betsy Tanner to EM
            (12-29-97).
page 227–28 Pat and the ice-making machine: Letter from E. G. McGrath to EM.

page 229   "Ed's health had taken a precipitous downturn": Letter from Pat to
             Carroll Sudler, Sudler and Company (1-26-69).
page 231   "The separation did indeed continue . . . without rancor": Letters
             from Pat to Michael Tanner; letters from Pat to Barbara Hastings;
             Louise Tanner to EM (3-22-98).

18. Life in Death Valley

page 233–34 Quotes from Alan Stark: To EM (6-10-99).
page 235–36 Pat coming out to Michael: Michael Tanner to EM (6-19-97).
page 236   "The affection that Pat sometimes had trouble expressing": Ibid.
page 236   Quotes from Carlisle Brazy (Connick): To EM (8-21-97).
page 237   Pat and his TV show: Letters from Pat Tanner to Barbara Hastings
             and Michael Tanner; James Harvey to EM (1-26-98).
page 237   "Pat soon grew bored with the inefficiency": Letter to Barbara Hast-
             ings.
page 237–38 "One of his most brazen escapades": Murray Grand to EM (7-2-97);
             Nina Quirós to EM (9-11-97).
page 238   "Another time, Pat went to dinner": J. B. Johnson to EM (1-23-98).
page 239   "Throughout all the madness in Mexico": Nan Badian to EM (9-29-
             97).
page 245   *"Paradise* was, in fact, optioned for the movies": Ray Powers to EM
             (9-22-97).
page 246   "Pat would often help little Clinton": Clinton Wright to EM (4-7-
             98).
page 247   "Pablo, to whom Pat had been like a father": Murray Grand to EM
             (7-2-97); Glendora Brazy to EM (8-22-97); E. G. McGrath to EM
             (9-18-97); Katherine Walch to EM (6-5-99).
page 249   "They offered an advance": Letter from Peggy Brooks to Pat (11-25-
             70).
page 249   "Peggy Brooks had some good suggestions": Ibid.
page 251   Pat and Nina's TV show and PR firm: Nina Quirós to EM (9-11-97).
page 253   "After one of those big Acapulco events": Ibid.

19. North of the Border

page 254   "Pat suggested that it was time": E. G. McGrath to EM (9-18-97).
page 254   Pat and the Hicks twins: Ibid.
page 255   Quote from Pansy Kimbro: To EM (1-25-98).
page 256   Pat's visit to The High Camp: E. G. McGrath to EM (9-18-97).
page 256   Pat and the customers at Gallery Victor: Ibid.
page 257   *New York Times* review of 3-D: December 10, 1972.
page 257   Quote from Peggy Brooks regarding 3-D: To EM (11-18-97).
page 259–60 Pat and Carmen Capalbo working on *Nymph Errant:* Carmen
             Capalbo to EM (10-9-97).

20. Serving Time

page 263 Quote from Abe Badian: To EM (9-29-97).

page 263 "Armed with a portfolio of references": Michael Tanner to EM (6-19-97).

page 263 "Pat announced his plans to Louise and his closest friends": Cris Alexander to EM (7-25-97).

page 263 Louise Tanner quote: To EM (3-22-98).

page 263 Susan Hastings (Sister Joanna) quote: To EM (7-4-97).

page 263 Joy Singer quote: To EM (8-7-97).

page 264 Peggy Brooks quote: To EM (11-18-97).

page 264 Background on Stanton Griffis: *New York Times* obituary, August 30, 1974.

page 265 Pat serving Charles van Rensselaer: Louise Tanner to EM (3-22-98).

page 269 Nan Badian quote: To EM (9-29-97).

page 272 The *Chicago Tribune* article: January 8, 1976.

page 274 Background on Ray Kroc: *Chicago Tribune* and *New York Times* obituaries, January 15, 1984.

page 277 Quotes from Betsy Tanner: To EM (12-29-97).

21. Paw in Paw down the Sunset Trail

page 279 "Pat had given up on the doctors in Chicago": Betsy Tanner to EM (12-29-97).

page 281 "Pat made sure that one of the last things": Michael Tanner to EM (6-19-97).

page 282 "Pat had asked his friend Dr. William G. Cahan": Dr. William G. Cahan to EM (10-97).

page 282 Pat's final words: Cris Alexander to EM (7-25-97).

INDEX

NOTE: "Pat" stands for "Edward Everett Tanner III" (pseudonym Patrick Dennis). Unattributed works are by Pat. Characters in works are given in reading order, e.g. "Agnes Gooch" (not "Gooch, Agnes").